Fraternity

Alexandra Robbins

Fraternity

An Inside Look at a Year of
College Boys Becoming Men

DUTTON

DUTTON

An imprint of Penguin Random House LLC
penguinrandomhouse.com

Copyright © 2019 by Alexandra Robbins
Penguin supports copyright. Copyright fuels creativity, encourages diverse
voices, promotes free speech, and creates a vibrant culture. Thank you for buying
an authorized edition of this book and for complying with copyright laws by not
reproducing, scanning, or distributing any part of it in any form without
permission. You are supporting writers and allowing Penguin to
continue to publish books for every reader.

DUTTON and the D colophon are registered trademarks of
Penguin Random House LLC.

LIBRARY OF CONGRESS CATALOGING-IN-PUBLICATION DATA
Names: Robbins, Alexandra, 1976– author.
Title: Fraternity: an inside look at a year of college boys becoming men /
Alexandra Robbins.
Description: New York, New York: Dutton, [2019] | Includes
bibliographical references.
Identifiers: LCCN 2018027905 (print) | LCCN 2018032943 (ebook) |
ISBN 9781101986738 (ebook) | ISBN 9781101986721 (hc: alk. paper)
Subjects: LCSH: Greek letter societies—United States. | College fraternity
members—United States. | Male college students—United States—
Conduct of life.
Classification: LCC LJ34 (ebook) | LCC LJ34 .R55 2019 (print) | DDC
371.8/55—dc23
LC record available at https://lccn.loc.gov/2018027905

Printed in the United States of America
10 9 8 7 6 5 4 3 2 1

Set in Dante MT Pro
Designed by Francesca Belanger

While the author has made every effort to provide accurate telephone
numbers, Internet addresses, and other contact information at the time
of publication, neither the publisher nor the author assumes any responsibility
for errors or for changes that occur after publication. Further, the publisher
does not have any control over and does not assume any responsibility
for author or third-party websites or their content.

To my family, past and present, with love

CONTENTS

Fraternity

Preface

IN THE YEARS since I wrote *Pledged: The Secret Life of Sororities,* which remains the most widely read of my books, I have spoken to thousands of fraternity and sorority members. As I became a go-to media pundit on Greek life, TV viewers and audience members at my high school and college talks often asked me about fraternities, which prompted me to return to this world. This book, however, is not *Pledged.* The surprise for readers of *Pledged,* in those years before universal social media, was that sororities, then viewed as bastions of pearls and purity, were not all good. Perhaps a surprise for the public in this book, then, is that fraternities are not all bad.

To find out what it's really like to be a fraternity brother in the twenty-first century, I contacted hundreds of current and recent brothers whose fraternity chapters didn't make headlines. Brothers who made me question whether the media had turned the system into a caricature—and who made the case that many fraternities can actually be safe spaces for men who fear they attend a school where guys cannot be themselves, will not easily find friends, or would otherwise slip, lost and invisible, through the cracks.

Readers might naturally wonder from the outset whether this book is pro- or anti-fraternity. The shortest answer is that this book is pro-students and the people who care about them. While fraternities are often either celebrated or demonized, the truth is much more complicated. Many fraternity chapters do what you'd want them to do: offer support, guidance, friendships, and training to young men who have never lived away from home. But others encourage the worst in the same demographic, too often with tragic or disturbing consequences. This book explains why and how this happens during an era in which the state of America's young men, and their interpretations of masculinity, concern us all.

To better portray fraternity perspectives, and to make this book more entertaining to read, I closely followed the stories of two real-life college boys for approximately one year. I chose Jake, a freshman searching for brotherhood, and Oliver, a sophomore striving for leadership skills, because they represented students missing from the media and contemporary literature: smart, good-hearted, self-aware, earnest fraternity members whom readers would root for. While I intended to capture undeniably positive experiences, both stories took surprising turns—and one had a stunning outcome that I could never have foreseen.

In the essay sections, readers will also meet Kirk, a transfer student who experiences his fraternity through two distinctively different chapters; Ben, who as a junior founded a South Carolina chapter of a national fraternity; Teddy, a working-class Oregon brother whose chapter is his "family away from home"; and several other fraternity members who want readers to understand the truth of their experiences.* Many of these brothers are former AP students or engineers, rather than the lunkheads depicted in fraternity movies. Some of them are the kinds of guys who mentioned to me without prompting that they are feminists. While I prioritized interviews with active and recent brothers because this is a book about current college life, I occasionally include the perspectives of alumni acting

---

* Some potentially identifying details and the order of certain events have been changed. Most names, including Town College, State University, and all Greek groups in Jake's and Oliver's stories, are pseudonyms. All events, dialogue, and thoughts are written as reported to or observed by me, except for details changed to protect identities. While this book does discuss black, Latino, Asian American, multicultural, gay/bi/trans, and other fraternities, unless stated otherwise, *fraternity* usually refers to a national, historically white, university-recognized social fraternity.

as advisors because their views reflect Greek experiences outside the bubble of a single chapter. The variety of stories provides a fresh look at issues that concern boys and their parents: seeking friendships and navigating identity, sex, social media, peer pressure, alcohol use, gender roles, social development, and even porn.

This book is about the alternately fraught and rewarding transitions from high school to college and boyhood to manhood. *Fraternity* includes the stories and explanations that both reveal to college guys and soon-to-be college guys the reasons behind their impulses toward certain behaviors and help their classmates, parents, educators, and sorority counterparts to consider the boys' perspectives. One of my intentions is to provide parents and students with a starting point for discussions so they can openly communicate about the meanings and pressures of masculinity, and about whether to join the Greek system or how to manage the culture. Readers of my previous books have said that by talking about the characters rather than themselves, students and parents have been able to have more open, in-depth conversations about school. Non-Greeks also will find much to learn, as I did, about what it's like to be a college guy today.

Someone must advocate for the boys who *aren't* causing trouble and for the parents who want to help and understand them. Someone must give them an opportunity to tell their stories in their own words. Today's young men are coming of age at a time when we are renegotiating what it means to be a man, which presents new challenges, reopens old wounds, and creates additional reasons for students to seek out brotherhood. It's imperative that we attempt to comprehend and alleviate the pressures faced by teenage boys in twenty-first-century America—and acknowledge that even fraternity brothers struggle with them, too.

CHAPTER I

Joining: Why Go Greek?

BEHIND THE GATE, the party raged. Jake had carefully timed his arrival: 11:00 P.M., not so early as to appear eager but not so late as to miss peak capacity. He was glad he had come with the three freshmen he knew from high school. Once they had walked through the double-arched white Gothic gates that flanked the campus entrance, and past a few bars and a gas station, the town became sketchy. Jake didn't know whether to be intimidated or comforted by the hordes of students streaming from various directions in groups of 10, 20, even 30. His first-ever fraternity party was going to be a memorable one.

When Jake's group reached the front of the line at the Delta Rho house, two fraternity brothers manning the backyard gate let the girls right in. Jake and his good friend Arjun tried to follow them, but a brother held up a hand. "Girls can stay but guys have to pay," he said.

That's terrible, Jake thought. Arjun and Jake each pulled out the five dollars they saw the older guys in front of them pay. *That's so arbitrary. It's a party! Why should gender matter?*

When the guys attempted to hand over their money, the brother stopped them again. "Guys pay ten dollars now." *No one's questioning how messed up this is,* Jake thought as he gave the brother another five. *Why do guys have to pay more the later the party goes?* The long line of students fidgeted behind him. Jake hurried through the gate without protest.

Thirty minutes later, Jake was packed elbow to elbow with hundreds of students gathered among the three bars set up around the yard. Most people seemed to be drinking Delta Rho's signature jungle juice, a strong, unidentifiable concoction. In a corner, a DJ spun loud dance music. The air, sweltering thanks to body heat and the August humidity, reeked of alcohol and weed. Standing next to Arjun, who was already on his third drink, Jake quietly surveyed the scene, holding a red Solo cup from which he planned to take one sip every half hour for appearance's sake.

In high school, Jake and Arjun had been straight-A students who were heavily involved in school activities and did not party. The two girls from their competitive high school who had also been accepted to the selective Town College (TC) were similarly inclined. All four of them had sat at the same cafeteria table, where they usually did their AP homework or played trivia games. On Friday nights, if they went out, they saw a movie or chilled at someone's house. On Saturday nights, Jake usually stayed home with his family. He was known in high school both for being the class overachiever and for his long blond sideburns. Classmates liked to joke that, at five foot eight, with wire-rimmed glasses and a smile that seemed to light up half his face, Jake resembled a bespectacled teenage Calvin without a Hobbes.

Arjun came from a staid Pakistani family that prioritized academics and shunned alcohol. When he had moved into his dorm last week, his parents asked Jake, whom they knew was not a drinker, to watch over their son. Unsure whether they were kidding, Jake had so far tried his best.

But how do you police friends who do not want to be policed? Already, Jake could sense the dynamics changing among his high school friends. Last week, his classmates had partied out of control. Arjun specifically had become almost a burden, drinking to excess until he transformed into someone whom Jake thought embodied "the stereotype of a frat bro." Jake would walk him home, even when Arjun didn't want to go, half carrying him for blocks.

"Woo! Party! WOO!" Arjun yelled now, to no one.

A gorgeous girl approached Jake and Arjun. "Hi! I'm an Epsilon sister and the girlfriend of the Delta Rho president," she said. "So are you guys interested in Greek life?"

Jake nodded.

"Hell yes!" Arjun said. He was dead set on rushing, lured by the hookup to parties, drinks, and girls.

"Which fraternities are you interested in rushing?" she prodded.

"Uh, I don't know if I want to talk about what fraternities I'm interested in while I'm at a Delta Rho party," Jake half joked. He hadn't expected to have this conversation so early in the semester.

She waved him off. "Oh, no. It's fine."

"Yo, def D-Rho," Arjun said, and listed a few other fraternities. Jake's eyes widened. Arjun had named only top-tier fraternities. Jake didn't have the heart to tell him he'd heard that top-tiers at TC rarely gave bids to minorities.

On many campuses across the country, students unofficially ranked fraternities and sororities, labeling them as top-tier, middle-tier, or bottom-tier chapters. Jake knew this because, like everything else in his life, he had researched it extensively. He had spent hours over the summer poring over message boards about TC fraternities, taking copious notes, as if familiarizing himself with campus Greek life were his first and potentially most important college homework assignment.

The sorority girl turned to Jake. "And you?"

"I have a few ideas. Kappa Tau, and this party's got me interested in rushing Delta Rho," he lied, to be polite. Jake was too intimidated to rush Delta Rho, or any other top-tier fraternity, because he wasn't, as he put it, "a party-hard, sports-playing dude who's like a total bro all the time." He planned to aim for middle-tier fraternities because he assumed they weren't as intense or competitive as the top-tier groups, he'd be less likely to get hazed, and he'd have better opportunities to meet kindred spirits.

He didn't tell the sorority sister why he was rushing K-Tau—or why a guy like him, who didn't consider himself "the fraternity type," wanted to go Greek to begin with. Jake's father, a former K-Tau chapter officer, had told him fraternity tales for years. He was over-the-moon excited for his son to be a part of his fraternity so they could share the secrets, that legacy, those stories. Jake was already close with his parents and his two younger sisters; he'd been surprised that he didn't cry when they said goodbye after moving him into his dorm. For Jake, the prospect of becoming even closer to his father through their shared K-Tau membership was irresistible.

If not for his dad, Jake might not have chosen to rush. He was scared of hazing. No matter whom he asked about which fraternities hazed and what kind of hazing they did, he couldn't get a straight answer. ("It's apparently a well-kept secret," he told me.) The idea of forced drinking terrified him. He had never been drunk before, didn't like the taste of alcohol or the way it made him feel, and didn't want to lose control of himself. He couldn't begin to fathom how he would handle being forced to do something against his will or to participate in activities that would make him uncomfortable.

But Jake's father, who wasn't a stereotypical frat bro, either, believed Jake could benefit immensely from the lessons and friendships that fraternities had to offer. He often said that his time in K-Tau was his most valuable college experience. At TC's prerecruitment meeting, Jake was reassured by the Interfraternity Council's statement that hazing was not a part of TC's Greek community. At TC, as at most schools, the IFC governed the predominantly white social fraternities. (Service, honors, professional, and religious fraternities are separate organizations.) IFC officers assured the TC recruits that they could choose how much time to spend with their chapter. It was like another class, they said, but a casual one. And much of that time, the IFC insisted, was spent on study hours and tutoring opportunities.

Jake liked the IFC officers' description of campus Greek life. Fraternity brothers had higher GPAs than non-Greeks, controlled the student government and some other major campus groups, were responsible for most of the college's charitable funding, and, as the officers kept hammering home, developed students into "better people." Jake had three goals for college: Get good grades, get involved in activities, and meet a variety of new people. A fraternity seemed like a great way to accomplish all three at once.

Even more, Jake craved the bonds of a brotherhood. For him, "the biggest allure of an all-male group is the idea that you have guys you could depend on for whatever, to be part of a solid group of people you can relate to and keep in close touch with." He wanted to feel that there was somewhere he belonged.

Jake also hoped that joining a fraternity would improve his social confidence. He called himself "the textbook definition of an introvert," prone to "awkward conversations and cringeworthy displays of social anxiety." He winced when he thought about his first-ever college social event. It was his second day on campus, before his high school friends had moved in and before he had met anyone at TC. (He had arrived early to give himself time to get acclimated and to claim the lower bunk in his dorm room.) A dorm on Central Campus was holding a pizza party open to all freshmen. Figuring he had to eat anyway, Jake psyched himself up for the chance to meet people and score some free food.

Because the dorm was farther across campus than he'd anticipated, he was 20 minutes late. Fifty students were already there, chatting in small circles. Jake took a slice of pizza and awkwardly stood alone in a space between groups, munching quietly while dozens of unfamiliar people mingled and laughed. For a while, afraid to make eye contact, he stared down at his phone, pretending to look preoccupied. Then he mustered the courage to attempt to join a group in mid-conversation. Hesitant to interrupt, he didn't introduce himself. The students were gossiping about mutual friends and last night's parties. Jake didn't volunteer his Saturday night activities, which had consisted of calling his parents and messing around online. He ended up uneasily listening to the group and occasionally laughing along with everyone else, until he understood that their odd glances at him signaled that he couldn't possibly get their inside jokes because he turned out to be the only person at the party who didn't live in that dorm. Somehow this level of social awkwardness was not unusual for Jake. He had made similar gaffes between then and tonight's Delta Rho party.

In the yard at Delta Rho, Jake was nervously chatting with Arjun when, without warning, the music stopped and the lights went out, leaving little visible save a third-story window of the house. Three brothers climbed out the window, shimmied onto the roof, and posed. "ARE YOU READY TO PARTY!" they yelled. The crowd erupted.

The brothers shot firecrackers into the air, raining ash and soot on many of the partygoers, who mostly seemed too wasted to care. *Whoa, whoa, what's happening?!* Jake thought, starting to panic. He didn't think the firecrackers had hit anyone, but he wasn't positive. A brother on the roof shook a champagne bottle, popped the cork, and poured champagne onto the students below. The crowd cheered again, the music resumed, the lights flicked back on, and the party raged even harder than before.

Wow, college is going to be interesting, Jake thought. *What am I getting myself into?*

An hour and a half later, he dragged a resistant Arjun out of the party. After downing five cups of jungle juice and who knew how many shots, Arjun was mumbling and could barely stand.

"Don't wanna leave," he muttered. "Party!"

"Okay, Arjun. All right. Time to go, man, time to go," Jake said.

A few blocks away, Arjun veered toward a bush and puked. Unfazed by the disgusted reactions of student onlookers, Arjun rallied, raising his arms in a victory sign. "PARTY!" he shouted, delighted. A minute later, he retched into another bush, then continued walking, beaming beatifically at everyone who passed by.

"Oh man, you're not going to like this in the morning," Jake told him.

Arjun stopped short at a lamppost, happy as could be. "Yo, man, I'm gonna climb this pole. Watch me!" Unaware that he hadn't left the ground, he humped the lamppost.

The next night, Jake again tried to party with his high school friends. Arjun again drank until he barfed. One of the girls drank herself out of her mind; she continually told anyone within earshot that she was ugly, and then tried to make out with the first guy other than Jake to disagree with her. "My friends have already changed since coming to college. These aren't the same people I knew," Jake told me later. "I'm not having a good time at these parties because I have to watch over these guys, and they're making no sense. I'm trying to meet new people, but I feel lonely because I'm the most sober person in the group."

He yearned for real friends more than ever, for confidants who viewed friendship as a two-way street, who would make this new, bewildering stage of schooling feel more like he was on a grand adventure with buddies than like he was peering forlornly through a window into a club full of people who knew better than he did how to have fun, how to be cool, and how to fit in.

Jake was, he now knew for sure, ready for fraternity rush.

Introduction: A Different Kind of Story About Boys in College

It's a tough time to be a college-bound teenage boy. Surviving an increasingly competitive high school environment is hard enough; today's young men are doing it during what has been called "a collapse in the American construction of masculinity." Unsure about what's expected of them, they're growing up in a world where women can be doctors, but men still face stigma for becoming nurses; where the majority of high school dropouts are male; and where experts point to "toxic masculinity" as a driving force behind everything from mass shootings to international terrorism.

With their support networks often reduced to the size, and depth, of a smartphone, boys may need some sort of "fraternity" more than ever. According to an American College Health Association survey of 28,000 college students, more than 50 percent of college guys "felt very lonely" in the last 12 months and more than 20 percent in the last two weeks. It's not always easy for boys to make friends. Worse, those who don't find the socialization and connections they yearn for could face dire consequences: Boys comprise 75 percent of 15- to 19-year-olds who commit suicide.

Greek-letter fraternities have long promised brotherhood and community to college boys, and in recent years, students have been signing up in record numbers. Between 2005 and 2015, the North-American Interfraternity Conference (NIC), which governs 66 fraternities, including all but four of the major historically white fraternities, reported a 50 percent increase in the number of new pledges. Today, there are about one million current undergraduate members of campus Greek-letter organizations, and one out of every eight American students at four-year colleges lives in a fraternity or sorority house. When those students graduate, they will join a group of alumni more than nine million strong.

Nonmembers know little about the secretive organizations that so many students have turned to for a constellation of friendship, social support, alcohol, debauchery, and postgraduation professional networks. Fraternities, an influential sector of Americana, occupy a unique place in the college landscape, both dependent on the university and separate from it. Each fraternity represents a series of long-standing traditions, specific value sets, and a storied history that together offer an anchor that many young men crave.

Yet shocking media headlines about fraternities have become so commonplace that they often don't shock us anymore. Between 2005 and 2017, at least 72 boys died in fraternity-related incidents. Well-established research shows that Greeks drink more heavily than non-Greeks. And sexual assaults among Greeks are so common that some researchers have concluded that it is specifically the fraternity experience that causes students to be more likely to rape.

High-profile deaths and scandals haven't discouraged students from wanting to join these groups, though. Even colleges that have had fraternity scandals don't necessarily see enrollment numbers dip. According to the most recent American Freshman Survey, distributed to more than 100,000 college freshmen, interest in joining a fraternity or sorority is the highest it's been since national data collection began in 2000. At DePauw University, 75 percent of male undergrads joined fraternities in 2016; at MIT, nearly 50 percent of guys were fraternity members. These all-male groups, many of them nearing two centuries old, are more widespread now, in twenty-first-century America, than ever before.

Given the ubiquitous negative headlines, why are students joining fraternities in droves, and why would parents want them to? Current brothers told me their chapter is "a second family" that provides invaluable emotional and academic support. These fraternity members, many of whom are sincere, intelligent guys who genuinely believe in the value of Greek brotherhood, described scandal-free chapters that helped them adjust to college, power through tough circumstances, make hard life decisions, and—a particularly common phrase—"become a better man."

The NIC trumpets flattering statistics: Fraternities raised $20.3 million for philanthropic causes in the 2013/14 academic year, and the all-fraternity GPA is 2.912 versus the 2.892 GPA of the general male college population. (It's worth pointing out that in many chapters, if a member doesn't maintain a minimum GPA, he's deactivated, which could help explain why fraternity GPAs are slightly higher than those of nonmembers; fraternity castoffs are dumped into the nonmember pool.) Some black Greek-letter organizations (BGLOs) offer merit-based scholarships to members.

Fraternities like to publicize that there were, for example, 36 Greek senators and 122 Greek representatives in the 115th US Congress, and that 85 percent of Fortune 500 executives are Greek alumni. Forty percent of US presidents since 1877 were fraternity members, as were 85 percent of US Supreme Court justices since 1910. BGLOs estimate that 75 percent of black leaders in business, government, science, and the arts are members of black sororities or fraternities; alumni include Martin Luther King Jr. and W. E. B. Du Bois.

But statistics and scandals don't tell students and parents what they truly need to know. This book is less about the "what" than the "why" of fraternities. Parents of high schoolers, for example, need to understand more about fraternities before they help their sons or daughters decide where to apply to college and whether to go Greek. And they must be able to distinguish the chapters and campuses that are safer for their children. Most universities are not providing this information. Neither are the fraternities themselves. Fraternity membership carries high stakes—financial, emotional, physical, academic—and it is hoped that this book will help parents and students choose wisely.

Media coverage may be misleading. An analysis my researcher

and I conducted found approximately 2,000 historically white social fraternity incidents publicly reported online (involving sexual assault, hazing, death, racism, noteworthy alcohol abuse, violence, and vandalism) between January 2010 and June 2018. Those incidents, which naturally generated plenty of headlines, were perpetrated by 1,338 chapters (including historically white NIC member organizations, plus Tau Kappa Epsilon, Lambda Chi Alpha, Kappa Sigma, and Phi Delta Theta). But these organizations have more than 5,600 chapters, which means less than a quarter of historically white chapters were featured in those headlines. Even if, between violations we may have missed and incidents that were not publicly reported, another, say, 500 chapters exhibited blatantly problematic behavior, more than two-thirds of current fraternity chapters—hundreds more if you consider nonwhite fraternities—did not commit major conduct or ethical violations in the 2010s.

It's no wonder many fraternity members feel they are under siege. Several brothers complained that when a major problem occurs in one campus chapter, universities are quick to suspend the activities of all chapters. But what then happens to the academic-focused and culturally based fraternities, the service-oriented chapters, the responsible drinkers, and the safe spaces for quirky, gay, and/or "good" boys who have broken few or no university rules?

Many chapters may be doing terrible things, but it seems that more chapters are not. The trick is to be able to distinguish them before it's too late. Typically, once a student is initiated into one NIC fraternity, he can't join another. "I wish people understood that there is significant variation in Greek life from school to school, from chapter to chapter, and even within one school," said a recent graduate of a New York chapter that emphasized academics and brotherhood over partying. "A lot of public attention toward Greek life is directed at large-school, party-oriented groups, which causes a mischaracterization of fraternity life. Large chapters at big party schools have the most alumni and the largest houses, they host the largest parties, and are most likely to do something that makes the news in the wrong way. But for every chapter that has 150 brothers and throws massive pool parties, there are two or three that have 30 to 40 members and truly encourage brotherhood, scholarship, and success."

This book does not dive deeply into the debate over whether fraternities should exist; the fact is, they do. Fraternities not only reflect but also provide insight into changes in American masculinity, and their metamorphosis reveals much about the bigger picture of American higher education. By presenting the realities missing from the headlines, this book should help readers determine how they wish to maneuver in this complex world, because it influences so many students' lives whether or not they are Greek.

During rush, Jake told me, "I hope this book helps future freshmen deal with what I'm dealing with now. There's nowhere to look this stuff up." This is intended to be the book Jake wished for: a different kind of story about boys in college. About boys who may be misjudged and misunderstood because of whom they choose to associate with. Boys at a vulnerable, formative age who are attempting to form friendships and decipher their identities in a climate that can stigmatize them merely for being male. And boys who are trying to forge a path to manhood while they are away from home, on their own for perhaps the first time, and, like Jake, searching for allies who can provide advice and support so they don't have to navigate this complicated coming-of-age journey alone.

Ω Ω Ω

Only a few days after classes began, formal fraternity rush was under way. Sunday through Wednesday, recruits could attend casual open houses during the day and formal rush parties at night. By

Thursday night, recruits would have to choose one house from the bids (official paper invitations) fraternities had offered them.

Jake was overwhelmed that rush was happening so quickly. He hadn't yet adjusted to his five-class course load, an unusually heavy schedule for a first-semester freshman. On Sunday, he decided to visit Mu Zeta Nu and Omega Phi during the day, two bottom-tier houses where he could ease his way into the process. He'd save the first night's rush party exclusively for K-Tau, where his father assured him he'd get a legacy bid. Jake hoped the early bid would be a confidence booster that would propel him through the rest of the week. While he was 95 percent sure he'd accept K-Tau's bid, he thought it wouldn't hurt to check out other chapters.

Jake liked MZN's low-key open house, where he pushed himself to make small talk with a group of approachable brothers. At Omega Phi, a brother immediately greeted Jake and introduced himself. "Quick, tell me your life story in 10 seconds," the brother said.

Jake blurted the first thing that came to mind. "Uh, my mom met my dad, and now I'm here."

"Welp, you definitely got the biological aspect of it down," the brother said.

After a friendly chat, the Omega Phi introduced Jake to other brothers, who told him about the chapter, gave him a tour of the house, and made sure he got a plate of food. Omega Phi was one of the smallest fraternities on campus. Neither MZN nor Omega Phi had drawn many recruits to their first open houses; Jake wondered if their bottom-tier status was already well known among freshmen. But he liked the guys—they were "chill and relatable," he said—and he planned to visit them again later in the week.

At K-Tau, Jake signed in at a front table and paused. Unlike MZN and Omega Phi, K-Tau brothers weren't greeting recruits or offering food or tours. As the house quickly filled with hepped-up freshmen,

Jake realized he would have to seek out conversations with the brothers. He wondered if K-Tau was at a higher tier than the mid-ranked status his research had indicated.

In the living room, Jake approached a brother wearing what looked like an expensive suit. The brother eyed him. "Quick, what's your favorite sex position?" the brother asked.

Jake's mind whirled. How was he supposed to know? He had never even attempted to get past second base, and that was more than two years ago. "Doggie?" he ventured, desperately hoping it was an acceptable answer.

"That's my favorite, too," the brother said, leaning forward. They chatted for a few brief minutes before the brother said, "It was really nice to meet you. Go talk to some of the other brothers around here."

Jake approached some K-Taus, who lobbed less invasive questions: "What did you do in high school?" "What are some of your hobbies?" "You play any sports?" Jake told them he went skiing every year, but he could tell that wasn't the kind of sport they meant. The brothers said K-Tau was one of the largest houses at TC, usually won the fraternity league football championship, and always placed members in TC's student government. Jake tried to work into the conversations that he was a legacy.

Fifteen minutes into the rush party, a brother shouted into a large megaphone that a freshman had accepted a bid. The K-Tau talking to Jake instantly left to join the other brothers, who cheered the new pledge as he ran down the hallway to the side door, followed by every brother in the house. Jake watched through a window as the brothers gave the pledge a T-shirt and took a group photo with him on the lawn. Jake assumed the freshman was a younger sibling of a brother, to have gotten a bid so quickly.

But shortly, it happened again. And again. About every five minutes, K-Tau announced a new bid acceptance, cheered for the recruit, ran outside, and took a group photo. Meanwhile, the brothers whom Jake approached asked him only a few questions before telling him to talk to another brother. *What am I doing wrong?* Jake wondered. He knew that small talk wasn't his strength, but he wasn't blatantly awkward one-on-one . . . was he? He reassured himself that the freshmen receiving bids must have already hung out with the brothers at the invitation-only parties before Rush Week.

Another K-Tau motioned to Jake. "Hey, you want to talk over here where it's less crowded?" the brother suggested, pointing toward a smaller, formal-looking room. In what became Jake's longest conversation of the night, the brother asked him about his high school years. Relieved that he and the brother were hitting it off, Jake relaxed. *This must be the room where they offer bids*, he thought. Mid-conversation, another brother peered through the doorway, made a quick hand gesture, and disappeared.

After a few moments, the brother Jake was talking to excused himself, and Jake looked around for another K-Tau. An affable-looking brother approached him. "Hey, man, what's your name? Nice to meet you," he said, shaking Jake's hand with a noticeably strong grip. "Can you come with me for a second?"

Jake was ecstatic. *Oh, man, this is it!* he thought. *I did it!* "Sure, that sounds great!"

The brother walked him to the front of the house. "Hey, man, the brothers and I have been watching you tonight, and we think you're overall a really good guy." Jake grinned at him. The brother added, "We just don't have any bids to extend to you tonight. Tonight was for guys who have been to our parties, stuff like that."

"Oh, okay, okay! I get it. Do you think I should come back tomorrow or the next day?" Jake asked.

"No, no, I wouldn't," the brother said. As Jake took a few moments to process what the K-Tau was trying to tell him, the brother continued escorting him to the front door. "Hey, man, this happened to me last year, when one of my first fraternities gave me this talk, too. I'm really sorry about this. We just don't have any more bids we're giving out tonight."

At the doorway, Jake stopped, numb. "It's all right," he said slowly, "but I really thought I'd try rushing here because my dad was K-Tau."

The brother shrugged. "Well, man, I don't know what to say. You seem like a great guy, and I sincerely hope you find a brotherhood in some form with another fraternity. Maybe MZN, Chi Iota, or Omega Phi?" All were bottom-tier chapters.

It wasn't all right. Jake was devastated. In a handful of conversations over the course of an hour, K-Tau had already judged him unworthy. He was sure this was the worst thing that could happen to him in college: He was rejected from his father's fraternity. As he turned to leave the house, the megaphone blasted to announce a bid acceptance—another bid that K-Tau did have to give out tonight, after all. The brother left the doorway to go celebrate the newest pledge, running with the other K-Taus to the lawn.

While trudging back to his dorm, Jake called his father. "Dad, I got rejected from K-Tau," he said, choking up.

His father was livid. "What?! How could that happen? You were a shoo-in! Un-fucking-believable. Jake, did you tell them you're a legacy? Did you tell them where I went?"

"Yes. And yes." Hearing how upset his father was made Jake feel even worse.

"God, I should call up Nationals. This is honestly unfair. This is not right. I'll send a grievance."

"No, Dad. Don't bother." Jake told himself to let it go. He didn't want to become a brother on a technicality.

"I can't believe this! When I was a K-Tau, we were practically looking for brothers! We were the small, nerdy frat!"

"It was a different time and place, Dad. Maybe your generation did everything right and made K-Tau into one of the biggest names here. Maybe it went too well." Jake found himself in the odd role of consoling his father even though he wasn't over the rejection himself. "These aren't the same guys you knew in the eighties, Dad. These are jocks, people who care a lot about partying. They don't exactly have the same tastes as us."

"I should complain to Nationals," his father said again.

"No, Dad. It's better for me just to move on and see if I get in anywhere else. I'm determined to find a place I can call home, to find some brothers who fit me."

At the prerecruitment meeting, the IFC representatives had told freshmen to visit every fraternity that interested them, and as often as possible. After his K-Tau rejection, Jake realized he would have to miss several classes this week to visit houses, and even then, he had time in the next few days to home in on only four chapters. He didn't know how he would also manage to complete the six class assignments he had due this week, but he never considered dropping out of rush.

On Monday, Jake returned to MZN and Omega Phi, and added Phi Rho and Zeta Kappa, lower-middle-tier houses, to his rotation. At those houses, brothers offered tours or handed him off to other members rather than leaving him to fend for himself.

At a Zeta Kappa open-house lunch, about half a dozen freshmen lounged in the dining room with Grant, the steward (who managed the kitchen), and Kevin, the academics chair. Grant explained to the freshmen that his job included "relegating positions" to brothers.

"You mean 'delegating,'" Kevin said.

"No, I mean relegating. That's legit the word for it," Grant said.

"Bullshit," said Kevin. "Look it up, look it up."

Grant read the definition aloud from his phone. "Oh. Right, okay."

Kevin rolled his eyes. "I swear to God, we're going to relegate you from steward to something you can actually do." Jake cracked up, pleasantly surprised that fraternity brothers would banter with wordplay.

The brothers told the freshmen that Z-Kap had a long-standing tradition for brothers who "lavaliered" a girl, Greek-speak for giving a serious girlfriend fraternity letters on a necklace, like a promise ring: The tradition was to throw rotten or smelly items into a trash can for a week—the last time they had done this, they said, one brother had urinated into the concoction, another vomited into it—and then to tie the offending brother to a tree and douse him with the contents.

Jake laughed along as the brothers told this story, but he told me later, "If they're willing to do something like that, I don't know if it's going to be too chill of an experience there. That kind of turned me off a bit."

That night, Jake vowed not to overstay his welcome at any house so that he wouldn't be rejected outright again. He watched wistfully as fraternities celebrated other freshmen who had accepted their bids.

The MZNs and Omega Phis were nice guys, but their rush parties were dead compared to the others; the brothers mostly just played Ping-Pong. The issue with both chapters was that most of the members seemed nerdy like Jake. Jake didn't have a problem with that—of course he didn't—but he realized that he didn't want to join a fraternity of brothers who were just like him. He told me, "I want to join the guys who I want to turn into in four years, the people who resemble the person I *want* to be."

Who did Jake want to be? He wanted to be more social, less awkward. He wanted to have more experiences and gain some confidence. He wanted to get to know more girls. But he didn't want to lose himself in the process: his values, his love for his family, his integrity, his intellectual curiosity. He wanted to be, he decided, like some of the brothers he met at Monday night's Zeta Kappa rush party. As soon as he signed in, a brother offered to give him an extended tour of the house. The Z-Kaps had an impressive four-story, white-pillared, redbrick fraternity house. The brother showed Jake the wall of ceremonial paddles, a well-stocked game room, large bedrooms, and a lush, green backyard with an expansive patio.

As he led Jake around the house, the brother asked if he knew about "the all-important ratio." Jake shook his head.

"Do you know how large the sororities can get?" TC had 22 historically white sororities.

"A hundred, maybe?" Jake guessed.

"More. Two hundred at some of the largest ones. And we're a midsize house with a hundred ten guys, so we get a good ratio at parties. It's a very important statistic to have."

When the brother returned Jake to the Great Room, a large den where ornate fraternity letters hung on the wall above one of the couches, he handed him off to Sebastian, a good-looking, friendly Canadian freshman who had accepted a bid the night before. Right away, Jake liked Sebastian, who eventually introduced him to Andy, the chapter president. After some small talk, Andy raised a question that came up at every house: "What do you want out of the brotherhood?"

By now, Jake's answer was well practiced. "Throughout high school, my dad hyped about how Greek life transformed him into a better person. That's all I can ask for. I see brotherhood as providing an experience where I can become a better person by the end of my four years here."

"Good answer," Andy said. "I like that. That's really the right reason you should be going into this. We don't hear that as often as you'd think. Some people come here for the free food and don't hang around for too long. That's something the brothers notice."

Jake had assumed his answer was what fraternities wanted to

hear, but it was also genuinely how he felt. He told me later, "I'm not looking to get shitfaced every day or fuck as many girls as possible. That's the least of my concerns, to be honest. I want to get to know the brothers, get connections, and get involved in the fraternity."

Andy took Jake to a part of the house he hadn't seen before: the Scholastic Room, which had shelves of files labeled by academic course. This room was far enough from the Great Room that Jake could barely hear the bid acceptances that were announced every 15 minutes. Andy didn't disappear to join the celebrations, instead peppering Jake with questions about his college aspirations and career goals. "I can tell you have a good head on your shoulders and you're definitely taking freshman year more seriously than I did. Zeta Kappa has really transformed me; it's made me think about the future more and made me get much more involved than I would have been. And it's really helped me expand my network," Andy said.

At midnight, the music stopped. "Oh sorry, it's twelve. This is the part where we kick you out," Andy said.

"Well, thanks. This was such a great conversation," Jake said. He meant it. This had been his favorite rush conversation so far, and he valued getting to know a brother beyond superficialities. "I really appreciate all the work the brothers have gone through to plan all these formal rush events," Jake said. (He told me later, "I'm learning to say the right things!")

"Hey, if you come back to formal rush tomorrow, look for me. I'd like to talk to you again and introduce you to other brothers," Andy said.

Zeta Kappa's lower-middle-tier status appealed to Jake because he assumed they were "pretty chill and not into hazing." He went to sleep that night thinking, *If Andy's the kind of person I can turn into after this, maybe that's the place for me.*

But after another night of rush parties, Jake began to worry that he wouldn't receive a bid. There was only one more night of formal rush. He wondered if he had made a mistake by not returning to MZN or Omega Phi, where he likely had better odds, or if he should have visited more houses to increase his options. Again, the bid announcements continued—the cheers, the claps on the back, the hallway runs, the photos—while Jake diligently mingled, meeting new people, saying what he hoped were the magic words that would gain him entry into a world that became even more enticing as his chances of getting in seemed to fade. *What am I doing wrong?* he asked himself over and over again. He began to consider backup plans in case he did not get a bid.

Ω Ω Ω

It was the fourth day of Work Week at the Phi Epsilon house at State, a large university on the West Coast. Oliver, a well-muscled brother with close-cropped brown hair and a dimpled chin, worked nonstop in every common room, laboring alongside his brothers as they spruced up the house this week, addressing their concerns and questions, managing paperwork, encouraging the pledges, and relaying information to alumni when necessary.

Oliver never would have envisioned that he'd have this role in college. As a child, he was shy, ducking opportunities for leadership roles, careful to stay within his comfort zone. He played soccer but didn't excel because he assumed he wasn't as skilled as his opponents, mentally removing himself from the game before he gave himself a chance. He was a good student but prone to self-doubt. He spent much of his time watching superhero cartoons and daydreaming about being Batman, fighting faceless enemies to protect the people he loved. He fixated on Batman because, he rationalized, "this guy surrounds himself with superpowered people and still ends up their leader despite the fact that he has nothing going for him besides money and a tough attitude. And everyone respects him! I wanted to be that level of tough and strong in every way."

In middle school, with his father's encouragement, Oliver left soccer to join a Brazilian jiu-jitsu gym, where he could strive for that fortitude. As a high school freshman, he joined the wrestling team, but the moment he stepped onto the mat, he convinced himself he was going to lose. Often, he did.

When Oliver was a sophomore, a young family friend in another state was hospitalized because his drunk father had beaten him and his mom. Furious, Oliver poured his energies into channeling Batman's strength. If he couldn't protect his friend, he could at least be a rock for the boy to lean on emotionally. He could be everyone's rock. Because he was focused on other people's emotions, he buried his own. After all, Batman never broke down.

Following a mediocre high school freshman year season, Oliver told himself that his wrestling opponents weren't necessarily better than him. Maybe they just worked harder. So he pushed himself to train more intensely, and placed in the county tournament the next year. Encouraged by his success, he continued to emulate his fictional role model, testing himself on the mat and in the jiu-jitsu gym to gauge how tough he could be. By the end of high school, between sports and a car accident, Oliver had racked up three concussions. Each recovery only increased his resilience.

Back then, it never occurred to him to go Greek. After touring colleges around the country, he knew he wanted to attend a large university with strong sports teams and major school spirit. It so happened that the colleges he got into were also big Greek schools. Oliver was hesitant to rush because he worried that the fraternity experience would be like the movie *Animal House,* which didn't reflect his values. At the same time, he was drawn to the idea that fraternities were founded on the concepts of brotherhood and loyalty. Because Oliver was an only child, "the idea of having this family of brothers around me was extremely appealing," he told me.

He was already accustomed to belonging to a tribe. Native American on his father's side, Oliver and his family appreciated the traditions, heritage, and culture of their community, though they didn't live on the reservation. Oliver's uncle was running for tribal office and his great-grandfather had been a notable figure in tribal history. The tribe would pay for much of Oliver's college tuition.

In high school, too, Oliver had already found a brotherhood of sorts. His tight-knit group of six friends had deep discussions about global events, girls, school happenings, and their dreams for the future. Christopher, one of Oliver's best friends, had joined the group because he was tired of hanging out with the clique he'd been stuck in, a group of druggies who pressured one another to party. He said he wanted friends who were more "real." Christopher and Oliver had vastly different personalities. Christopher leaped before he looked; he followed his whims, thinking nothing of skipping school or trying a new drug. Levelheaded Oliver, by contrast, assessed several possible outcomes before making a move. As seniors, the boys strengthened their bond when they both dated junior girls.

One of Oliver's most memorable outings with Christopher happened a few weeks before a junior class dance to which they were the only two seniors invited. They spent an afternoon hanging out at a park in Christopher's car, eating fast food and discussing whatever came to mind. Christopher confided that school was challenging because he had anxiety issues. Oliver confessed that he was struggling with his college decision because he wanted to be near his girlfriend. Christopher had told him, "Go with your heart." Oliver followed his advice and stayed close to home, not just because of his girlfriend—they broke up several months into college—but because of the region: He appreciated both its progressiveness and its climate. He enrolled at State U with no second thoughts.

During Oliver's last month of high school, a friend who was a State freshman convinced him to check out his fraternity house. Oliver was surprised that the brothers he met were laid back and kind. He liked that the fraternity valued individuality and offered to improve multiple aspects of members' lives. The chapter's rush process also defied stereotypes. Rush at State was informal and continuous. At any time after February and before the fall pledge period began, brothers could introduce a recruit to the house. There wasn't even a vote; barring strong objections, an interested recruit backed by a brother would get a bid. If brothers didn't like the recruit or thought he wasn't "the right fit," they simply told him, "I don't think this will work out." Oliver was relieved the process wasn't the intense cattle call that he had heard existed at other colleges.

Oliver's parents didn't object. His father, who had grown up in poverty, had attended college for one quarter; his mother had enrolled for a few years but didn't graduate. "I thought I'd get backlash, like 'You're just going to party all the time,' but my mom was cool about it. She said, 'You're going to make good friends, so make sure you choose the right fraternity for you and focus on what's important.'" Christopher, always supportive, was thrilled that Oliver, who was usually reserved, sometimes to the point of brooding, was putting himself out there, meeting new people, and doing something "kind of crazy" for him. None of their other close friends had gone Greek.

Oliver knew he had made the right choice during his freshman year Work Week. He was cleaning the back parking lot when a brother poked his head out a window and yelled, "My God, what is that smell?"

Geoff, then a sophomore, stuck his head out another window and shouted, "It smells like a used diaper filled with Indian food!"

Oliver laughed. Movies were Oliver's comfort zone, and *Anchorman* was his favorite. He often watched and discussed movies with his parents. When he was stressed, he tried to get to a movie theater, his happy place. Hearing his new brothers quoting *Anchorman* validated his decision not only to become Greek, but, more pointedly, to join PhiEp.

This year, every member of the chapter was working hard to get the four-story house into shape. On Monday, the brothers focused on removing clutter and scrubbing the house clean. Tuesday through Friday, they tackled renovation projects. They repainted and reorganized the bar room at the end of the main hall where the chapter held its parties. They weeded the lawn and planted sod and shrubbery. Today, several brothers and pledges worked in the basement, where they threw out old weight room equipment and prepared to lay down new floorboards.

With a few dozen rooms for about 75 of the chapter's 90 brothers, the PhiEp house was one of the smallest on campus. The freshmen slept in the top-floor "sleeping porch," a common Greek house arrangement in which the pledge class lived in a giant beds-only room to promote bonding. In Oliver's house, each freshman—30 could fit in the porch—kept all his clothes in a dresser in a current brother's room, a directive intended to nudge them to talk to brothers with whom they wouldn't normally interact.

On the main level, the Formal Room resembled a fancy living room, with couches, a big-screen TV, and a piano that several guys could play proficiently. Throughout the school year, brothers would wander in to play anything from Bach to pop. The chapter, which was about 10 percent nonwhite, had a reputation on campus for being offbeat; not the only offbeat house at State U, but definitely the quirkiest. Some chapters called the PhiEps hipsters or intellectuals. Others referred to PhiEp as "the gay fraternity" because several recently graduated brothers and a few younger members were gay or bi. The chapter wore this banner proudly, but the relatively liberal student body wasn't usually the type to use that label pejoratively anyway. PhiEps, who liked to joke that they were "a lower-tier fraternity on the rise," didn't care how people labeled them. Most of State U (apart from a few sororities) was too laid back to put much stock in the rankings. The school's Greek system was relatively healthy, with only a few negative fraternity headlines in the last five years despite thirtysomething historically white national chapters and nearly a dozen BGLO and other fraternities.

Rather than push members to conform to one standard, the State U PhiEps liked to say, "Keep PhiEp weird," which meant "Make sure we have interesting people who have a full range of diversity, and learn to appreciate relationships outside the house, too," Oliver said. PhiEps truly valued that everyone "brings something different to the table." One brother was an accomplished trumpet player who had turned his love of music into an award-winning DJ side gig. Another brother had completed the university's computer science track in only two years. Another was a graphic designer who created artwork for brothers who needed it; he designed the DJ's logo, for example, and was helping Oliver design his first tattoo, based on his Native American clan symbol. One brother was obsessed with *Overwatch,* a video game; a few brothers were passionate about *Star Wars.*

And Oliver, of course, had his superheroes. Now known as "the Batman of the chapter" because of his martial arts skills and dedication to helping people, he had a Batman blanket on his bed, a Superman poster painted by a PhiEp alum on his wall, and an Arrow bobblehead on his nightstand. As a teenager, Oliver had come to love Arrow as much as Batman, "because he's human, he gets to where he is by working hard and being a general badass, and he wants to actually make a difference in every aspect of his life. He's not just going out at night fighting crime, but also striving to make people's lives better as mayor of his city." Oliver had even found a fellow PhiEp who was equally as besotted with superheroes. After first-semester finals freshman year, the two of them spent the day binge-watching every holiday episode of *Arrow* and *The Flash.*

Work Week was an effective way for the brothers to bond and get to know the 28 freshmen who had rushed before non-Greek students had even arrived at school. This year's freshmen reminded

Oliver of his own pledge class: outgoing, bold, and goofy. During these early days before classes began, the PhiEps typically didn't shave. This year's pledges enthusiastically participated in the tradition; there were more exaggerated mustaches in the house than anyone could remember. The only reason Oliver shaved was because of his part-time job as a file clerk at a local law firm, where he felt it would be disrespectful to sport unusual facial hair.

This was the most productive Work Week in recent memory. Every brother pitched in for the good of the house. When Oliver told the guys, "We need your help," they helped, no excuses. Every day, the guys worked from eight or nine in the morning until late afternoon. Then they played dodgeball in the parking lot in front of the house. Dodgeball had been Trey's idea. Trey, the chapter president from two years before, was a large guy with a large personality—a charismatic leader, enthusiastic, passionate, and well-spoken. He was one of the most successful PhiEp chapter presidents in history, having won for State U the national fraternity's most coveted award: the Most Outstanding Chapter Award, which was announced at Phi Epsilon's annual national fraternity conference.

Before school began, Oliver had called him to ask why the chapter ended every Work Week day with dodgeball. Trey said, "It's a little something to boost morale, to bring the house together. It's an icebreaker for the new freshmen and a fun way to show them we know how to have a good time. It's a small thing, but it brings people together and shows them we're not all about drinking."

As Oliver asked a bunch of guys to help him rip out the old, nasty carpet in the basement, he marveled at how he had gotten to this point. Near the end of Oliver's freshman year, his pledge class had held a meeting to discuss their goals for the house. The pledge class resembled the rising seniors, the group of devoted guys who had supervised their rush and pledge processes. These brothers were nothing like the rising juniors between them. As one of the rising seniors had explained to Oliver's class, there are horses and there are carts. "You can either be a horse that's pulling everything along or the cart that's being pulled," he said. Oliver's class fell into the horse category, "constantly working toward a better tomorrow," as Oliver put it. (In conversations about fraternity life, he often reverted to clichés, like a pro athlete giving a postgame interview.) The rising juniors were mostly carts. Heavy carts.

When the older brothers refused to handle responsibilities, with excuses such as "I already paid my dues," Oliver's class lost faith in them. It wasn't uncommon for older students to begin to distance themselves from their fraternity. But too many rising juniors didn't seem to embrace the values of the brotherhood as wholeheartedly as Oliver's class did.

This was why, at his rising sophomore pledge class meeting, Oliver's class decided to nominate an all-sophomore slate for the Executive Council (EC) officer elections. With an all-sophomore lineup, they, rather than the apathetic juniors, would be the role models for the incoming pledges. They wanted to show the pledges that, as Oliver put it, "the hard work never stops."

The rising seniors had reminded them throughout the year that everyone in the house had the ability to make a difference. "We were very inspired by them. Sure, some of them could be idiots, but they all embodied the values that make a good PhiEp. They were loyal, really supported community service, academics, and leadership, and valued individuality," Oliver told me. "We wanted to not only strive to do what they did, but to be better. An all-sophomore EC hadn't been done before."

One of Oliver's friends turned to him. "You should run for president, Oliver. It's probably not something you were thinking about, but you'd do a great job." Other pledge brothers agreed.

"Hey, thanks. That's nice of you to say," Oliver said. "I'll think about it." However cool it would feel to be chapter president—and as a sophomore, which was practically unheard of—he was daunted by the prospect that most of the brothers would be older than him. He didn't think it could actually happen, anyway. He was too young for the position and didn't have experience in leadership roles other than as a member of the chapter's Judicial Board, which consisted of two delegates from each class who assigned punishments when members were accused of various infractions. Compared to the current president—and even more, compared to Trey—Oliver was drastically underqualified. Besides, he told a friend, "I'm not a forefront, leading-the-charge type of guy. I'm not a vocal leader; more 'lead by example.'" He had expected that as a junior he'd run for pledge trainer: the brother who helped the pledges navigate their first 10 weeks, teaching them about the fraternity's values and about the type of men the fraternity hoped they'd become. He wanted to be in an older brother role, "building close personal relationships, guiding people through their struggles, and helping out as much as I can."

When Oliver's pledge brothers continued to push him to run, he sought out Diego for advice. Diego, now a senior, was the person Oliver most admired in the house. The pledge trainer for Oliver's class, Diego was the most driven, dedicated person Oliver knew, and one of the best leaders. He was a hard-ass, but he pushed the freshmen to handle their responsibilities, not because their pledge trainer told them to, but because they wanted to be good people. When pledges missed a chore or skipped a party, Diego often talked about efficient use of time. He'd say, "Everyone else has done it. I've done it. It's possible. You just need to manage your time correctly. Sure, it's going to be hard, but you can do it. You just work at it."

Diego's pep talks resonated with Oliver because Diego motivated people in a way that wasn't warm and fuzzy but still earned their respect. "He had very clear expectations. There's no reason you shouldn't be able to do whatever task," Oliver told me. "He has a similar opinion as me on mental toughness, the idea that I'm not going to stop before I accomplish this task and do it really damn well. I'm not making excuses. If you have to stay up all night, then you do. One of my favorite quotes I always listened to before wrestling matches was a speech about mental toughness. It said, if you don't want to wake up early and work out, then you need to wake up early and work out. Doing things you don't want to do that are hard—that's how you build a mentally strong person."

Oliver and Diego had become close that year. Diego was the brother Oliver went to for advice and serious conversations—about girls, partying, time management. Diego was an ROTC member, fit and strong, positive and inspiring, and Oliver's favorite workout buddy. By trying to keep up with Diego in the gym, Oliver had thrown up more times during workouts than he had because of drinking.

Diego told Oliver that the presidency would be time-consuming and difficult, especially because he was younger than most of the brothers. He would also have to give up much of the fun during parties because he would be responsible for the brotherhood. "It will be really important for you to manage your time right and stick up for what you believe in," Diego said. "I trust you. I think you should go for it. The worst that could happen is you don't win, and you go back to where you are right now. So you might as well try."

While not all the sophomore nominees won the election, Oliver became the first sophomore chapter president in recent house memory. When he was elected, he announced that his goal was for the chapter to be so successful that it would win the Most Outstanding Chapter Award. Oliver set this objective because the award was the highest recognition he could aim for, and if under his command the chapter won it, he could prove that young officers could be just as effective as older ones, that the Greek hierarchy didn't have to depend on age, and, more personally, that a quirky introvert could learn to be an influential leader like Trey. Immediately, the doubters spoke up. The brothers didn't think they could win the award again so quickly. Some of them privately voiced concerns that Oliver was too young to be president, and that the juniors would walk all over him. He wasn't Trey.

Trey's were big shoes to fill. Now Oliver was still trying to adapt to the challenges of balancing his social life, academics, fraternity life, and presidential duties. And as Oliver looked around at the 18-year-old pledges cheerfully helping him roll up the carpet, he was still struck by the enormity of the responsibility for the safety, academics, and success of the 90 college boys under his command. He desperately wanted to take good care of the pledges and to do his brothers proud. But how could an inexperienced leader accomplish even that at 19 years old? And what did it take to be a fraternity leader in the first place?

How Fraternities Became Dominant in American Culture

Ben was a college junior when he and his roommate, aided by alumni, petitioned the headquarters of a major national fraternity to found a chapter on his South Carolina campus in the 2010s. Ben hadn't rushed his school's existing fraternities because, as a football player, he had been hazed and didn't want to risk going through that again. But he was drawn to the idea of a close brotherhood and, he said, "I liked the idea of leaving the place a little better by building something shaped differently, to show you don't have to follow a single narrative to build respect for a fraternity, like: 'If you don't throw the best parties and have relationships with the best sororities, you're going to fail.'"

Ben spent endless hours filling out paperwork and navigating college bureaucracy, then recruited 19 guys to form a "colony," or conditional chapter. The group got together for a heart-to-heart about what they wanted out of the fraternity. The answer they settled on was "shared experiences that can give a foundation for lifelong friendship." Instead of hazing, the group designed events at which members would have to collaborate to solve a problem or achieve a goal. They planned to encourage brothers from disparate backgrounds to "learn about each other and learn to trust each other, a foundation to help them through the rest of college and even their lives," Ben said.

Ben, who eventually graduated summa cum laude, told administrators that his chapter would be the antithesis of stereotypical "frat bro" culture. "My reputation, my academics, and my career are on the line," he told them. "I'm giving you my word: If something goes wrong, I get in trouble." He successfully convinced university authorities and fraternity officials that his chapter would be a positive addition to campus life.

Convincing the students was another story.

College in the 1700s and early 1800s was an austere life of prayer, recitation, and study, with dull drills intended to train students to become ministers, though many students would not follow that path. At the turn of the eighteenth century, wealthy families increasingly began sending their sons to college. These students did not take well to the strict regimen.

The resulting uprisings at most colleges led to high expulsion rates; in 1806, Princeton expelled more than half its students. To deter students from rioting, college presidents agreed not to admit students who had been expelled from other schools. The only exception was Eliphalet Nott, the president of Union College, who accepted the protesters. Interestingly, the five former members of an organized military company who in 1825 formed the Kappa Alpha Society, the first social fraternity, were seniors at Union College.

Originally, students formed fraternities not only for the camaraderie, but also to assert their independence from college administrators and professors whose rigid discipline left little time for socializing. Colleges typically had nonexclusive student-run literary societies that encouraged reading, debates, and speaking competitions. Fraternities distinguished themselves from other college clubs with their secrecy, exclusivity, and (something non-Greek campus secret societies didn't have) ties to chapters at other schools. They used Greek letters because the students, who studied Greek, believed the names made them seem more elite. Their secret passwords, handshakes, and rivalries mimicked the secret clubs many students had formed as young boys.

But fraternities were much more meaningful to their members than childhood clubs. College students were younger then than they are now; they were teenagers when they graduated. As fraternity brothers, they turned to one another to form a surrogate family. Members got together frequently for meals and trips into town. They swore initiation oaths to treat brothers with kindness and goodwill. By the mid-1800s, nearly every college campus in New England and the Mid-Atlantic had a Greek-lettered fraternity chapter, and some had spread to the South and the Midwest. Members were white and Protestant.

Fraternities' priorities and activities both followed and represented the standards of masculinity at the time, according to historian Nicholas Syrett. In the mid-1800s, when public speaking skills were considered a demonstration of manliness—literary societies battled each other in debate competitions—fraternities, too, engaged their members in debates. Fraternity brothers met to prepare for careers other than the ministry and to talk about subjects their professors didn't teach them. Modeled after the literary societies, fraternities required members to write and present essays, perform extemporaneous speaking, and/or discuss literary works. To be manly was to set oneself apart from boys; fraternities emphasized autonomy, confidence, and intelligence, without appearing too studious, as manliness also entailed a disregard for college rules.

Thus, from the very beginning of Greek life, members who wished to embody the Fraternity Man had to grapple with competing ideas of masculinity. Much as today's fraternity brothers attempt to balance the warring images of beer-soaked partiers and upstanding gentlemen, boys at the dawn of fraternities had to walk the fine line between succeeding in an academic system that prized rules and appearing to rebel against those rules.

Fraternities' very existence as secret societies violated college protocol, a deliberate rebellion against school administrators, who unsuccessfully tried to shut them down. By joining an organization that most colleges outlawed, students asserted their independence and, by extension, their masculinity, defying the faculty that treated them like children. Sometimes their meetings included drinking, smoking, and profanity.

After the Civil War, as the United States found industrial success, "manliness" in college also came to signify money. Fraternities sought to recruit wealthy students who could afford expensive clothes, travel, and entertainment, and who presumably could help fund the fraternity houses that rising numbers of Greek alums and actives (current brothers) were building. Alumni of these now-national organizations gave preferential treatment to members seeking jobs. They expanded this early professional network with national conventions, alumni associations, fraternity magazines, and directories. By the late 1800s, fraternities were of such widespread interest that major newspapers covered fraternity conventions, including their elections and delegates' names. Competition for recruits was so intense that the groups developed strict rushing and pledging rules. At some schools, students began to rank fraternities by their wealth.

In the early 1900s, to gain prestige and respect at college, students were expected to excel at sports and other extracurricular activities. Fraternities duly shifted to prioritize athletes during recruitment. Rather than requiring debates and literary exercises, chapters focused on parties and other social events. Fraternities used their recruitment strategies and connections to dominate college politics, athletics, activities, and honors, ensuring that brothers remained the Big Men on Campus. By the 1920s, fraternities flourished even in Canada, with 42 chapters at the University of Toronto and 23 at McGill. In the United States, 11.74 percent of male college students at traditional four-year colleges belonged to a fraternity, a figure that included students at colleges that had no Greek system.

As networking became more valuable to a man's prospects than grades, fraternities, having founded powerful networks decades earlier, were well situated to place brothers in leadership roles. Members reached prestigious, powerful positions in US politics, business, medicine, and law, where "fraternity masculinity has set standards for life beyond the college campus," Syrett wrote in his 2009 history *The Company He Keeps*. To retain their high status and elevate their members in society, these white Protestant groups took pains to keep others out of the network. As colleges diversified their student populations, fraternities added clauses to their charters that excluded nonwhites, Catholics, and Jews.

If they had the means, students who were excluded from one fraternity started a new one. Students at what's now DePauw University formed the first university Greek-letter fraternity for women in 1870. The first Catholic fraternity was founded in 1889, the first fraternity founded by Jewish students in 1895, the first Chinese fraternity in 1916, and the first Latino fraternity in 1931. Special-interest fraternities sprouted as well, such as Phi Mu Alpha Sinfonia, a music fraternity (1898), and Alpha Kappa Psi (1904) and Delta Sigma Pi (1907), now coed business fraternities. Alpha Phi Alpha, the first intercollegiate black fraternity, was founded in 1906, beginning the formation of the Divine Nine, a group of five African American fraternities and four sororities.

When fraternities were founded, they didn't focus on women at all. Even when women were first admitted to the larger universities, fraternity members refused to interact with them. But as increasing numbers of women enrolled in college in the 1920s, masculinity came to be defined in opposition to femininity and, by extension, homosexuality. Because fraternity brothers lived, ate, and slept together in close quarters, outsiders began speculating that fraternities were dens of homosexuality. To prove they weren't gay (though some were), members loudly boasted about their dating lives and heterosexual conquests. This reaction fundamentally changed the nature of fraternities: Chapters sought to recruit students who were popular with women, and members gauged their masculinity—now associated with power, aggression, and heterosexuality—by their ability to seduce women.

Fraternity members weren't the only students treating young women like sexual objects and pressuring them to perform. But fraternity brothers were more successful with girls than the typical college guy; they were more sexually active and the most popular campus dates, thanks to their unsupervised, private houses; their access to money for entertainment, alcohol, and cars; and, most notably, their status. "A college man who did not belong to a fraternity was not regarded as quite as collegiate as his Greek peer," Syrett wrote. "The pressure to belong was thus felt not only on campus but also at home from families, friends, and perhaps former high school classmates. Local and national newspapers annually published the names of the men who had been selected for fraternity membership. . . . The young man who returned home at Christmas of his first year at college without a fraternity pin on his lapel often did so under a cloud of disgrace."

The 1920s were a particularly influential time for fraternity dominance, considering that many colleges doubled their enrollments during that decade. The media glorified college students as if they were celebrities. Historian Beth Bailey noted, "While their numbers were relatively small, the doings of college youth carried much symbolic weight with adults and their nonstudent peers, who viewed youth culture sometimes with suspicion, sometimes with envy, almost always with fascination." The public considered fraternity men to be the most glamorous students of all.

This focus on prestige spawned a practice that I believe is a major reason that many fraternities today are unfairly stigmatized—and why the media and the public mischaracterize the good chapters with the misbehavior of the bad chapters. As fraternities became a new shorthand for this kind of status, Greeks became obsessed with finding partners who wouldn't bring them down. In what Willard Waller, a prominent sociologist at the time, called the "Rating and Dating Complex," students rated members of the opposite sex on their appearance, fraternity or sorority membership, wealth, and extracurricular participation. "Members of leading fraternities are especially desirable dates; those who belong to fraternities with less prestige are correspondingly less desirable," Waller wrote. Female students "wonder to what degree they are discussed and are constantly afraid of being placed on the black list of the fraternities."

Brothers in the top-ranked fraternities dated the girls from the top-ranked sororities, and so forth, particularly in state universities with a thriving fraternity system. Social psychologist J. K. Folsom, Waller's contemporary, observed that women who wanted to "retain Class A standing" had to consistently date Class A men. "The fraternities and sororities apply considerable pressure to the 'dating' of their members. One gets merits, whether formally recorded or not, for dating with a coed of a high-ranking fraternity, demerits for association with a non-fraternity person."

By the end of World War II, when increasingly visible gay communities were accused of Communist connections, members of all-male groups drew suspicion, which likely increased sexual aggression on campus, Syrett wrote. "In order to prove themselves as men, many fraternity men were increasingly forcing themselves on their female classmates."

Meanwhile, though many undergraduates were willing to admit minorities, fraternity alums, accustomed to defining their identity by what they were not (boys, feminine, gay), resisted. Even when in the 1960s the Civil Rights Act required universities receiving public funds to desegregate, some national fraternities continued their discriminatory policies. Others changed the language in their charters, but privately ordered active members to admit whites only, an unofficial mandate that, for some Greek groups, lingered even into the twenty-first century. By 1970, fraternity membership had dwindled to only 4.8 percent of male students.

Then *Animal House* changed everything.

The movie, screenwriter Chris Miller's 1978 sex-and-drinking fictionalization of his Dartmouth fraternity days, led to a major comeback for fraternities. Many students came to college expecting to party hard. The alcohol industry "saw an opportunity and aggressively ramped up marketing on campus," said Lisa Wade, author of *American Hookup*. "They started advertising in school newspapers, erecting massive inflatable beer cans at sporting events, promoting drink specials at nearby bars and clubs, and hiring students as representatives of their brands to give beer away for free. They spent millions in the 1980s to convince students that 'it's naturally part of college life to drink.'"

In 1984, when the legal drinking age was raised to 21, underage students moved their partying from bars to private houses, which changed the Greek experience profoundly. Now that fraternities had disproportionate control over the college party scene, they played an even more dominant role on campus. By the early 1990s, 86 percent of fraternity brothers were binge-drinking.

The late twentieth century also saw the proliferation of many new fraternities, such as ethnic, multicultural, gay, religious, and coed fraternities. Delta Lambda Phi, a fraternity for gay, bisexual, transgender, and progressive men, formed in 1986 and is welcomed as an equal member of the IFC at many schools.

If the first college fraternities sought to provide a support network for boys at universities underprepared to meet the needs of a new wave of students, today's BGLOs and Latino Greek-letter organizations (LGLOs) are serving the same purpose. The widening gap in graduation rates between white and minority students can be partly attributed to inadequate university guidance and support. Most ethnic and culturally based fraternities, which can help to fill that gap, do not have the resources of predominantly white NIC fraternities, which often have relatively large membership numbers, private fraternity houses, a gender-specific Greek council, and wealthy alumni. But their brotherhoods nevertheless are sound.

Today, approximately 13 percent of male students enrolled full time in all public, private, and nonprofit four-year colleges—including those that do not have Greek systems—are social or cultural fraternity members. Studies show that Greeks tend to have a higher social status on campus than non-Greek students and continue to wield more power. Researchers have called fraternity houses "socialization sites," where new freshmen "observe the behavior of upperclassmen and learn what is normative on campus." Members are still more likely to be white, wealthy, and conservative than the rest of the student body, signs of privilege that partially explain these institutions' success in the political and business arenas. Predominantly white fraternities and sororities own at least three billion dollars in college student housing and manage several hundred million dollars in annual revenue and foundation assets.

And among current Greeks, the ranking system, an objectifying tradition so powerful that it is the driving force behind most of the damaging elements of Greek life, has a stronger hold on students than ever before.

Fraternities and sororities, it turns out, never completely abandoned the rating-and-dating complex of the 1920s. For many reasons, the tier system not only thrives on today's campuses, but also often dictates a fraternity's behavior, parties, and recruitment strategies and success. (Recruitment processes vary greatly by campus.) "There's pressure to be in higher tiers," said a recent Delaware brother. "Sororities and fraternities took the lunch table concept of high school and built houses on top of them: Jocks in one fraternity, hipsters in one, nerds in one." In this era in which teenagers are pressured to overachieve, students place even more weight on perceived prestige. Much as the *U.S. News & World Report* college rankings disastrously skewed the education landscape, Greek rankings have sent many fraternity and sorority members into a dangerous frenzy.

"The idea of tiers is one of the more destructive things that fraternities and sororities face. When I was an undergraduate, we were obsessed with what other fraternities and sororities thought of us. If we'd used a fraction of that energy on something more productive, we could've made such a difference in the campus community," said Nathan Holic, a University of Central Florida chapter faculty advisor and former national fraternity leadership consultant. "A chapter officer [just] vented to me about this very issue, how much time his brothers were wasting by trying to become a more popular fraternity in the eyes of the Greek community. It broke my heart then, and it breaks my heart now. These men should be thinking, first and foremost, about who they are, and about what they want to be, and why it matters. That identity shouldn't be determined by some sort of tier system that, once they reach a certain step in the ladder, suddenly bestows upon them value and importance."

Rising attention to social media and ranking apps and websites have made students on many campuses hyperaware of a chapter's tier. Even if students take Greekrank.com and the popular TotalFrat Move.com (TFM) with a grain of salt, they are still influenced by the content. Not unlike the media's glorification of youth culture in the 1920s, today's social media glamorizes Greeks, separating the haves from the have-nots with prominent group photos emphasizing who belongs where, further delineating tiers with posts, pictures, and videos of their parties, houses, functions, and friends. Just as the college rankings have stripped schools down to names, numbers, and scores, so, too, has the tier system reduced fraternity boys to their wealth, alcohol supply, and looks.

Sororities' tiers are often determined by how attractive the sisters are and how willing they are to party. Fraternities are ranked by "looks, partying hard, money, and hookups," a Florida sophomore said. "A big factor of top tiers is the parties they throw."

On some campuses, fraternity tiers are determined by the size of a chapter. The more members, the more money. "This money can be used to make the house nicer or bigger, [for] large donations in sorority [fundraising] competitions, larger and more attractive recruitment events, which bring in more members, and of course, larger and more parties," said Teddy, an Oregon junior. "Competitions often pair houses, and the houses that win tend to be large and powerful. So it's important, as a middle-tier house, for us to associate with higher-tier houses. And alumni take great interest in the house's power and recognition on campus, so they'll donate and help the house much more, ironically, when the house demonstrates it doesn't need it."

Many Greeks are taught that the higher your tier, the more likely that opposite-gender chapters will interact with you, and the more impressive your social schedule, the more attractive your chapter will be to recruits. Because fraternities' tiers can depend on how often and which sororities interact with them, and vice versa, developing a relationship with a higher-tier group can improve a chapter's rank. Campus status can be all-consuming because, as a sorority advisor explained, "Everything in Greek life deals with which chapters hang out with each other because that determines the tiers, and the tiers ultimately decide how well chapters do in recruitment and their reputation on campus."

The emphasis on tiers depends on the campus. Some campuses, such as Oliver's, are more laid back. A recent graduate of a top-tier Washington, DC, fraternity, by contrast, said that when his brothers were invited to lower-tier sorority formals, they'd worry about what the rest of the Greek system would think. Greeks gossiped in perplexed amazement when a sorority sister dated a member of a lower-tier fraternity, he said. And when he visited a Georgia chapter of his fraternity, his friends questioned, "Why are you visiting that chapter? It's middle-tier there. The party will be better at one of the top-tier chapters." The brother explained to me, "Everyone's competing for recruits. To put it one way, there's not much difference between Yale and Harvard, but when you drop off to the eighteenth-ranked school, that's an issue."

When Ben founded his South Carolina chapter, the students' tier system was his most difficult obstacle. He had diverged from the status quo by promoting collaboration within the chapter rather than hierarchy; also, nearly a quarter of his first pledge class were minorities, which was unusual on his campus. "It's very important: Are you considered first tier, second tier, or third tier? When your fraternity can only throw four or five big social events a year, you need a reputation to get people to come to those in the first place," he said.

Ben's new chapter even had trouble scheduling philanthropy events. "Philanthropy can be hard because you need other fraternities and sororities to participate in your event. The other fraternities knew the more events they participated in, the more prestige that would give me and that could potentially negatively affect them. Unless I had close personal relationships with people in the chapter, other fraternities were very unwilling to help. It was no secret: They were trying to say their fraternity was better because they were more established."

Consequently, Ben worked hard to encourage his brothers to charm sorority sisters. "I pushed a lot. I'd sit back and critique how our members would interact with women. If I saw something disrespectful, I'd intervene. If someone was hanging back or too scared to talk to anybody, I'd help that person engage." But sorority social chairs continually rejected the chapter's invitations to cohost mixers and other events until another fraternity was kicked off campus and Ben's chapter moved into its house, which was near the football stadium. "That's when we were finally able to get a higher-tier fraternity to partner with us, because they wanted the prime location for tailgates. The petty politics!" Ben said.

One Maryland school is so caught up in the rankings that stories circulate about sorority sisters sleeping with top-tier fraternity brothers "just so they can say they fucked a Kappa Tau," a junior said. Once, when his lower-middle-tier chapter was partnered with a top-tier fraternity and a top-tier sorority for a function, he initiated a conversation with a sister. "What fraternity are you in?" she asked. He answered. "And she just turned and walked away!" he told me. "Half the girls did that to our guys! They only wanted to talk to guys in the top-tier fraternity."

Because the public is inundated with images and headlines from the biggest or most well-known chapters, the top tiers, the holdovers from the rating-and-dating era, we assume their behavior represents all fraternity chapters. It doesn't. Not all chapters are consumed by the rankings. And I'd argue that those chapters that, like Oliver's, aren't willing to push for higher status at all costs are often the most supportive and the least toxic.

So we don't necessarily hear much about the brothers who are in the system for the right reasons, or about the brothers who choose to associate with people because of their character rather than their tier. Teddy works as a paid houseboy at a sorority house, where he washes dishes, mops floors and performs other janitorial work, occasionally assists the house chef, and buses tables during formal dinners. The sorority is a lower-middle-tier chapter on an Oregon campus that ranks sororities by their looks, "but I think of them as a top-tier sorority because their members are kind and courteous. They are always friendly to anyone. I wanted to work there for a reason," he said.

The difference between tiers on some campuses is akin to the difference between being liked and being "popular." Studies have shown that among students, popularity equates with visibility rather than likeability. Similarly, top-tier fraternities may be the most visible chapters on campus, but they're often not the most liked. Indeed, every sorority sister I asked told me that at their school, the fraternity chapters with the nicest, most respectful guys are middle- to bottom-tier groups.

Social media plays a major role in perpetuating the tier system. Not only do social media sites punctuate Greeks' status, but also fraternity members who engage in inappropriate, boneheaded, or criminal activities are more likely to be caught. Each publicized instance adds to the country's general impression of fraternities. And the posts most likely to gain traction, the ones that will be the most visible, are not the posts made by low-status chapters, which might address more positive activities.

By connecting people remotely, social media has also increased a feeling of disconnectedness among teenagers. It is particularly hard for boys to make friends, harder still to find intimacy among a large group of guys. Many fraternities continue to offer a cozy environment in which boys can share confidences, seek comfort, find help, and feel heard. "I wish people would understand that it's not just a drinking club or 'paying for your friends.' Our house was a place for guys to escape the stress of college or real life," a recent Pennsylvania grad told me. His NIC chapter had members who were black, Hispanic, Korean, Syrian, Indian, gay, straight, and bisexual. "Sure, people drank, but most of the time it was a place for brothers to just relax, hang out, play Xbox, talk about the week, complain about their girlfriends or roommates, and study. Where freshmen could escape dorm life, almost like a sanctuary, with no judgments or prejudices."

Just as the first fraternity brothers, in a new setting a long way from home, sought a surrogate family at school, so, too, are many of today's young men drawn to a group that's so devoted that its members swear oaths to support one another. Fraternities exist, faculty advisor Nathan Holic told me, "to give young men a sense of family and community as they start their new lives in a place far from their own homes and families. A lot of them become something worse, but there are so many of them that simply serve that essential need." He said, "Too many national fraternities overwhelm their members with programming, and the fraternities become something other than what the members first wanted. And too many of the undergraduate members romanticize the past. They binge-drink and haze, all to make it like it was. But it doesn't ever need to be like that. Every time there's a new movie about a college party or fraternity party, students aspire to that lifestyle. The movies are reflecting what is happening, quite often. But then real life imitates the cinematic portrayals, too. It's a cycle that feeds on itself."

Yes, the system must reform, in several ways, and soon. Yes, many chapters should be shut down because they've shown they can't escape the grip of a long-standing culture steeped in prejudice and vice. But perhaps we should not automatically deny all boys— those in earnest chapters that don't care about tiers; close-knit houses that treat people right; companionable chapters providing safe spaces that enthusiastically welcome boys of all types—the opportunity to experience the intimacy that is the secret life of college brotherhoods.

Ω Ω Ω

On the last night of recruitment, Jake spent the hour before the rush parties nervously pacing his dorm room and sprucing himself up. Instead of wearing the unofficial rush uniform of a polo shirt and shorts, he wore a button-down shirt, slacks, and nice dress shoes. *Yeesh, it feels like I'm rushing a sorority, trying to make myself look nice,* he thought.

As he walked to the Zeta Kappa house, he reviewed his game plan. If Zeta Kappa didn't give him a bid, he would go to Phi Rho, MZN, and Omega Phi, in that order. If he didn't get any bids, he resolved, "I'll figure out what I can change over the next few months, and rush again in the spring." It was hardly consolation that Arjun, whom he had managed to check in with once this week, hadn't yet received a bid, either. Arjun had rushed only top-tier fraternities.

Jake took a deep breath as he walked alone through the Zeta Kappa pillars. As soon as he stepped inside the door, a few brothers greeted him. "Hey, what's up, man!" "Glad to see you again."

"Glad to be back!" Jake replied.

He served himself a plate of food and sat down at a table between two freshmen who had already accepted bids. "Man, it's Wednesday, and Zeta Kappa already has more than 40 guys in their pledge class," one freshman said. "I feel bad for people who don't have bids because if it doesn't work out today, they're done." Jake didn't mention that he was the only person at the table who had not received any bids.

Shawn, an older brother, interrupted the conversation. "Hey, Jake, good to see you again. You want to come with me?"

Shawn led him toward the front door. *Oh God no, please don't let this be like K-Tau,* Jake worried. But Shawn walked past the door and led Jake upstairs to the library, a well-appointed room with mahogany bookshelves and several tables. Andy, the chapter president, sat at the head of a table between two other brothers; all three wore formal suits.

"Hey, Jake, I guess you can kinda figure out what's going on here, but we'd like to ask you a few questions first," Andy said. "First question: A fraternity is a two-way street. Anyone who joins will receive a lot of benefits from us. We would like to know what we will receive from you."

Jake told the brothers he would be an involved member of the fraternity, that he wanted to work hard for their philanthropy and join the student government, where he could be an advocate for Greek life.

"Good answer," one of the brothers said. "Second question: What does a brotherhood mean to you?"

"Trust," Jake said. "I'd want to demonstrate to my brothers that I'm a trustworthy person, and vice versa. I believe this is the foundation of creating brotherhood and family."

"Okay," Andy said. "Here's the final question."

Jake exhaled. *Make-it-or-break-it time,* he thought.

Andy pointed to the brothers next to him. "Okay, Jake: Fuck, marry, or kill?" The brothers cracked up.

Jake pointed to the brothers in order, left to right: "Okay. Fuck you, marry you, and kill you."

"Yeah!" the fucked brother cheered. "Three for four! I'm three for four!"

"We thought you had good answers," Andy said. "These questions were just to make us certain this is the right decision on our part. As you may have guessed, we would like to extend a bid to you. You can decide to accept now or hold it until tomorrow night." He handed Jake a piece of cardstock. *It's personally signed and everything! It has my name on it!* Jake thought, giddy.

"I'm honored," he said. He was strongly tempted to take part in a bid acceptance tradition, running through the house, feted by brothers. But the week had been such a whirlwind that he thought he should hold on to the bid and "think about what I'm getting myself into, just in case," he told me later. "Mainly to take a step back, sleep on it, and decide whether, after all this, I really want to dedicate four years of my life to a fraternity."

"I'm going to hold it," he told them.

"That's fine," Shawn said. "Are you coming to our Bid Dinner tomorrow? That's the time when you'd formally accept the bid."

"I'll definitely come to a decision by then," Jake answered.

"Great," the brother said. "Do you have a date?"

Jake thought he was joking. "Uh, nope." Having spent all his time this week with fraternities, he hadn't even properly met any girls.

The brother explained that Zeta Kappa hoped to match each pledge with a sorority girl for the dinner. "Hey, you want me to ask this girl I know if she would be interested in matching up with you?" he asked.

This was happening too fast. "Yeah, sure, okay!" Jake said. The brother sent a text as Jake started to leave the room, thanking the Zeta Kappas on his way out.

"She's busy, but we'll work on it," the brother called to Jake. From the hallway, Jake could hear the brothers listing other sorority sisters, debating their looks.

The moment Jake came back downstairs, brothers congratulated him, clapping him on the back. The recruitment chair gathered together Jake and a few other freshmen. "So we'll see you tomorrow," he told them. "And then Saturday we're throwing a huge party. There are going to be a hundred and fifty girls here, and it's going to be insane."

Another brother snorted. "Oh—and say goodbye to your liver."

That night, Jake was the happiest he'd been since starting college. "I feel so great. I'm on such a high right now!" he told me when he got back to his dorm. "I finally don't have to worry about the possibility of not getting a bid. It's this enormous weight off my shoulders. It's been a crazy experience. Just, like, think about this: What if I told you that at college there's a program where for a week you're meeting several hundred guys and everything you say and do is judged. And some guys are impressive enough to receive a secret paper to join a secret club that revolves around letters. Taken out of context, it's just such a weird concept."

At the same time, he was disenchanted by the all-consuming whirlwind of Rush Week. Because he'd spent so much time rushing, he'd missed the deadlines for other extracurriculars he'd hoped to join, including the literary magazine. "I really hate the whole process. It's been brutal. It's good in some aspects of meeting people, but I have to catch up on so much homework," he said. "It sucks how it's taken such a toll on me. And my emotions! This has been one giant emotional roller coaster. Sunday was one of the worst days I had in a while, and today was one of the best. High school was like a consistent 'eh.' In college, the highs are higher and the lows are lower."

He had no inkling that Rush would turn out to be one of the easiest, and least dangerous, weeks of the semester.

CHAPTER 2

House and Hierarchy:
What Happens Behind Closed Doors

JAKE'S FIRST OFFICIAL fraternity function was not what he envisioned. He showed up alone, in a formal suit as instructed, expecting to be seated for a couples' dinner for which he did not have a date because the brothers hadn't found him one. Instead, he awkwardly stood in the foyer, overhearing guys and their dates partying in the bedrooms.

Within minutes, a brother swooped in and brought him upstairs, explaining that Zeta Kappas pregamed everything, including dinner, and that Jake was the last freshman to arrive. The two-hour pregame (or preparty) would be followed by dinner and a trip to a club. Only one other pledge besides Jake didn't have a date, but that was no big deal, the brother told him. He didn't need a date to drink. The Zeta Kappas were spread out among bedrooms, avoiding front windows to drink unseen. Jake's heart raced. *A big drinking night already? No one warned me. I'm not ready for this.*

As the brother led him down a hallway, Jake saw hordes of people squeezed into bedrooms, drinking hard liquor. Everyone seemed wasted already. The brother deposited Jake in a room where Shawn drunkenly waved a bottle of tequila. "Hey, you fucking killed me yesterday!" Shawn exclaimed. "You gotta drink up for that!" He poured Jake a shot.

Jake wasn't sure how to do a shot. He tried to sip it, but Shawn steeply tilted the glass into Jake's mouth. Shawn made sure Jake downed every drop and then poured him a second shot. The tequila burned. When Jake finished the shot, Shawn gave him a thumbs-up.

Jake, who hadn't eaten, felt the effects quickly. He stumbled into another bedroom to join a group of fellow pledges with their dates. He tried to sober up by talking to them, but brothers kept stopping in with bottles of whiskey, rum, or vodka, and ordering the pledges to take a pull.

Jake spent much of the evening talking to Ty, one of the less extroverted pledges, whose date had gotten sick and left early. Jake thought Ty didn't look like a fraternity brother any more than he did; he didn't have that cool, effortless vibe that so many brothers projected. Jake liked him immediately. He suggested they look out for each other, "to make sure we both don't get so shitfaced that we pass out before the club."

Jake was chatting amiably with Ty when Grant, the chapter steward, came into the room with another brother. "Pledges!" Grant cackled. "I love making pledges drink!"

This guy creeps me out, Jake thought. Grant held a dark bottle first to Ty's lips and then Jake's. "Take a three-second pull!" Grant demanded. As the boys drank, Grant bragged, "I'm staying sober so I can watch everyone else get drunk."

Jake could barely walk straight as it was. Worried he would black out, he tried to fool the brothers. He held the bottle as if he were chugging, but took only occasional sips, blocking the aperture with his tongue. He fake-drank for five seconds instead of three.

"Yeah, man, I respect that," Grant said.

"Nice job," said the other brother. They insisted that Ty drink again, this time for five seconds, to match Jake.

"Hey, look, even though I'm making you guys pull this stuff, no brothers are going to make you get to the point where you're going to vomit," Grant assured them.

Jake was consoled by this. He said to me later, "I appreciated that because it gave me some idea like, okay, these guys want to get us shitfaced, but it isn't to torture us. It's just all in good fun to celebrate so we can feel really good tonight, like them." At the same time, he added, "But as I was drinking, I felt my liver aching, and I knew *Oh God, it's falling apart the more time I spend here.*"

As the group finally gathered in the dining room, Ty brought Jake, the last uncommitted recruit, to Andy, the chapter president. "I'm accepting my bid tonight," Jake said, and gave Andy the paper.

"Congratulations! Enjoy the dinner," Andy said, patting him on the back. Brothers shook Jake's hand. Ty clapped him on the shoulder, and Andy began a speech to welcome the pledge class.

After dinner, as people resumed drinking in the bedrooms, someone passed around a bong. Jake was uncomfortable, but yearning to fit in, he told himself that while he would not smoke, he would at least continue to participate in the drinking. He noticed that brothers weren't targeting the pledges exclusively; they ordered around other brothers, too. The brothers explained that each member had a "BN," which stood for "bond number." The number, their BN for life, was assigned to them at initiation. Brothers with lower BNs, meaning they had been initiated earlier and had seniority, could make demands of those with higher BNs. If an older brother said, "BN!" before issuing a command ("Change the channel!" "Clean that shit up!"), the higher BN was expected to comply. That evening, Jake heard many shouts of "BN: Drink!"

As the night wore on, increasing numbers of pledges passed out on couches and floors. By 1:00 A.M., Jake was drunk enough to forget his fears about drinking. He and Ty headed into the Great Room, where several other guys surrounded a brother playing "Piano Man" on a guitar, sloppily singing along. Jake and Ty swayed and sang, too, so engrossed in this happy, bonding moment—for Jake the best part of the night—that it took them more than five minutes to notice the pledge slumped across the table from them, covered in vomit.

Jake and Ty got on the last bus to the club with mostly older brothers and their dates. Jake had never seen a party bus before. Students sat on cushioned benches or fooled around on stripper poles in the aisle, belting out the words to a sexually explicit song Jake hated that pounded from the bus speakers.

At the club, the bouncer didn't care that Jake had no ID; everyone on the party bus was allowed inside. The club experience itself was anticlimactic. Jake and the other pledges danced halfheartedly while looking over the balcony railing at the main floor, where older brothers danced, drank, and made out with their dates. Occasionally, brothers stopped to congratulate the few pledges who had made it to the club instead of passing out at the house. "Hell, yeah. You were able to hold your liquor!" one brother praised them. "You got through the party. You did well," said another. But other brothers scolded them. "Pledges, you disappointed us because you didn't pass out," said Tanner, a brother who had enthusiastically forced pledges to drink at the house. "Obviously you didn't have enough to drink. When I was a pledge, I woke up in the fucking toilet stall the next morning."

Jake lurched into his dorm room that night thinking, *It's a miracle that I managed to get back to my own dorm. I don't think I should be doing this.*

"I guess that's what you call hazing, when a brother forces a drink on you?" Jake mused to me later. "I guess so. You're in a closed room, and they definitely insist that you drink it. They're not going to let you off until they feel you've had a lot to drink."

The next day, Ty told Jake that his friend in K-Tau had endured a much more difficult first-night "celebration." The K-Tau brothers supposedly had locked the 30-odd pledges into a room, refusing to let them out until they'd finished 200 cans of beer and 30 bottles of vodka. "I am so fucking glad they didn't accept me, because they seem like assholes here at TC," Jake said. "Thank God I dodged that bullet."

Ω Ω Ω

By 10:30, the PhiEp Tuesday night house party was just starting to pick up. About a hundred students were drinking and/or dancing to the music blaring from the speaker at the far end of the bar room. Oliver wasn't sure why State U Greeks traditionally threw parties most Tuesday and Thursday nights. PhiEp's parties were relatively small for State U, with about 200 to 300 attendees. Before the parties, like most fraternities on campus, PhiEps pregamed with a sorority.

PhiEps believed they were one of the most vigilant chapters on campus when it came to risk management. When a party started, usually at 9:30 or 10:00, four sober brothers would take their designated positions, one manning a small window in the front door, one in the Formal Room (a good vantage point from which to view whether students or police officers approached the door), and two at a table just inside the door. The brothers stationed at the table and Formal Room took turns rolling through the bar room every few minutes to make sure guests were safe. In addition, one exec was assigned to "float" at each party. This "sober exec" was tasked with ensuring the party ran smoothly. He monitored guests, assisted with door duty, and escorted police during their occasional party walkthroughs, a routine campus procedure. The PhiEps's strategy worked. Their parties usually didn't get out of control.

The brothers at the door were the gatekeepers who allowed every girl in, without question. Guys had to be on the guest list to enter. The first brothers to text the risk managers their male friends' names got them on the list, up to about 10 to 15 people. The number of non-PhiEp guys was capped because, Oliver said, "it tends to be other guys who have more destructive attitudes. When we have a party with other fraternities, a lot more stuff gets stolen, broken. They have the attitude that they can do whatever they want because it's not their stuff getting ruined."

Every other week, instead of one of their house parties, PhiEp cohosted a larger party with one or more fraternities. At these parties, to which no other guys were invited, the host fraternity hired security while the cohosts paid for the alcohol. PhiEp used funds collected from members' social dues. Because State U fraternities handled all costs, they didn't charge guests a cover. State U required that security guards be present at parties with more than three fraternities; the guards were stationed in the bar room, on the deck, and at points around the house where uninvited guests might sneak in.

Oliver was hanging out in the bar room when another sophomore came to get him: Campus police officers were knocking. Oliver was not the sober exec on duty tonight, but he was the closest officer to the door.

He wasn't fazed. State U required fraternities—as far as Oliver knew, the only campus groups subjected to this rule—to register their parties with the school's Interfraternity Council at least four days in advance of the event by submitting a form detailing the date, time, and expected number of guests. Campus police often stopped by parties to check the bartender's ID and do a walk-through of the party. The campus officers were usually casual about it, sometimes even joking around with the partygoers, and generally giving the PhiEps the benefit of the doubt.

Oliver opened the door. Three police officers stood on the walkway. "Is there a party tonight?" one asked. The door to the bar room was closed, as usual, but there was no mistaking the dance music reverberating down the hall.

"Yes, there is," Oliver answered. "Would you like to do a walk-through?"

"Your party isn't registered," the officer said.

Oliver distinctly remembered signing the registration form the social chairs had given him. "I'm pretty sure I had us signed up," he said.

"Well, you're not," another officer said. "So we're going to have to write you up."

Oliver sighed in frustration. This would not look good for a new, young chapter president. The IFC would notify PhiEp's Alumni Board, and Oliver would have to explain the irresponsibility. *What a pain,* he thought. *It'll look like I'm a clueless idiot.*

"We're going to have to ask you to shut the party down. If you don't, you'll face further violations," the officer continued.

"Okay, I'll take care of that," Oliver said. He wished them a good night.

The officers waited outside as Oliver threaded through oblivious dancers and yanked the speaker plug out of the wall. The partygoers looked at him, perplexed. "Party's over," Oliver said. "Sorry, that's the way it is. Hope you have a good night."

After the inevitable chorus of *Aws*, the guests cleared out, and the brothers bombarded Oliver with questions. "What went down?" "Are we okay?"

Oliver gathered the brothers together so that he would have to explain the situation only once. "Hey, so our party wasn't registered, apparently," he said. "I'm not entirely sure why, and I'll stop by the IFC office tomorrow. For the most part, I think we're going to be fine. It was probably just a mistake in communication, and I'll go figure that out. Stand by for more details."

As the group dispersed for the rest of the night, Oliver pulled aside the two older social chairs. PhiEp traditionally had four social chairs, two older and two younger. The older chairs were supposed to handle event planning while the younger chairs observed them and managed the grunt work. "Hey, when was the form turned in?" Oliver asked. They shrugged. That was the younger chairs' responsibility.

The next day, Oliver walked to the IFC office in the middle of campus. The State U Interfraternity Council included one representative from every historically white chapter. The director was an adult hired by State U. Given that the officers were fraternity brothers, the IFC was relatively lenient, looking out for fellow Greeks as best it could.

"Hey, we had a party registered, but the cops came and said it wasn't," Oliver told the director. "What happened? Did we turn in the form?"

The director tapped his desktop keyboard. "Yeah, you turned it in, but it was a little late, so it didn't get sent to the police in time. Don't worry, I'll go clear it up for you. You at least registered the party."

Back at the house, Oliver found the two younger social chairs. "Hey, why didn't you tell me the form was turned in late?"

"We turned it in the day before the party. Sorry, man. We totally spaced; that's our fault," one said.

"We probably should've told you, but we didn't know when it was due. We thought maybe it was fine, since we got the form in."

"Come on, guys. It's a super-simple, small task. It's not that hard. Just get it done," Oliver said. He added, to soften the blow, "I should have followed through and made sure you were doing what you needed to do." As president, he firmly believed that "pretty much all responsibility falls back on me at the end of the day."

The IFC took care of the issue, PhiEp's Alumni Board was understanding, and Oliver brushed it off, unaware that this was only the beginning of the trouble he'd experience throughout the year—trouble that would jeopardize both his chapter and his health.

Ω Ω Ω

Initially, life as a Zeta Kappa pledge seemed relatively innocuous. The pledges met Greg, their new member educator, or "pledge master," an easygoing guy who usually sported a backward baseball cap. Greg's job would be to guide the freshmen through the 12-week pledge process. He explained that the pledges were expected to attend tailgates and to clean the entire house, an activity that Jake enjoyed because it gave him time to bond with the other pledges, "working together on something other than getting shitfaced." Even when Jake and Ty were assigned to scour the filthy microwave, Jake didn't mind it so much. Ty, who was from Manhattan, was a cheerful, understated guy who didn't seem rattled by anything. The two chatted quietly about their lives before college and how their high school friends had changed in the months since graduation. Jake hadn't heard from his old friends, including Arjun—who hadn't received a fraternity bid—in days.

While Jake gravitated toward Ty and Sebastian, whose Canadian accents intrigued him, he also spent time with other new friends: Jamal, a quiet, genuinely nice guy from Boston; a smart pledge the brothers called Black Sam, to distinguish him from a white brother also named Sam; and Logan, a driven pledge with wavy red hair who looked like Conan O'Brien and who already knew he wanted to be chapter president someday. Not every pledge was endearing, though. Quinn, book smart but lacking common sense, was overexuberant to the point of annoying. And Bryce was a loud, crass freshman who tried to get other pledges to cover his chores. When the pledges were ordered to clean the basement at 5:00 A.M. one day, Bryce was the only one who didn't show.

Before the pledges' first ceremony, Greg gave them a warning: They were not allowed, under any circumstances, to look at the officer sitting to the right of Daniel, the chapter vice president. That was Brother Zeta, or "Z," Greg said, and if pledges were caught looking at or speaking to him, there would be consequences. Jake already found Daniel imposing, with his buzz cut and ever-present Ray-Ban aviators. *Now there's a secret brother who's even more intimidating?* Jake thought.

After leading the pledges through a traditional induction ritual, the officers laid out the rules. The pledges were to keep their fraternity pins on them at all times. Their fraternity activities, including Tuesday pledge meetings and Thursday Education Program sessions (EPs), would be announced on the pledges' Facebook page. To enter the house, pledges had to use the double doors in the backyard and wait downstairs in the basement; they weren't allowed to come through the main entrance. They also weren't allowed in the official chapter room. Pledge meetings would be conducted in the informal chapter room on the second floor.

When pledges tried to peek at Z, brothers scolded, "Don't fucking look at him!" Jake forced himself to stare at the floor for the entire ceremony, except during a brief PowerPoint presentation titled "What to Wear." The officers instructed the pledges to don formal fraternity attire—a full suit and tie and boat shoes—every Tuesday, all day long. (Jake would have to spend a few hundred dollars on blazers and shoes.) On other days, the pledges were expected to wear a collared shirt with khakis. Sneakers could be worn during sports activities, as long as they weren't Vans or Chucks. Also—and this was a tough one for Jake—on no occasion were they permitted to wear cargo shorts.

The list continued: No graphic tees or sleeveless shirts. "I do not want to see a wifebeater in this fraternity! If we see it, we'll cut it off you!" an officer said. No color matching. "It's cool if you want to wear opposite colors on the spectrum, like orange and blue, but if we see two related colors, like blue with violet, we will burn at least one of those items."

"And one more thing," Daniel said. "Everyone has to look well groomed. So all of you with goatees, sideburns, or hair past your collar, shave or trim that shit by Thursday's EP."

Some of the pledges knew that Jake's sideburns were his signature. "Even Jake?" Ty asked.

"Even Jake."

Oh man, Jake thought. In high school, he was well known for his 'burns. His high school friends had constantly told him how much they liked the look; it made him look older, they'd said; it made him look cool. Shaving them would be a big deal. But he didn't object.

At the end of the ceremony, the pledges had to recite an oath of secrecy, vowing to "ever conceal and never reveal, whether by verbal means or written word"—not to parents, nor siblings, nor friends— what happened in Zeta Kappa.

At the first Tuesday pledge meeting, the pledges made several mistakes. Jake wore socks with his boat shoes because his feet were sweaty, but the brothers said socks were unacceptable. They didn't penalize him because they were impressed that he had already shaved his sideburns. Every brother he saw told him the clean-cut look was an improvement. One even called him a "pussy magnet," a phrase new to Jake.

In any case, other pledges had made more egregious errors. Quinn was the only pledge without a tie, and he wore dark pants instead of khakis. When Greg, the pledge master, came into the basement, he spotted Quinn and looked pained. "Are you fucking serious, Quinn? We went over this!" Greg ran out of the room and, moments later, chucked a spare tie through the doorway. He asked another pledge to help Quinn, who didn't know how to tie it, and then disappeared again. A few minutes later, he returned with Matthew, the shortest pledge and the youngest—he had just turned 18 in August—who had forgotten the rule not to use the front door. "Okay, I get it. It's an honest mistake to make," Greg said, harried. "It's a learning process, but I better not see this happen again."

Soon, the basement door opened again and Greg dragged in Wes, a pale, freckled pledge who seemed extremely confident despite his mistake. "Okay, that's two. That's *it*," Greg said, and slammed the door.

The pledges yelled at one another. "We have to stop fucking up!" They berated Quinn for not dressing appropriately and shouted at the boys who'd come in the wrong door. When Greg brought the pledges upstairs to the meeting, Jake tried not to look at Z, but the rule was like telling someone, "Whatever you do, *do not* think about purple elephants." He couldn't help it. He caught a fleeting glimpse of floppy black hair before he quickly looked away.

"It's so tough to understand this," Jake told me later. "How am I supposed to hide from someone I'm not allowed to look at? I don't know who I'm supposed to be hiding from." On the framed composite photos in the hall, one brother's photo was always covered with black fabric.

At the meeting, the officers assigned pledge chores in addition to the regular kitchen-cleaning tasks. Jake's was to sweep the main hallway. Grant, the steward, warned the pledges, "If you miss your chore or don't get someone to cover for you, you will get more chores."

Then officers doled out punishments. As Daniel, the VP, announced Quinn's transgression, the brothers trash-talked him, raucous and unrelenting. They slow-clapped when Greg presented a dog collar that Quinn would have to wear for the entire week. Quinn took it all in good humor. Although his exuberance could grate sometimes, Jake noticed that Quinn was good at socializing with the brothers, and he didn't seem to mind their ribbing. The officers also gave Quinn an extra pledge duty: As "wiki pledge," he had to look up the answer to questions any brother asked or texted him at any time, day or night. For coming in the wrong door, Wes was now the "weather pledge," who would go outside at 6:30 every morning to check the weather and post it to the Z-Kap Facebook page.

Minutes after Jake returned home from the meeting, Greg posted to the pledges' Facebook page that all pledges were to report to the house later, at exactly 12:30 A.M. You can't be anywhere in sight of the house at 12:29. You need to start running then. Don't walk, run. And don't be late. The pledges' group text lit up. Oh shit, they commented, here comes the hazing.

The pledges decided to meet two houses away at 12:15. Jake suggested that they form two orderly lines and run in at the same time, with two pledges sacrificing themselves to open and shut the backyard double doors for the rest of the group. At 12:29, the pledges at the front of the lines began to run. "Don't go in yet!" the other pledges shouted. "It's 12:29!" The group waited 20 more seconds. Jake and Logan manned the double doors, the last pledges inside.

As the pledges raced through the hallways, brothers stared at them silently. Greg and other officers stood in the Great Room. "Get in alphabetical order," Greg said quietly. The pledges scrambled to get in line. When they had finally arranged themselves, Greg said, "That was pathetic. You guys need to get that down faster."

Then came the lecture. "Some of you pledges have fucked up," Daniel said, exasperatedly running a hand through his buzz cut. "If this happens again, there will be issues. If you don't dress right, there will be issues. If you come in the front door, there will be issues. If you try to look at Z, there will be issues. Just don't fucking do that."

Greg distributed to each freshman a pledge book, a spiral-bound handbook containing the fraternity history and symbols, and information including the Greek alphabet, a list of the officers and their positions, the creed (a three-paragraph oath), the fraternity prayer, and descriptions of the three core values of Zeta Kappa: truth, honor, and trust. The book also included a list of every brother in the chapter. The pledges were expected to interview each brother to earn their signatures in the space next to their names in the book. "You'd better know this book inside out," Greg warned.

"Yes, sir," the pledges replied.

Greg told them to return to the house at 8:00 P.M. on Thursday for the first of their weekly EPs, the sessions during which the officers would teach them about the fraternity. "Bring a pillowcase," Daniel said, "and a six-pack of beer. A nice beer, the kind you'd share with your dad or girlfriend."

Jake panicked. He didn't know the "nice" beer brands, and he worried the brothers would make fun of him for not knowing. "If anyone's too uncomfortable getting beer because you're underage, tell me now. I'll get it for you, and you can repay me," Greg said.

Jake meekly raised his hand. He didn't even have time to research the brands before Greg asked what kind of beer he wanted. "Um . . . Corona?" Jake asked, then exhaled with relief when no one mocked him.

That Thursday, at the first EP, the officers led a session about truth. Afterward, the pledges were deposited in the basement, where Greg distributed practice interview pages: lined paper with room for several brothers' signatures. He instructed the pledges to drink one or two of their beers and trade the rest for brothers' autographs, a one-night speed rehearsal for pledge book interviews. For the first half hour, the brothers quizzed the pledges on pledge book minutiae before they agreed to sign their paper. The pledges, who mostly didn't know the answers, had to find another brother who would agree to help them.

As the brothers got drunker, they turned the interviews into a hazing game, refusing to provide their signature unless the pledges completed an arbitrary, inane task. They told Jake to run into each bedroom and yell, "I didn't vote for Andy." Another pledge crept on all fours down the hallway. One had to yell, "Grant has smegma!" And brothers ordered a few pledges to answer the question "Who has curry dick?" sending them from room to room until they found the guy with the Indian girlfriend.

When the pledges were relaxed and tipsy, Daniel suddenly yelled, "Give me your pages and get into the basement!"

Instead of waiting quietly, the pledges decided that practicing the creed would please the brothers. It did not. Daniel barged into the basement and ripped off his Ray-Bans. "Shut up! Shut up, all of you! You guys don't know how badly you fucked up! You have just opened the gates of hell!" He slammed the door.

The pledges moved their conversation to their group text, where they wondered what was going on. After a while, Greg came in, divided the pledges into groups of four, and told them to bring their pillowcases. He led them single file to the Great Room, where brothers put the pillowcases over the pledges' heads and shoved each group out of the house and into a waiting car.

As soon as the car doors closed, the brother driving Jake's group blasted earsplitting, screechy techno music. *Oh God, now we're really going to get hazed,* Jake thought. The brother drove unsafely, swerving, speeding, knocking the silent pledges against one another. Jake closed his eyes. *I am actually scared for my life,* he thought.

After what seemed like an eternity, the car stopped. Another brother opened the door. "Oh my fucking God, Tanner. You made them listen to this?" he said, laughing at the music. He addressed the pledges. "Take your pillowcases off."

The pledges were standing in front of a large off-campus house where several senior brothers lived. When they heard dance music, they looked at one another in relief. They had been played.

Inside, the house was crammed with brothers drinking. "Ahaha, you guys fucking got us," Jake confessed to the brothers closest to the door. Once the pledges were assembled, the Zeta Kappas gave them beers and reminded them about the favored "ratios." Alpha Rho, the sorority that would be arriving in half an hour, had 150 sisters, the brother said. To Jake, the implication was clear: Get with them.

Instantly, two brothers flanked Jake. "Time to get skull-fucked!"

one announced, brandishing a tubed funnel in the shape of a skull. The other brother handed Jake the end of the tube. "Pledge! Chug!" Jake put down his empty beer can and complied.

The brothers had Jake chug the equivalent of two beers, and gave him a fist bump and the look of acceptance that Jake craved. (When I asked Jake later why he obeyed, he said, "For their approval, it was better to just go ahead and go through with it. I've made a lot of progress! Three months ago, I had my first beer of my life and couldn't even finish it because it was so disgusting to me. Now I'm able to chug them. I did want to get pretty hammered anyway, though, because I wanted to be able to talk to girls.")

Jake was playing beer pong when the busloads of sorority women arrived. *Tonight I'm going to man up and actually try to get with one of them,* Jake decided. He turned to his beer pong opponents. "Screw this, you win. I'm going to go talk to girls now."

Spotting two girls wearing Metallica shirts, he called out, "That's one of my favorite bands! You guys like Metallica?"

"No. We're pledges, and they told us to find matching shirts," one said.

"Ohh," Jake said, and struggled to fill the uncomfortable pause.

He thought he was striking out until he spotted a girl in a mini-golf shirt. "I love mini-golf, but where I'm from, we call it putt-putt," Jake said, and introduced himself.

The girl, a freshman with bouncy brunette curls, seemed almost as drunk as he was. She laughed. "I'm Laura. Why would you call it putt-putt? It's mini-golf! I fucking love mini-golf!" They debated in jest for a while, and before Jake knew it, they were wrapping their arms around each other, swaying to the music.

"Can you get me a drink?" she asked.

"Sure, I can get you a drink, but I don't want to force you to do anything," Jake slurred, his conscience making unfiltered leaps through his drunken haze.

"Oh my God, thank you for understanding!" she said, squeezing his arm.

Wow, this is going well, Jake thought on his way to the punch bowl. *It may actually work out with her.* As he returned to Laura with a cup of jungle juice, Henry, a Zeta Kappa senior, cut in with Rob, a pledge with a chiseled jawline. Both were tanked. "Heeyy, this is Rob," Henry said, introducing the pledge to Laura. As Henry prodded Rob to talk, Laura gradually turned away from Jake, their conversation dying.

When Henry detached himself, Jake followed him. "Yo, I was trying to get with Laura. Why'd you introduce Rob?" he asked.

"Aw, sorry, man, I didn't know. I'm just trying to hook up everyone tonight," Henry said. "Look, I'ma help you out. I'm gonna make sure you have sex tonight. You're going to have a much better first mixer than I did when I was a pledge."

Jake inwardly face-palmed. *It was happening so naturally with Laura,* he thought. *I don't want it to come down to a brother setting me up.* Jake had had one long-term girlfriend in his life, an aloof girl who seemed merely to tolerate him throughout sophomore year of high school. When he had envisioned meeting girls in college, he hoped to connect with someone in class, have an engaging conversation, find a shared interest, and go from there. Or maybe their eyes would meet over their laptops as they studied across the table in the library, "like a naturally forming relationship," he told me later. "But in fraternities, relationships seem very set up with sorority sisters. There's a very different feel. Like when the brothers were trying to find us pledges dates for Bid Dinner, they were talking about girls like items on a menu, judging them based on their looks and trying to get a girl for everyone around the table. Hopefully through this I don't turn out to be some guy who judges girls on their looks. That's just not me."

"Oh! I know the girl you should have sex with. Come on," Henry said, dragging Jake toward a knot of partygoers. "She'll want to have sex with you if you don't say you're a freshman," he advised, and introduced Jake to the group as a sophomore. He pointed Jake toward a sorority sister who was already talking to Preston, the Zeta Kappa treasurer. *This is not going to go well at all,* Jake thought. *This is not how I want it to happen.*

Jake looked at Henry as if to say, *What the fuck?*

"Okay, I got an idea," Henry said. "We're going to Duane's room to get a Bud from his fridge. You're going to give the beer to her and tell her it's the last Budweiser in the house. Come on, tell her you're getting her a drink." Jake complied, but when Henry lumbered away, he turned to the girl and said, "I apologize. He's drunk, and I'm not going to lie: I'm actually a freshman, and he's trying to set me up."

The girl barely looked at him.

"Hey, while you're there," Preston said, giving Jake his empty cup, "fill me up."

Jake followed Henry upstairs and into a bedroom, where Henry gave him a Bud. "See this room?" Henry said. "You're going to have sex in this room tonight."

Jake did not say what he was thinking: *One, I'm not going to have sex in Duane's room; two, I'm not going to have sex with that girl; and three, you stopped me from hooking up with Laura in the first place, so I'm already hating you.*

Back downstairs, when Jake gave the beer to the girl, Preston glared at him. "The fuck, man, where's my goddamn beer?" Jake looked down. He was still holding Preston's empty cup.

Preston started to rebuke him when Henry stepped in. He had seniority over Preston. "I'm watching over Jake tonight," he told him, "so you're not going to fuck with him, okay?" It was the one good thing Henry did for Jake that night. Preston mumbled to himself as Jake backed away.

Jake ended up playing beer pong with a cute freshman girl against Eric—who had one blue eye and one brown eye and whom Jake thought was the funniest pledge in his class—and a sorority sister who let Eric feel her up between tosses. Jake made every cup. He was used to over-studying for and acing every test, and beer pong was no exception. After Bid Dinner, when he realized beer pong would be a frequent chapter activity, he'd conducted extensive research on the rules and best strategies. But he didn't make a move on the sorority sister. It didn't feel like the right thing to do.

The crowd in the party room dwindled as the pledges went elsewhere to hook up, go out, or sleep. Three pledges would report the next day that they accompanied some Alpha Rhos to an off-campus apartment where, to their bewilderment, the girls just took selfies and then asked the guys to leave.

In the main room, Jake ran into Ty, who was so hammered he could barely stay upright. He told Jake he had struck out with the Alpha Rhos, too. "Well, since we're not going to get any action tonight, we might as well do a good deed and clean up," Jake suggested. They began throwing out red Solo cups and retrieving the blue beer pong balls.

To Jake, this final activity pretty much summed up his evening. "Hey, Ty," he said, holding up two of the balls. "These are my blue balls tonight."

What It Really Means to Represent the Letters

Non-Greeks, or "GDIs" in Greek-speak (Goddamn Independents), often judge fraternities collectively by headlines, snapshots, or viral videos of individual chapters, a practice that can infuriate Greeks because they know that fraternities are not all the same. But many fraternity brothers, too, don't realize until they're initiated exactly what it means to be a member of their specific chapter.

Kirk, a college debate team captain with a 4.0 GPA, decided to rush a fraternity because, after a lonely freshman year, he craved a "sense of closeness and brotherhood." He found a casual camaraderie in a chapter at his southwestern university. But it wasn't until he transferred to a school in the Northeast, and its corresponding fraternity chapter, that he found the deeply connected brotherhood he had been searching for.

At Kirk's first university, conversations with his fraternity brothers mostly revolved around "the three Bs: booze, basketball, and bitches." All the brothers drank, he said, and were expected to attend a party every Saturday, plus one or two mixers per week. If a member had a test the next day and said he couldn't go out, the brothers would pressure him: "Come on, you can show up drunk to the test; we all do that." At Kirk's current university, he told me, "that just wouldn't fly." Seven of his brothers are nondrinkers, and though the chapter does party, partying isn't the focus of its program.

While Kirk's former chapter, considered one of that school's most diverse, was approximately 90 percent white, his current chapter is about 40 percent white and includes gay brothers, nonbinary brothers, and a large international, religiously diverse contingent. These brothers are proud to be known on campus as "the guys you can introduce to your parents. We're genuinely good guys. We're not stereotypical 'frat boys'," Kirk said. "One of the biggest challenges administrations and universities across the country face is separating the good fraternities from the bad. Which are good fraternities that really foster brotherhood between the brothers, foster goodwill, are philanthropic in nature, and have support networks? Which are bad and support racism and misogyny? It's hard to separate the two."

Distinctions among houses are largely missing from media accounts of fraternity life. The low-risk chapters, the ones that better represent a fraternity ideal, usually fly under the public's radar. The priorities in a house of studious brothers might dramatically differ from those of a house of partiers. Activities also vary by region, campus, and chapter. "At regional conferences we'd realize how different the groups are. There's a very different mentality depending on university support. There's not as much pressure in small liberal arts colleges as at large schools," an East Coast chapter advisor told me. Even the geographic layout of a campus can affect fraternities' interactions with other students. At several schools, Greek houses are separated a substantial distance from dorms, which leaves them more isolated and insular.

At Kirk's current university, he treasures a chapter tradition: the brotherhood's weekly three- to four-hour "deep talks." The fraternity supplies chips and ice cream, and a member leads a probing conversation on topics such as, in recent months, "The value of an education," "Race, religion, and you," "Fraternity men and alcohol abuse," and "Are you happy?" As a conservative in a liberal chapter, Kirk values these discussions, which "expose me to ideological, racial, national, and religious differences I'd never encounter elsewhere. My brothers constantly challenge my deeply rooted convictions, and I leave as a stronger individual. They help me be a more intelligent, helpful, trustworthy, and responsible person."

Kirk's first chapter didn't have this tradition. Kirk differentiates among *traditions,* which he said develop at a chapter level; *rituals,* which are activities that all chapters of a national fraternity are expected to follow, though their execution can vary; and *Ritual,* standardized, scripted ceremonies and lessons about the fraternity's stated values. Most fraternities have a ritual book that describes these activities.

Part of sustaining a brotherhood involves these activities. This is the innocuous explanation for many of the secrets that fraternities hold close. As a fraternity risk-management and insurance guide instructs, members are expected to "Obey the law and live the Ritual." For sure, secrecy can be unhealthy, particularly when students are asked to keep secrets from their parents. One fraternity's ritual book explains that "the color of the shield signifies the secrecy and mystery of our brotherhood. The Skull and Bones indicate the penalty for the violation of your Oath of Obligation," which includes a vow of secrecy.

But are fraternity secrets worth the pains Greeks take to hide them? One fraternity's secret handshake involves interlocking pinkies, and its secret motto, "Phi Alpha," means "Brightness from obscurity." Another major fraternity gives brothers titles such as conductor, guard, sentinel, worthy high master (the chapter president), and worthy master (the vice president). Some of that fraternity's ceremonies involve intricate gowns, altar tables, kneeling cushions, a candelabra, and a salt cup. Initiates take a vow of "eternal secrecy."

Yet another large fraternity's secret motto is "Holy friendship forever." Its password is *Mizpah*, Hebrew for "watchtower," which refers to the biblical line "The Lord watch between me and thee, when we are absent, one from another." This fraternity's ceremonies also have brothers in the roles of guard and sentinel. Initiates, who must take an oath of secrecy, are instructed, "The secrecy that surrounds us is not an idle pretense but a veil to hide from the outer world our proceedings that they may not be misinterpreted or corrupted, and that our pure ideal may not be dishonored." They are instructed to strip off their shirts. Eventually, the senior marshal strikes each initiate on the chest with the flat side of a sword to "shatter the fetters of cynicism and selfishness."

Various secrets have overlapped since fraternities' earliest days, and many of their traditions and rituals are similar. In one major fraternity's "Firing Squad" tradition, the brothers circle a member and take turns telling him how they feel about him. The student must stand silently until each critique is finished before he can respond. Real-life examples include critiques that began with "You're not as involved as you should be," "I feel like you betrayed me when you . . . ," and "You're in charge of finances, and we feel like sometimes you're incredibly hard on us." One Pennsylvania participant told me, "It's honest but respectful, and we sit together and discuss the issues afterward and ask, 'What did you get from this?' It's about opening a dialogue. If we're going to be a family, we need to learn how to resolve things. You're not going to like everybody in your chapter, but you learn to respect your differences."

Another major fraternity conducts a ritual called the Eye of Wooglin. Like Firing Squad, the ritual places members one at a time in the center of a circle. In some chapters, the brothers take turns criticizing the member. He's not allowed to respond, and no one can speak about the comments afterward. "There are some harsh criticisms about people's characters. For a week, some people won't talk to someone," a New York brother told me. A different chapter's Eye of Wooglin simply gives each member two to four hours to tell the group his life story—and "then everyone drinks," a member said. "When I did this with my pledge class, we grew the closest we'd ever been."

Rituals, which are often intended to build character or forge connections, usually don't make headlines. But for many Greeks, the rituals represent one of the most important aspects of the brotherhood. Regardless of the nature of the secrets, merely by having them, fraternities bond their members. And in groups with such relatively rapid turnover, the secrets ensure that a sense of continuity is shared with the alums of the past and the undergraduates of the future. Recently in one chapter, a ritual helped members cope when one of their brothers died. At every chapter meeting, an officer called roll; each brother responded with his assigned number, for example, 987. After the student's death, the officer continued to call his name, and the brothers answered together with his number.

A problem in some chapters, and one of the reasons fraternities can differ so drastically, is that teenagers are put in charge of these activities—and one another, which can lead to arbitrary and sometimes dangerous power and punishments. Chapter traditions, education programs, and rituals aren't necessarily presided over by trained adults. "Something many young student leaders lack, especially in Greek life, is maturity. I was 20, leading a group of students, making decisions and dealing with more money than most 20-year-olds ever dream of seeing at that age," said a recent Florida chapter president. "We get thrown into this role with intense responsibility, and realistically we have no experience beyond some charisma we displayed in a speech against the guy that got nominated because he's a poli-sci major and wants to go into politics one day."

Fraternity members are often expected to hold one another accountable to the fraternity's policies, standards, and values. This is one of the challenges for chapter officers: how to discipline their friends. The Florida president, who was juggling MCAT prep, a job, and a full course load, made clear to members that he "held every brother to the same standards I held myself; if you have time to party and play around, you better make sure your schoolwork's complete and you'll make it to mandatory events," he said. "One of the toughest things a fraternity president deals with daily is the balance between friendship and business. The line can easily get blurred between what's best for the chapter and what's best for the friendship."

Ben's South Carolina fraternity held disciplinary hearings;

offenders were usually temporarily prohibited from attending social events. Because he was the president and founding father, he said, "People don't want to tell on their brother and don't want to tell me." In one case, Ben heard about a brother who allegedly was trying to haze pledges. Ben announced to his chapter that the brother was "putting our members in jeopardy," and he moved to deactivate him. "It was incredibly difficult to say that in front of him, but it's not about the feelings of one person. It really is about the organization set up to help a group of young men who are willing to help each other."

While the situation was uncomfortable for Ben as a student among students, he didn't consider informing an alum or national rep. "If I had felt he would freak out, I could have gone to our chapter advisor and say, 'This kid's going to get someone hurt.' They would immediately come in and take over. But the problem is they typically go too far and do a member review." During membership reviews, fraternity reps interview brothers to decide whether to suspend or deactivate certain members. At the time, Ben's national headquarters recently had reviewed a chapter at a neighboring school, Ben said, and kicked out half the members.

Ben's chapter voted to remove the brother. "When I agreed to found a chapter, I didn't recognize the full breadth of responsibility I had undertaken for 70 people's well-being. But I counteracted that by recruiting people I thought would help pull this organization forward."

Many incoming college students initially are unaware of the responsibility that comes with fraternity membership. Brothers speak about the allure of "belonging to something larger than yourself." But joining that broader group means being held accountable for its reputation. A current fraternity brother whose school recently experienced a series of campus Greek scandals put it this way: If a Google employee sends a racist email during his free time, the employee is fired, but "you don't see Google being persecuted for that." If a fraternity brother sent that email, the entire fraternity would come under scrutiny. "You do have to ask yourself whether the fraternity's culture contributes to that brother [feeling] freer to use that language around their brothers," he said. "The natural GDI proclivity is to say it's the fraternity's fault and they deserve to be punished. But we don't all contribute to the bad things. Individuals make the mistakes, but GDIs strip away members' agency."

In 2016, the president of Cornell's Psi Upsilon chapter was accused of attempted rape; he subsequently pled guilty to a misdemeanor sex offense. "Everyone hated" the fraternity then, a brother of another Cornell chapter said, and a top-tier sorority dropped Psi Upsilon from their social calendar. Two months later, when a Cornell basketball player was arrested on charges of first-degree rape and three counts of first-degree criminal sexual assault, the student body didn't criticize the basketball team, the brother said. "They just said, 'That guy's a creep.' But they all criticized the fraternity. There was a clear divide."

There are divisions among fraternities, too. In an interesting study from 1996, researchers compared parties at fraternities that campus women classified as high risk (dangerous places for women) to those at low-risk houses (safer for women), as well as to the scenes at two local bars. The chapters characterized as high risk, the researchers learned, also had more members, more severe and frequent disciplinary incidents, and more reports of property damage than the low-risk houses. Brothers in low-risk chapters were more likely to play intramural sports while brothers in high-risk chapters were more likely to be varsity athletes. More of the low-risk house members attended a campus rape-prevention program.

The researchers found that a typical party at low-risk houses had an equal gender ratio, a clean women's bathroom, more conversations, and an atmosphere of general respect toward women. Parties at the high-risk houses had uneven numbers of men and women, with a filthy bathroom and an environment in which men joked about or degraded women behind their backs. Drinking dominated the high-risk parties, which typically didn't offer nonalcoholic alternatives. Conversations among mixed-gender groups were rare at the high-risk houses; the music was too loud and there were few places to sit down.

Current brothers told me that the distinctions made in that study have mostly held up over time, and that top-tier houses generally are more likely to be high-risk environments than lower-tiered houses. Several brothers theorized that this was because higher-tiered houses typically have more money, so they can furnish more alcohol, hire entertainment (such as DJs), and invite more guests.

At a southern school, parties at top-tier houses draw several hundred people while low- to mid-tier parties host about 100. At high-tier parties, "there's a lot more drinking, louder music, and a lot more risk. There are more people, but not enough people to cover security, to make sure people don't get hurt or alcohol poisoning," said a member of a mid-tier house on that campus. "The loud music plays a factor. You're either outside at night or in a dark hallway or room, so it plays into how you interact with girls. People go to a higher-tier party to get some. At our parties, a lot of girls are friends with the guys and are there to mingle. So as opposed to getting lucky, you get their number and you follow it up. It's a little more of a process."

A Virginia brother said his low-tier house offers seating and space away from the main party room, and at least two sober brothers patrol all parties (three or four at larger parties) so that women feel safe. His chapter serves drinks next to a sink with drinking water and, unlike other houses on campus, has a separate bathroom for women. Another difference he noticed among tiers was the access to drugs at higher-tiered houses.

Do fraternities deserve their bad reputation or has the media unfairly branded them? The brothers I spoke with mostly offered variations on "We don't deserve the bad reputation, but some chapters do." A Missouri brother said, "You only hear about fraternities in the media when members die from drinking, get arrested, or rape girls. So the assumption is that's what everyone does. The truth is the majority of people don't do that, and the majority of Greek experiences are positive. People build strong friendships, they change and develop fundamentally as people, and have some of the most memorable moments of their college careers thanks to Greek life. That story doesn't get told in the media. That being said, some stereotypes are true. I wasn't hazed, but many fraternities do haze and do crappy things to pledges; fraternities do throw really fun parties and binge-drink too often; and fraternity brothers do get really caught up in fraternity loyalty and pride."

Many brothers struggle with the resulting stigma of the letters. Students warned one Maryland brother to avoid wearing his letters to certain classes because the professors were known to dislike fraternities. Ben brought up a recent hazing death in one of our conversations. "Those instances do happen, but do they define the Greek system as a whole? The character of the millions of people in Greek life? The answer is unequivocally no. *Fraternity* has become a bad word," he said. "I'm very hesitant to say I was in a fraternity because, to certain people, that will mean I was in a culture that promoted sexual assault, I partied my whole way through college, I had no responsibility, and I'm a privileged Caucasian kid who had everything handed to me. That stigma is incredibly incorrect, but it's promoted nonetheless."

A New York chapter president said that fraternity membership instead should signal to people that "you developed key social skills, learned how to work as a team, and have a group of people behind you that support you."

In the study about high-risk versus low-risk fraternities, there was a line that I found striking. The researchers observed that many of the same students attended parties at both the high-risk and the low-risk houses—and their behavior shifted with the setting. Certainly, it is possible to interpret the data as proof that some fraternities enable dangerous behavior. But we should also note that the low-risk fraternities created an environment that encouraged better behavior. Establishing a set of social norms and learning to follow and drop cues about what behaviors are and are not appropriate— that's part of becoming an adult. Fraternities have the potential to solve entrenched, long-term campus problems that top-down policy changes have failed to fix. And if universities could expand the influence of and glorify the chapters that are doing it right, then maybe the headlines could change.

Ω Ω Ω

Jake got to his Psych 100 lecture hall early for his first-ever college quiz. He slipped into a seat in the front row, organized his things, glanced at the student next to him, and did a double take. She was beautiful, with cascading strawberry blond waves and pale green eyes behind purple-framed rectangular glasses. She was looking over her notes and tapping a pen on her chin—a Pentel EnerGel-X BL 107 retractable, the same pen Jake used religiously.

Jake turned toward her and held up his own. "Hey, nice pen!" he said.

She smiled. "Look at that! I haven't met anyone with the same pen before," she said. They fell into the typical self-deprecating student chatter about how they weren't ready for the exam and would probably fail (though Jake had never earned worse than a B+ on any test in his life).

During the quiz, Jake occasionally peeked at her paper—not to copy (he was crushing the test), but to get to know her better. He could tell she was a good writer, had neat handwriting, and was obviously smart and articulate. After the test, he made sure they walked out of the room at the same time so they could introduce themselves properly. He waited two days before sending Beth a Facebook friend request. He hoped he'd be allowed the time during pledging to get to know a GDI.

That night, the pledges were again summoned to the house at 12:30. All the pledges gathered in the basement except for a pledge who said he had a fever, and Bryce, who was inexplicably absent. Greg led them to the informal chapter room, where the brothers sat in a broken circle on the floor. The pledges filled in the rest of the circle as Greg passed out candles, lit one, and turned off the lights. "This is called Light the Circle," Greg explained, taking off his baseball cap and placing it behind him. "When the person next to you lights your candle, you tell an embarrassing or funny story about something that happened to you. Then light the candle of the person to your right."

The brothers went first, their faces intermittently lit only by the flickering candles. Almost all their stories were hilarious anecdotes about sex or drugs. One brother described a night when he was so drunk during foreplay that he couldn't get a boner. He tried to save face by helicopter-dicking, wildly spinning his penis for the girl's entertainment. As the candles increasingly illuminated the circle, Jake dreaded his turn. He had no sex or drug stories. He had never even been drunk before he joined Zeta Kappa, and he still hadn't been drunk outside Z-Kap functions. The other guys were laughing their heads off at even the pledges' stories. Ty, for example, described a high school Beach Week night when he chivalrously placed his shirt on the sand to make a girl comfortable during sex. But he didn't know she had her period—and now his shirt had red stripes.

Finally, Wes, the pale, freckled pledge, lit Jake's candle. *I have nothing,* he thought. He told the fraternity the only story he could think of from the last time he had a girlfriend. He and 20 kids from school were playing in an unofficial Nerf War. Even though Jake had never played before, in the first game he had the third-highest number of hits. "So for the second game," he told the guys, "I figured I should make it my goal to get the top score of the day. That led to me becoming so obsessed with Nerf darts that I went berserk." Midway through the game, to maximize his score, he found his girlfriend, pinned her to a corner, and aimed his Nerf gun at her, racking up the points. "She was a little pissed off because she was in it to win it," he explained to the brothers—and then he tried to make the story sound funnier and more momentous. "But I wanted the points, so I Nerf dart–raped her."

Jake had never said—had never even thought—the phrase "Nerf dart rape" in his life. As soon as it came out of his mouth, he was horrified at himself. But he couldn't take it back. The Zeta Kappas flipped out, laughing uncontrollably at that phrase in that story from that pledge. "Nerf dart rape!" a brother yelled in a nerdy, nasal voice. "Nnnnerf dart rape!" another brother echoed. Jake's story became the moment of the night. From then on, whenever another pledge told a story, someone would interrupt: "Yeah, but did you Nerf dart–rape her?" After each story, the group erupted into "Nerf dart rape! Nerf dart rape!" chants, always with the nerdy voice. One pledge told a wild story about an acid trip gone wrong, but after the story ended and the guys laughed, someone said, "Yeah, good story, but there was no Nerf dart rape." And the Nerf dart rape chants began anew.

Oh no, Jake thought, laughing along but still mortified, *this is going to stick.* Within minutes, someone had changed the name of the pledges' group text to Nerf Dart Rape Fall '17 Class.

At the next pledge meeting, as soon as Jake entered the Great Room, brothers shouted, "Nerf dart rape! Nerf dart rape's here!"

Daniel, the chapter VP, slugged Jake on the arm. "Congratulations, man, you made a name for yourself here. I hope you enjoy it, because it's not going away." ("It's become a meme. *I've* become a meme," Jake told me. "I don't know if that's good or bad. But I wish I'd never come up with it.")

Occasionally throughout the meeting, a brother would yell, "Nerf dart rape!" for no reason. Brothers and pledges would join in, as if they were howling at the moon.

The officers announced that the pledges had continued to screw up. The pledge who had skipped Light the Circle because of a fever had lied; a brother had seen him afterward at a campus bar. Zeta Kappa kicked him out. A few other pledges had dropped out on their own; the pledge class was now down from 43 to 39 pledges.

Some pledges were on thin ice. Eric had lost his pledge pin. And at lunch that day, Quinn had sat next to Z, whom the pledges now knew was the chapter's chaplain, tasked with the care and guard of rituals. (Quinn didn't even know it was Z until brothers yelled at him to move.) Chase, the social chair, emphasized the severity of this transgression to the pledges, then explained, "Look, when I was a pledge, I didn't understand either why I wasn't allowed to look at him. But you will absolutely understand later when we tell you as a brother why we do all this." This explanation only deepened Jake's curiosity. He was dying to know who this guy was and what made him so untouchable.

When it was Z's turn to speak, even the brothers hushed. The pledges tried to look at anything but him. "Would pledge Sam please stand up," Z said.

Sam stood.

"Please recite the fraternity prayer."

Sam couldn't do it. "Sit down," Z said, disgusted, and turned to the next pledge. "Would pledge Matthew please stand up."

Matthew didn't even try. "I don't know it," he said, shrugging.

Z called on two other pledges, neither of whom had fully memorized the prayer. "If you wish to be a brother at this house, you'd
better know some fucking history," he said, sounding angry without
raising his voice. Jake's heart pounded as he worried that he would
be put on the spot, too. Normally he would have overprepared for a
moment like this, but he had studied for an exam that afternoon
instead of reading his pledge book.

Perhaps that had been a mistake, he thought now. When Z asked
the group to recite the creed, only Logan, the overachieving Conan,
and Jamal—an earnest pledge and one of three minority pledges—
knew it. Like the other freshmen, Jake mumbled, trying to keep up
with them, shaking his head at himself and feeling pathetic.

After the meeting, the pledges trudged out of the house, convinced they "deserved to be punished" for not knowing the material. "We're fucking up so badly as a pledge class," someone said, and
everyone agreed.

Jake felt guilty for not memorizing the creed the day he received
his pledge book. He believed the slipup was the only blemish on
his record. "Other than that, I feel like I have a pretty decent reputation of following orders," he told me. Thus far, he had faithfully
completed his pledge chores and study hours, and had attended all
meetings and activities, except for a few parties.

I asked him how it felt, talking to me outside the fraternity bubble, to say that he was or was not "following orders" given by teenagers and young twentysomethings.

"I continue to ask myself that because it's tough to reflect that I'm
forced to follow rules. Rules are in place and just asking for us to
fuck up. But I guess because all the brothers act so serious and upset
about, for example, looking at Z, it makes us believe this rule has
some weight to it," Jake said. Then he defended the brothers. "But
they don't physically punish us; they're reprimanding in a way that
leads us to want to change ourselves for the better anyways. I think

that's pretty good. They're not like [a top-tier fraternity here] that's torturing their pledges. Yeah, sure, we're ridiculed and shit on a lot, but we're not tortured. All I know is if I want to keep going through this, no matter how weird the rules sound, I've got to follow them."

Within days, his perspective would change.

CHAPTER 3

Pledging: "Earning" the Letters

A FEW HOURS before the second Thursday EP session, Greg posted to the pledges' Facebook page that they had to complete four interviews for signatures in their pledge book before 7:00 P.M. Each brother would decide when a pledge had shown sufficient interest in him to deserve a signature. Jake liked doing the interviews. He found that if he asked the right questions, some brothers shared interesting stories. And when a pledge was pressed for time, some of the nicer brothers only quizzed him quickly on pledge book information: the bond numbers of famous alumni, the traditional names and roles of each officer, the colors, history, and symbols of the fraternity.

Greg also told the pledges to bring a sleeping bag and sleepwear. *Oh God, what are they going to do to us?* Jake fretted. As soon as he saw the post, he wrote the pledges on their group text; typically, the first pledge to see Facebook orders relayed the message to the entire class ASAP.

The pledges instantly replied with their concerns. No one wanted to sleep at the house. Several had exams the next day. Jake had two, and one of them was in his most difficult class, a physics course. Several pledges didn't know where to get a sleeping bag.

I'm not planning on staying the whole night, so you can have the bag I use when they decide to let us go, Jake texted.

The others agreed. Of course they didn't have to stay overnight, they reasoned. Jake would later laugh at his naïveté, telling me, "As if we had an option to leave."

Jake spent an hour trying to memorize the creed before going to the house to get his pledge chores out of the way. As soon as he stepped into the Great Room, the shout-outs began. "Nerf dart rape's here!" "Nerf dart rape! Nerf dart rape!" For Jake, the joke had gone too far; the Z-Kaps were calling *him* Nerf dart rape before he could even say hello.

When EP began, Greg explained that tonight's values lesson was about honor. One of the brothers led a discussion about how the pledges thought they should treat the brothers and how the brothers should treat them. "You're new members of this fraternity," the brother said. "If a brother treats you like an asshole, you have every right to call him out for it."

"Does anyone feel like they've been disrespected so far?" asked Daniel, the VP with the buzz cut.

Jake was the only one who raised his hand. "Okay, I get it. You have a very good reason I know about," Daniel said, then talked about "the golden rule" without addressing Jake's concern. After Daniel's spiel, Greg distributed pledge book tests.

Jake panicked. *If I get any wrong, I'll get wrecked by the brothers,* he thought. So he did something he had never done before on any test, ever: He peeked at the paper of the student seated next to him and copied the answers to the prompts he didn't know.

When Daniel looked over the papers, he sneered. "This is pathetic. I can't believe none of you know what the fucking creed is. You better know this before your next pledge meeting. Go to the basement."

In the basement, the pledges were silent, afraid the brothers would yell at them again if they spoke.

Jake texted the group, Please call me Jake, not Nerf dart rape. Definitely my bad for saying it. But I don't want to walk into the house and immediately be called Nerf dart rape before I get the chance to talk to anyone.

It felt good to get that off his chest. When the pledges checked their phones, they gave him nods of acknowledgment. Someone changed the group text name from Nerf Dart Rape Fall '17 Class to Z-Kap Fall 2017 Class.

Sam followed Jake's lead: I do not like to be called Black Sam, he texted.

The pledges nodded again.

Chase, the social chair, came in and gave each pledge a numbered sticker. "Okay, guys, we're going to do some speed dating. Take a seat, talk to whoever's in front of you, and when we say, 'Switch,' switch seats." He led them to the Great Room, where several sorority sisters and a few brothers waited in a row of chairs.

Jake took a seat in front of a brother, who spoke in falsetto. "I only look for three things in a guy: money, good looks, and a huge dick." Jake laughed. He didn't know what the goal of this exercise was. *Am I supposed to convince them to give me their phone number, or just not look bad?* To play it safe, he tried only to make small talk.

Afterward, the pledges were debriefed. The purpose of the activity had been to see how well the pledges handled themselves in a dating situation, Chase said. Each "date" had ranked the pledges and commented on their appeal or lack thereof. The girls watched, amused, as Daniel read some of the comments aloud:

"Number Five was Gucci."

"Number Twenty-Nine talked about himself the whole time."

"Number Eleven asked for mouth-to-mouth."

At that, the brothers erupted in applause. About half the pledges, including Jake, weren't mentioned. *I guess I didn't shine,* Jake thought. *So I was average, but at least I didn't fuck up.*

"Okay," Chase said, "I need everyone to back up because we need space for a runway. Pledges, it's time to check if what you're wearing is 'frat' or not."

He ordered Eric, the goofball with the unusual eyes, to model his outfit in front of the room. "If it flies, it dies!" brothers yelled. Apparently, Eric had made the grievous mistake of wearing American Eagle brand clothes. "You have to have a high-end polo, either a good name like Ralph Lauren or a polo that doesn't have a brand name on it," Chase explained. "But you can't wear anything that has something that flies."

As the brothers critiqued more pledges in front of the girls, Jake whispered to Jamal, "Jeez, are we in a sorority? What's the big deal about fashion? Why does it matter so much what we wear?"

The brothers called up Logan, who confidently wore khaki shorts, boat shoes, and a blue button-down Ralph Lauren shirt that paired nicely with his red hair. "That is totally frat," Chase said. "That's like the perfect trifecta right there. That is 'frattire.'"

But when Chase summoned Wes to the runway, the brothers protested. "Noo!" "I can't look!" "What are those! What *are* those?!"

Wes looked down at the floor, his freckled face reddening. "Need I say more, ladies and gentlemen?" Chase said. "Not only are you wearing cargos, but they're patterned!" (Jake said later, "They didn't even give a reason why it's so awful. I didn't think they looked that bad.") The rest of the pledges escaped judgment.

Even though he was dressed appropriately, in boat shoes, khaki shorts, and a Ralph Lauren polo, Jake was relieved to evade the spotlight. After the girls left, a few brothers produced neckties and taught the pledges how to tie a Windsor knot.

The brothers left the pledges in the Great Room alone, wondering what was to come. "Do you guys know if there's any way I can talk to one of the guys here and tell them I have to go? I have exams tomorrow and can't really do this," Jake asked another pledge, who shrugged.

A few minutes later, Bryce retrieved his backpack from the foyer. A brother called out from the stairway, "Where do you think you're going, huh?" Bryce sat down. *Uh-oh, none of us is leaving,* Jake realized.

When Greg finally came downstairs, he said, "Okay, guys, bed-time. Use the bathroom downstairs. You can get undressed or do whatever you usually do before you go to bed. Set up in the Game Room." Between the pool table and the foosball table, the 39 sleeping bags had only a few inches of space between them.

Jake and Sebastian put their sleeping bags underneath the pool ta-ble. It was 11:30 P.M., and no one was tired. Greg and Daniel turned off the lights. "Nighty-night, guys, gotta go to sleep. Turn off your phones."

The tiled floor was cold and uncomfortable. After about 30 min-utes, Greg walked in. "Quinn, I swear to fucking God, get off your fucking phone, and that goes for all of you." He left the room.

The room was dead silent. A brother dressed in a hooded black robe perched on a barstool next to the pool table, facing away from Jake. "Go the *fuck* to sleep," he said.

Hidden beneath the table, Jake made eye contact with Sebastian. Sebastian rolled his eyes and mimed shooting himself in the head. Whenever someone made any sound, even just the rustle of a repo-sitioned sleeping bag, the robed brother bellowed, "SILENCE. Sleep!"

Jake couldn't. He hadn't brought a pillow; no one had. He lay still, his mind whirling as he listened to some of the pledges snore. *Maybe at midnight they'll let us go,* he thought. He had spent so much time studying his pledge book that he hadn't finished studying for his Psych 100 and physics exams. Midnight came and went, and still, every slight stir earned a "SILENCE. Sleep!" Jake checked his watch. By 1:00 A.M., he was losing hope that he'd be able to go home.

At 1:30, the door opened. Two hooded brothers tiptoed into the room, one holding a pillowcase, the other a flashlight. The flashlight blinked on and off into the eyes of the pledge sleeping closest to the door. Jake wondered how many others were awake and watching. Sebastian was sound asleep. The brothers threw the pillowcase over his head, lifted his arms over their shoulders, and lugged him out of the room.

At first Jake was relieved. *Maybe he did something wrong, and once they bring him back, all of us will be free to go,* he thought. But about five minutes later the brothers dragged the pledge back to his sleeping bag. His head was bowed, as if in exhaustion. They removed the pillowcase, whispered something in his ear, and woke and hooded the pledge next to him.

Now Jake was scared. The brothers returned every few minutes, moving down the rows of pledges, sometimes taking two boys at a time. Jake agonized about what the brothers could have done that would leave the freshmen so limp. He worried that they were stripping the pledges naked and beating them with the paddles hanging in the hallway nearby. He was wearing only underwear and shorts. *This is terrible,* he thought. *Right after they talked about honor, they're hazing us!*

After an hour, the robed brothers came for Jake. He pretended to sleep until the flashlight glared in his face. A whisper: "Wake up. Wake up now." A pillowcase, hot and stuffy, covered his head. Barefoot, Jake blindly tripped over sleeping pledges' legs as the brothers maneuvered him out of the room.

Once the door closed behind them, the brothers ran Jake down the hall to the staircase and dragged him, stumbling, up four flights of stairs to the hall outside the sleeping porch, where the freshmen would live next semester. The pillowcase lifted. Jake was in front of a pillar bearing a candle lamp and a goblet of what looked like wine. The flame illuminated a figure in a black robe. Afraid to look up in case it was Z, Jake gazed at the floor.

"KNEEL!" the brothers at his side commanded. Jake dropped to his knees, hyperventilating. What were they going to do to him? The not knowing tormented him. The brother in black intoned, "The obligations of membership are sacred and enduring. If you desire to assume these responsibilities, your journey will become more difficult. Sacrifices will be made."

When he finished his speech he ordered, "Go!" and extinguished the flame with his fingers. The brothers flanking Jake put the pillowcase back on his head, lifted him by his shoulders, ran him down to the other end of the hallway, and spun him in circles a few times before sprinting back to the sleeping porch. They lifted the pillowcase. "KNEEL!" they demanded again.

Jake fell to the ground, nervous and disoriented. A brother in a white robe stood at the pillar. In the candlelight, Jake could see Greg beneath the hood, his baseball cap uncharacteristically absent. Greg's message was more optimistic: If the pledge followed the fraternity's values, his journey would be successful. When Greg extinguished the candle, the pillowcase once again sheathed Jake's head. The brothers ran Jake downstairs and retraced the path to his sleeping bag, again tripping him over pledges' legs. Before they set him down, one of the brothers whispered, "Ever conceal and never reveal, by verbal means or written word." And then they woke up Sebastian.

For the next hour, Jake watched silently as, one by one, every remaining pledge was pillowcased and dragged out of the room. When the last pledge returned, Jake waited for the brothers to tell them to go home. Instead, the brother sitting at the bar bellowed, "SILENCE! Go the *fuck* to sleep." Little chance of that. Jake put his shoes underneath his sleeping bag to prop his head off the floor. He was dizzy and dehydrated, but too scared to ask if he could get water. He and the other pledges remained still and silent, afraid of the brother at the bar. Except for one: A freshman named Isaiah turned on his phone's flashlight, stood up, and left, taking his sleeping bag with him. To Jake's surprise, the brother at the bar said nothing. Isaiah did not return.

Jake gave up. He wasn't leaving. He tried reviewing exam prep in his head, but he felt borderline delirious. He was accustomed to getting a decent night's sleep. He lay there for two more hours, after which all the lights went on at once. "Get the fuck up, everyone! Get in line in alphabetical order now!" a brother hoarsely instructed. Jake didn't think he had seen this brother before. He was stocky and imposing, with floppy black hair.

The pledges fumbled around, barefoot and in shorts or boxers, half-asleep and blinking in the sudden brightness. "Hurry the fuck up, everyone! Come on!" the brother commanded.

When the pledges were lined up, the brother continued: "You were shit trying to get yourselves in alphabetical order. First and foremost, you all better know who I fucking am by now." Jake looked around. All the other pledges' heads were bowed. *Oh, shit, it's Z*, Jake realized, and snapped his head downward. "You guys should know how much you fucked up recently. You're not supposed to fucking sit next to me at lunch! You've also fucked up because you haven't learned the creed yet. That's a fucking disgrace on our fraternity. Now, who doesn't have a pin? I know one of you doesn't fucking have a pin on you."

Eric raised his hand. "All right," Z said, more calmly now. "One of you lost your pin, good." Daniel came into the room and gave a brick to Z, who dropped it at Eric's feet. The pledges didn't make a sound. Z returned to the front of the room. "Eric, you will now carry the brick everywhere you go. You'll fucking sleep with it. A brother can text you anytime to ask where the brick is, and you have to take a selfie with it," Z said. He turned to the group of pledges. He did not raise his voice. "You all don't know how fucking nice we've been so far with all the times you guys have been fucking up. You guys know you don't have to be here. You could just leave whenever you want. But if you're planning on becoming a brother, you're not going to do that. You're not going to skip events we spend hours planning out for you, and you're certainly not going to become a brother by not doing your pledge chores or study hours. I'm your goddamn ticket into this fraternity, and I will remove you without any hesitation if I see another fuckup. You understand that? Does everyone understand that?"

No one moved. "I'll take that as a yes. Get your stuff and get the fuck out of here. Leave."

The pledges, demoralized, remained frozen until Z was out of the room. Later, when they checked their phones, they saw that Daniel had posted a message to the pledges' Facebook page: **If you see this before 3:30 A.M., you're out.** And soon afterward: **Hell to pay, Isaiah.** Isaiah, a nice guy who had obeyed all orders until he had looked at his phone, had either been kicked out or had quit in the middle of the night.

Back at his dorm, Jake desperately gulped from the water fountain. He tried to study for his exams, but he couldn't concentrate. To him, Z's speech had been brutal. *I guess we haven't been doing our stuff right, and a few of us have been bringing the whole group down. We must be fucking up, because it took a full confrontation from Brother Zeta himself, so you know it's bad,* he thought.

Eventually, he fell into such a deep sleep that he missed his alarm. He awoke with a start and looked at the clock: 9:00 A.M. "Oh shit!" he yelled, and scrambled out of bed. There would be no last-minute studying, no breakfast, no shower. Still exhausted, he had 30 minutes to get to his first exam. He had not studied at all for his second.

When I talked to him after the tests, Jake was furious. Now that he had some distance from the evening's events, he didn't think his class deserved the mistreatment. "We've been doing pretty good, getting pledge chores out of the way," he said. "But that was definitely hazing! I feel kind of betrayed. They were just talking about honor, and how respect is a part of that. I don't like these rituals where we have to lie down on the ground and not talk or move for hours! It's awful!" He was shouting now. "There's no reason to have us try to pretend we're asleep when clearly no one's fucking asleep! Why is this a thing? I get it, okay, maybe Z had to step in and talk to us. Maybe he could've done that late at night or something. But having to lie on the floor for so many hours is the worst! Why should a fraternity have to carry out traditions like this that don't benefit us or them? It all just sucked."

By the next day, a conversation with his father had changed his tune. Jake didn't share details with his dad, only that "there was exhausting hazing last night."

His father said, "I'm disappointed to hear you had to go through that, but I can cheer you up." He told Jake about a family friend who had been in a fraternity in the 1980s. The brothers had driven that year's pledge class to a different state, dropped them off, and left them to find their way back to college alone in a pre-cell-phone era.

"Damn, that gives me some perspective," Jake said to me. "What we just did is definitely hazing, but I'm still on campus. I haven't been physically harmed. I still have my phone and personal belongings. It was exhausting, but I just have to remember that our family friend had it worse than me and he turned out all right. All the other brothers have done this before. This ritual probably happens to every single person. It's going to be okay."

Jake would also end up rationalizing the B on his second exam, which was the worst test score he had ever received. "I could have done better. But realizing how much work these courses are with everything else I have going on, I've kind of lowered my standards a bit."

The last weekend in September, Jake's parents and sisters came to visit. This was a relief to Jake: He needed to escape the Greek world for a while, to remember the person he was before he started down this road. It had been awkward around the fraternity house after the hazing, "knowing that the people who surround you had just participated in some satanic ritual the night before." The pledges walked on eggshells, careful not to discuss what had happened because they had been ordered to "ever conceal and never reveal."

Jake's parents asked him about the fraternity, pressing him on what he had experienced and whom he had met. He didn't divulge specifics. It felt strange holding back from them. "I used to be open about everything to them, but I was very hesitant to tell them about the inner workings about the fraternity and specific things that we've done," Jake told me later. When I asked him why, he said, "I don't know. In fear that it could get out, that someone could overhear? And I've been taught not to talk about this stuff."

Once his family stopped questioning him, he relaxed in their company, strolling around the city, staying in their hotel, chatting about college in general and the goings-on back home. He felt like a kid again for the first time since he had arrived at college. This time, when his family left him at his dorm, as soon as they were out of sight, Jake cried.

Ω Ω Ω

The new pledge class was integrating well. For Oliver's PhiEp chapter, the pledge process was a low-key effort to help the freshmen adjust to college and Greek life. "You come to college shell-shocked. Then, when you pledge as a freshman, in addition to school, you have all the chores of cleaning the house, studying pledge materials and other things you're expected to know. And you need a presence at parties to meet people. It's oftentimes very difficult for people to handle all that," Oliver told me.

The pledges were strongly encouraged to move into the house. Most of them did. Officially, the pledge period lasted 10 weeks, but only five of those weeks included official activities. Some activities were led by the brothers (Work Week, Scavenger Hunt, fraternity history lessons and pledge tests, dodgeball games against other houses), and some were delegated to the freshmen to manage independently (planning creative Homecoming decorations and week-end events for brothers and alumni, running their own weekend pledge retreat whenever and wherever they wanted).

The brothers taught pledges about fraternity history and values, as well as "how to be gentlemen." The first speech Oliver had given the pledges centered on the chapter's good-guy reputation. "We've worked really hard to build a reputation as a house of nice guys. If you endanger that reputation, you'll immediately be kicked to the curb," he told them. "That's not the kind of people we want. We're not the douchey frat house. We're not here to 'get bitches and get fucked up.' We're here to learn how to grow up a little bit. And with that comes learning how to be a nice human being, how to look out for each other, for guests, and for girls, and how to properly treat girls. If you're consistently nice and respectful, you're going to build a good reputation, and that's going to help you a lot in life."

This was a credo Oliver truly believed, because his parents had raised him "to always be the best person you could be and always try to make a difference in the world around you." His parents led by example, going out of their way to help people. If someone needed assistance crossing the street, his mom ran to help. If a driver had a flat tire, his dad pulled over with tools.

The emphasis on niceness seemed to work. Since this PhiEp chapter had restarted in the 2000s, there had been no major scandals. It had no history of racist incidents because none of the members, minority or not, would have stood for it. And the brothers didn't believe in hazing. Instead, they encouraged the pledges to connect by designing their own bonding experiences.

When Oliver was a pledge, his class had opted to schedule reg-ular Sunday night pledge class dinners. "We're not about hazing 'education.' That's something I have a big problem with. If I was being messed with when I was a pledge, I would have left, because I don't like the idea of big groups picking on smaller, weaker groups,"

Oliver told me. "We're trying to build friendships and family. It's way easier to do if you're not being a dick about everything. Yeah, some things are going to be hard. We expect a certain GPA. We have high standards, and there's a lot of pressure to get to those standards sometimes, but no one's going to be a huge jackass. We just expect pledges to participate in the things we have going on and to put in a lot of work getting to know people and representing us well."

Scavenger Hunt, one of Oliver's favorite pledge activities, perhaps came closest to the definition of hazing, but pledges said they enjoyed it. Many of the items on the list were, in Oliver's words, "absurd tasks with absurd objects," such as making a video of pledges doing pull-ups on a bus. The chapter expected the underclassmen to attend parties both for their sake and for the sake of the fraternity. Because freshmen and sophomores were underage, Oliver explained, "they can't go to bars. So parties are essentially for the younger guys to meet girls, hang out with friends, and make new friends. Also, if you have a party and the freshmen aren't there when the girls are over, that makes that pledge class look bad. My pledge class kept each other accountable. Even if you had to study, you took a little break."

By living together in the sleeping porch, pledges were supposed to get to know one another well. Some of Oliver's fondest fraternity moments were the mornings after a party. A couple of guys would laugh about the night's craziness, the rest of the group would wake up and join the conversation, and the entire porch would go out for breakfast.

At the pledge retreat, "Hot Seat," the only mandatory activity, usually lasted between six and eight hours. With one pledge in the "hot seat," each of the others around the circle revealed what he liked about him and what part of his personality he needed to work on. Typically, the guy in the hot seat, who was permitted to respond to the criticism, ended up sharing his backstory, which was one of the points of the exercise. Oliver had never heard of a year when the discussion didn't work out. The pledges were respectful, and their criticisms were constructive. An example during Oliver's pledge year: "I noticed that a lot of the time when we're at study tables, you're on Netflix when you could be spending that time studying for your tests. I'm noticing that because you said you're not doing very well in class, so that would be a good place to start."

When it was Oliver's turn in the hot seat, back when he was a pledge, many people complimented him on his maturity level or the way he carried himself. The criticisms mentioned that he wasn't around the house as much as they would have liked, because he traveled home so often to see his girlfriend.

Phi Epsilon wanted its members to bond through shared experiences rather than shared hardship. The PhiEps's pledge schedule consisted mostly of helping one another study for pledge tests, attending mandatory library hours to study for their classes, and finding time to hang out as much as possible. Oliver went to the movies with brothers whenever he could. When he was a pledge, he invited a pledge brother who was into fashion to go downtown with him. They had brunch, went shopping, and "had a fun 'bro date,'" Oliver told me. "At brunch we just hung out and asked each other, 'What makes you tick?' Things like that. You go do things that aren't dependent on alcohol to have a good time. That gets you close."

It wasn't unusual for pledge brothers to have a few beers on the lawn or while watching a movie. But "drinking isn't the foundation of our relationships, because we first bonded without alcohol. These are some of my best friends. These are my guys!" Oliver said. "Guys from other houses have told me they're envious that we're all super close and such great friends. They don't feel like they are because all they did was get fucked up, so they didn't have time to get to know each other."

PhiEp had started a tradition the brothers called Fourth Quarter:

After a pregame, party, and afterparty, the handful of guys who were still awake would gather to discuss their lives, girlfriends, or stresses until they were ready to go to sleep. Oliver was so accustomed to bottling up his own feelings that he didn't contribute; he merely gave advice and offered comfort to the others. As a freshman, he had sought guidance only from Diego, who was gracious about being his mentor and sounding board. Sometimes Oliver confided in his parents, who were unwaveringly supportive, but he didn't like to burden anyone else with his troubles.

Whenever Oliver felt like going out, though, he knew he could send a group text invite and at least six brothers would say yes. The chapter also had a "brotherhood chair," whose job was to plan two or three "Brotherhoods" per quarter. Brotherhoods were nights when the guys closed the house to nonmembers and did something fun to blow off steam. Sometimes the activity involved alcohol (they designed and competed in the Beer Olympics), sometimes it didn't (they set up a fortress and a maze inside the house and chased one another through it with Nerf weapons). Whatever they did, brothers often ended up chatting. "We're open with each other. We give each other shit, but people are able to speak their mind and at the end of the day, we're all here to support each other," Oliver said.

But good intentions and camaraderie within a fraternity are not always enough to change the perceptions of the people outside it. Two days after the "unregistered party" violation, the chapter got in trouble again. The members were scheduled to cohost a party with two other fraternities at another house. At 9:00 P.M., PhiEp started pregaming in its own front yard with a sorority.

Oliver was skipping the pregame to study for a midterm in the house library. He loved living in the fraternity house, but the environment wasn't always ideal. It could be hard to find a quiet space to study in a house of 75 guys. During one finals week, Oliver's last exam fell on a Friday, but from Monday onward his sleep and productivity suffered increasingly each night as more and more brothers shifted from studying to celebrating.

In high school, Oliver had been a 4.0 student. In college, his GPA hovered around 3.6; he particularly exceled in economics, English, and political science courses. He expected his GPA would drop further as presidential responsibilities ate up his time. He was at peace with the tradeoff because he found that he enjoyed "serving the people," as he put it. He liked being the guy who checked that the windows and doors were locked at night; the house was in a relatively dangerous part of town. He didn't mind working hard every day to handle small business management, wade through IFC paperwork, oversee the chapter's website, and make sure the PhiEps were doing their jobs.

He was determined not to let his brothers down. As a freshman, during a deep talk with a few other freshmen about their lives and what mattered to them, Oliver told the group about his work ethic and his goal to make the world a better place. "Damn, man," one of his pledge brothers said, "you really are Bruce Wayne."

At that moment, Oliver had felt like something clicked. He was where he was supposed to be, and he was becoming the person he wanted to be. "Even though most people think Bruce Wayne is a huge tool, he uses his money and power to fund projects to help people, like paying patients' hospital bills. He's totally willing to hurt his own reputation to ensure that no one suspects his true identity. All he wants to do is help people," Oliver told me. "His sense of a constant mission and not resting is also something I wanted to focus on. When Batman puts a criminal away in jail, he doesn't go celebrate at the bars with Robin. He moves on to the next mission." The pledge brother's observation only made Oliver more determined to emulate Batman's fierce loyalty, unwavering commitment to the cause, and mastery of preventive measures.

Close to 10:00, when the PhiEps were planning to go to the party, a brother found Oliver. "Yo, the police are here. Can you come outside?" Oliver followed him, puzzled. The party was registered and the pregame, which included only about 80 people, was almost over. *What now?* he thought.

In the doorway, the same officers from Tuesday night looked exasperated. "Are you having a party again?" one asked.

"No, we're not having a party here tonight. It's somewhere else," Oliver said, mystified.

"Why don't you come look at this." The officer led Oliver outside. Chaos. At least 200 people were dancing in the yard or grabbing drinks from a table laden with beer cans. The chatter of the crowd was almost as loud as the music. "That, by any definition, is a party."

Incredulous, Oliver watched PhiEp brothers unsuccessfully try to usher people away from the house, even as hordes of students continued to arrive.

"We're going to have to write you up," the officer said.

"But we really don't have a party. I've been in the library studying for a test, and I will deal with this, but I'm very confused as to what's happening," Oliver said, trying desperately to piece together how a medium-size pregame could have exploded into this blowout.

"Sorry, but that's the nature of the beast. You can expect an email from us in the next few days."

When the police left, Oliver wondered aloud, "What just happened?" As he walked toward the speakers, brothers gave him the recap. Apparently, the police had shut down a party at the fraternity across the street. A stampede of about 120 sorority sisters from that party then charged the PhiEp lawn, where they could hear the music and see the drinks. The police officers followed them over. It had happened so quickly that the PhiEps didn't have time to turn students away.

Oliver pushed through the crowd as members of multiple sororities continued to stream toward the beer. Most people hadn't yet noticed the police in the pandemonium. Oliver pulled the aux cord from the speakers. "Pregame's over, guys. Everyone head over to the party," he announced.

Oliver returned to the library to resume studying. His midterm was for his management class, of all things. He tried to compartmentalize his frustration. The alumni would again receive an email from the police; on paper, it would look as if PhiEp had committed two violations in three days. And even though Oliver hadn't been involved, as chapter president, he would again shoulder the blame. *They're going to think I'm lying because we have all these super-ridiculous situations,* he thought. *It's going to sound like I'm making up stories to avoid responsibility.*

Within an hour, his phone dinged with an email from the board. The alumni were furious. "What the hell?" a board member wrote. "What could possibly be going on?" The police had cited the chapter for both hosting an unregistered party and providing alcohol to minors.

Oliver slumped. There was no way he'd be able to concentrate on studying now. *These incidents make me look like I have no idea how to captain this ship,* he thought. He tried to explain the situation to the alums. "Hey, all these girls stormed from another house to ours and we had very little time to react. I understand this is not a good situation to be in, but we tried our best to resolve it, and it just didn't go well."

The alumni called the next day. Their patience was wearing thin. There are things you could have done to prevent this, they chided. Don't play music so loudly. Don't have alcohol out in plain sight. Oliver did these things already for PhiEp parties, but tonight's function had just been a casual pregame, and the time between the sorority scrum and the officers' arrival had spanned mere minutes. He didn't bother arguing with the alums.

Oliver scored a 56 percent on his exam.

Ω Ω Ω

As the pledges waited in the basement to be summoned to their Tuesday night pledge meeting, Jake suggested they line up in alphabetical order. He noticed someone was missing. He texted Jamal to ask where he was.

Initiation dues are today, Jamal replied. **Can't afford $500 so I dropped.**

Jake was disappointed. He liked Jamal. "After all we've been through already, to be done in by not being able to afford it, even though he was doing well with chores and memorizing stuff? That's sad. And they don't even have a scholarship fund or anything," Jake told me later.

When Greg led the pledges into the informal chapter room for their pledge meeting, they automatically turned their heads away from the officers to avoid accidentally spotting Z. The officers went through their business: The following week was Homecoming Week. Matched with the Beta Sigma sorority, the brothers would escort the sisters to a club, Poker Night mixer, ballroom party, and Heaven and Hell mixer at a bar. For Poker Night, the fraternity would provide every brother and pledge with twenty dollars to gamble. It did not escape Jake that just a fraction of that money would easily have covered Jamal's initiation dues.

"We'll have a good ratio all week: almost two-to-one girls to guys. It is going to be lit," one of the officers said. The chapter's expectation of the pledges at these functions was unmistakable, Jake said later. "Obviously they want even the pledges to really get with a girl at one of the events. I hope I don't get drunk-cock-blocked again."

Then Daniel relayed the bad news. "You pledges are still fucking up," he said. Because Quinn still wasn't dressing appropriately, a brother had snapped a naked photo of him in the bathroom and posted it to the chapter's private Facebook page. Quinn and JB, a smart and relatively large, out-of-shape guy, had left their pledge books at the house, a major mistake because pledge books were supposed to be secret and sacred. The officers ceremoniously returned the books, which brothers had defaced with Sharpie-drawn penises. Greg assigned both pledges extra duties: Now JB was the weather pledge and Quinn, still the wiki pledge, was also the mail pledge, responsible for sorting and distributing the mail for the brothers who lived in the house.

Because several of the pledges hadn't completed four interviews and the required weekly study hours, Kevin, the academics chair, announced, "We're going to have a study session Thursday morning at five forty-five. Put your pins in your pocket and wear comfortable shoes. Pledge Eric, what time are you going to be at the house Thursday morning?"

"Five thirty-five," Eric said.

The brothers applauded. "Good answer," Kevin said.

Greg added that because the brothers believed the pledges weren't working out often enough, they now had mandatory gym hours. Every week, they would have to spend four hours at the gym, Snapchatting Greg when they arrived and left. This was a blessing in disguise, Jake thought. He needed the push to stay in shape. But how were pledges supposed to find the time? Gym hours would be on top of study hours, pledge chores (and extra pledge duties for some), EPs, pledge meetings, Homecoming activities, the study session, interviews, and the hours the pledges needed to study their pledge books, not to mention classes and coursework.

Worst of all, Greg told the pledges to bring the same items to this week's EP that they'd brought the week before. *Oh, shit, does he mean the sleeping bags again?* Jake thought, and saw on his pledge brothers' faces that they feared the same. "Make sure you sleep in tomorrow, boys," a brother said, laughing. "It's probably the last bit of sleep you're going to get."

At 5:35 Thursday morning, Jake waited with the other pledges outside the house. Every pledge was present except for Bryce, who had somehow continued both to weasel out of pledge activities and to get his pledge brothers to cover his chores. The winds had picked up, and an early frost dotted the lawn. The boys shivered.

Kevin and a few other brothers came outside to greet the pledges. "So this isn't really a study session. You won't be expected to study while you're jogging," Kevin said. "Here are the rules. You will jog in a single line two miles to the basketball court on Third." Jake grimaced. The road was hilly, and the steepest incline would be in the middle of the run. He hadn't jogged since middle school. "If any one of you stops jogging," Kevin continued, "we'll make you all do 10 push-ups. And you have a time limit to beat. We're being generous about your time: You have 24 minutes to get every pledge to the court or you'll have to do the jog again."

As the pledges lined up, Kevin instructed them to jog "at the pace of the slowest person in the group." When he shouted, "Go!" the pledges at the front of the line took off quickly. Jake and Logan called to them to slow down; if this was a team-building exercise, the pledges had to work together. Kevin and a few other fit brothers ran alongside them, yelling at the pledges.

Half a mile in, Jake was still feeling pretty good; the empty road at this hour was peaceful. And at least he wasn't Eric, who had to do the entire jog while holding his brick. Wes, who had knee problems, was starting to fall behind, shuffling instead of jogging. "Come on, Wes, come on! Stay in line!" the pledges urged him. Other pledges, too, were beginning to slow down and switch places with the pledges behind them. JB, already breathless, had drifted to the back of the line.

At the midway point, when the group started up the incline, Jake pulled a quadricep. The pain reverberated through his leg. He limped, then hopped, trying to massage the muscle. If ever he had an opportunity to take a breather, this was the time, he thought. Who would blame him? On paper, he was a devoted pledge. Yesterday, he had tried to fulfill most of his obligations for the week: He worked out at the gym for two hours, finished all his weekly pledge chores, and completed five interviews. He had even skipped a class to fulfill his cleaning duties.

But as he had listened to other pledges talk about a party that he had missed to catch up on homework and sleep, he worried he wasn't bonding enough with the brothers. It seemed that the other pledges were forging friendships, creating inside jokes, and generally climbing the Greek social ladder, while he was just trying to survive. Even Quinn, who screwed something up every other day, had scored more interviews than any other pledge because he attended every social function. Some brothers had even invited Quinn to extra outings, where he was the only pledge.

Jake liked the interviews because they were a non-awkward way for him to connect with brothers under the pretext of learning about the fraternity. To ensure the pledges earned their signatures, some of the brothers hazed them, making them do push-ups, drive them around campus, or perform a silly task. Others were more lenient. One day while doing his chores, Jake informed Kevin, "Have you ever noticed that when you stand up, one of your balls hangs lower than the other, and it's always the ball that's opposite to your dominant hand? It's not a joke; it's a fact." Intrigued, Kevin stood up, reached into his pants, and confirmed that Jake was correct. They discussed this phenomenon until Kevin wiped his hand on his forehead and realized, "Oh, wait, that was the hand I used to touch my balls." When Jake asked him for an interview, Kevin gave him a break: "Nah, man. We just talked about balls for 10 minutes straight. I'll just give you a signature."

The interview conversations could be educational. Two brothers told him about the "families" within the fraternity; Big/Little Reveal was coming up, the night when pledges were assigned to their Big Brothers (chapter mentors) and, by extension, their dynasties (the "families" of Bigs, the Bigs' Bigs, etc.). Some of the chapter's families had better reputations than others. The dynasty known as Red Rum played beer pong every night. Orange Crush was known for smoking weed and drinking. Green Lantern was a powerful dynasty with several chapter officers. Jake hoped he got into that one.

When Jake interviewed Steven, a compassionate junior, he was surprised by his candor. Steven told Jake that he sometimes felt like the odd man out in the fraternity. He had joined as a second-semester freshman; he'd probably gotten a bid because a brother was a good friend. While he didn't regret joining, he told Jake he believed there were a few brothers who "absolutely hated" him because the fraternity was mostly conservative, while he was Jewish and liberal.

"I'm liberal," Jake said.

"Good. We need more of you around here. Most fraternities are conservative," Steven said. He was tired of the anti-Semitic remarks that some of the brothers made toward him. "I'd say ninety-five percent of the people here are absolutely great. It's just the five percent who hate my guts that I worry about."

Now, in the light of daybreak, Jake wondered, *Is someone going to hate my guts?* He'd kept his political views quiet. He weighed whether he should bow out of the two-mile run.

He did not. He kept going, his gait uneven, until Kevin jogged in front of the group. "So none of you noticed you're missing a pledge?" he asked. Apparently, Wes had paused to rest his knee. "Everybody stop and give me ten," Kevin ordered.

Jake's push-ups were wobbly and slow. The other pledges finished quickly and were instructed to jog in place until Wes caught up and completed his push-ups. The moment Wes finished, the pledges took off again. Midway up the incline, Jake's side cramped, and he doubled over in pain, but did not stop. The brothers led the pledges away from the road, up a rocky hill. Jake nearly couldn't take it anymore; the pain in his side was excruciating. He thought he might pass out.

About 20 meters from the basketball court, Kevin turned around, easily jogging backward, and yelled, "Everybody sprint to the far basket!" Nauseated, Jake pushed harder, feeling as if every vein in his head would burst. He had not come this far to fail. Finally, he reached the basket. "Good job, Jake. Walk it off," Greg said, and gave him a congratulatory swat with his baseball cap.

"You'll be all right, Jake. Put your hands on your head and lean back," Logan murmured. "Let your lungs expand and contract."

Kevin looked at his phone. "You got 20:58. Well, you guys made it. But you left a man behind." The pledges looked around, surprised. Wes was there, stretching out his knee. But JB wasn't. Several pledges raced to the edge of the last hill to see JB crawling up. Ten of them carried him to the basketball court. He looked like he had already fainted; he couldn't raise his head. When the pledges set JB on his feet, Jake propped him up on his shoulder. As the brothers distributed bottles of water, Kevin cleared his throat. The pledges watched him with dread. Would they have to run it all over again?

"You got 23:57," he said. The pledges cheered. "But you're not done yet. Now you're running suicides. Line up, sprint to the cones, sprint back, sprint to the half-court line, sprint back, then sprint to the end and back. And then do them all again. Ready, go."

As much as Jake had been an overachiever in high school, he forsook that ambition now. His pledge brothers left him in the dust, but he decided he didn't care. There were no threatened punishments for slow suicides. He finished near last, with only JB huffing behind him.

"Now you're done—for this week," Kevin announced. "You'll be jogging every Thursday at five forty-five, and each week you'll have to beat your last week's time."

When the brothers left, Jake told the pledges he'd wear a stopwatch for the next jog so he could help them beat the time limit, but not by so much that they'd have difficulties beating their time the following week.

Afterward, Jake and JB went to the library for study hours. "I feel really bad," JB said, slumping miserably in his chair. "I almost made everyone else jog two miles again." He told Jake he didn't understand why they were forced to run. "Jogging was supposed to be punishment for not doing study hours, right? But by making this a weekly thing, there's no motivation to do study hours," JB said. "There's no reason for me to stay if they're just going to make us do shit like this for no apparent reason."

Jake could see JB's point, but he didn't want another pledge to quit. "Well, you can leave at any time, but I think we jog so we bond," Jake said. "Maybe we'll get better at teamwork and coordinating things. I think it's supposed to teach us that we're one class and we all have to look out for each other, just like we looked out for you."

"Yeah, but aren't there other things we could do for team building instead?" JB asked. Jake didn't have an answer.

That night at EP, Greg tested the pledges on the officers' titles and BNs. He was pleasantly surprised that they got more than half of the answers correct. But like the week before, the brothers told the pledges to get ready for bed. Again, they turned off the lights in the Game Room, where a black-robed brother repeatedly intoned, "Go the *fuck* to sleep." Again, Jake lay sleepless for hours on the cold, hard floor. And again, the pledges were pillowcased and led out of the room to be spun about the hallways, this time holding a dildo for the entire ritual. The black-hooded brother's speech warned, "If you fuck anything up, the consequences will be severe." And even though they were down two pledges—Bryce and Wes said they were sick—the pledges had to remain still for the same amount of time.

Jake had gotten to know Wes better recently. Wes acted much more confident than he actually was. He told Jake he also had gone to Kappa Tau the first night and had been roundly rejected. The brother who walked Wes to the door had said, "This ain't working for you. Don't show up here again."

"At least my guy was considerate about it," Jake told his dad when he recounted that story. "K-Tau must be really exclusive. Being in Zeta Kappa is helping me become a better person."

"I can tell," his father said. "It's helping to smooth out your rougher edges."

"Whoa, hang on," I interrupted Jake as he relayed this conversation to me. "You're a great guy. What rough edges?"

Throughout high school, Jake explained, his father told him he had awkward mannerisms that a fraternity could "fix." A fraternity would teach him how to hang out with people, his father had insisted. None of the other three Town College students from his high school—not even Arjun—had kept in touch with Jake this semester. "When I talk to people my age, I usually look down instead of making eye contact. I mumble," Jake said. "Now there's a much bigger emphasis for me on what you wear, how you work out, how you socialize. It's a mixture of telling us how and throwing us into these situations, like surprise parties, that's helping me especially in talking to girls and learning how to drink. Being in a fraternity has definitely helped me build up a better tolerance for alcohol. And I'm much better at standing the taste of it. That's not something you can learn in a classroom. All my life, I've been used to learning every-thing in the classroom, so this is a changeup."

Outside of fraternity functions, Jake had developed platonic friendships with a few of the girls in his classes, including Beth, who always sat next to him in Psychology. But pledge life left no time for him to socialize with these girls, or with any other non-Greeks, when he wasn't in class. He barely knew his own roommate, a GDI.

Somehow, Jake managed to make it to most of his classes, even if he did occasionally fall asleep in them or drunk-post on class dis-cussion boards. He fell into the habit of drinking daily espresso shots to stay awake in class. In his English section, he commiserated with a sorority freshman who said pledging was "killing" her, too, what with pledging activities, sleep deprivation, and frequent hookups. Jake was the only fraternity brother in the small section, which con-sisted of selected honors students. He wasn't accustomed to being viewed as the class partier rather than the class brain. In English 101, he was known, in his words, as "the guy who's hungover and tired every morning, the guy who parties every night." He even wrote and submitted an entire essay at the last minute while drunk (and got an A). He wasn't yet sure how he felt about this change.

But he told me his father was right. "Before, I didn't really have a nice group of guys I could call friends. So even though pledging's been exhausting, and filled with chores, lots of drinking, and the craziest weeks of my life, I think it's helped," he said. "I sound crazy saying that, I now feel like I have a whole group of guys I can call my friends that I feel comfortable around, or I'm at least starting to."

Because he was in a particularly introspective mood, I asked Jake how he felt now about the forced drinking that had so terrified him before rush. "Forced drinking kind of goes along with any parties because of peer pressure. Even if they're not holding a bottle to your lips, there's a lot of pressure to have you drink as much as possible, especially when they're drunk, too, and can't tell you when to stop," he said.

"Would you consider that to be hazing?" I asked.

"I definitely think the drinking games are hazing, and at Bid Dinner there was a lot of forced-drinking hazing going on. These sleeping events are hazing. Jeez, man, we're forced to lie on the ground for hours just to be essentially kidnapped from our sleeping bags and thrown into this weird ritual. The jogging is hazing, I guess, too," Jake said. "But here's something I've gathered. Because I'm not the only one going through this, I can see how they can argue that these activities are meant to create a bond with your class. And it's worked. That's how I've gotten to know my pledge class much better: because we've struggled together. So I can't say that 100 percent nothing good has come out of hazing. And it sucks I'm actually defending hazing, but it's for one reason only: It's helped to create bonds."

Jake not only defended the hazing; he defended the hazers. "I've also got to consider the perspective. This stuff is relatively tame comparatively," he said. At the last EP session, he said, Greg told the pledges that the Beta Delts made their pledges eat an entire onion before each meeting. He described another chapter in which a brother wouldn't give signatures for interviews unless a pledge threw a bottle of beer at the wall and slurped the beer from the floor.

At the same time, Greg had explained that, unlike at pledge meetings, the Zeta Kappas never discussed chores and certain other tasks at the brothers-only chapter meetings because an alum always attended—and Nationals prohibited these activities, which were considered hazing. Jake deduced, "I feel like Greg's completely aware there's some hazing-like stuff that goes on. The fact that he puts stuff in perspective, like the guys eating onions, makes me think they're

making an effort not to haze us really hard. I feel like there's definitely some character to Greg and the officers in preventing unnecessary hazing. I dunno, I'm very mixed about this."

The Secret Reason Hazing Continues

Hazing, as practiced in most places, is wrong, it is unethical, it is
dangerous, and it is a crime in 44 states and Washington, DC. Yet 73
percent of Greeks are hazed, according to the most recent large-scale
hazing study. Binghamton University was so plagued by hazing
complaints in 2012, including allegations that fraternity brothers
were waterboarding pledges, that the school's former assistant director of Greek life told *The New York Times*, "My entire tenure from
start to finish, I was scared to death that someone was going to die."
Sure enough, in 2017, freshman pledge Conor Donnelly fell to his
death while trying to climb a balcony at an Alpha Sigma Phi party.
(Investigators ruled that while hazing was not involved, alcohol was
a factor in his death.)

Between 2010 and 2017, at least 17 pledges died from hazing by
university-recognized fraternities and at least two more in under-
ground or local fraternities, according to hazing expert Hank Nuwer's extensive research. The most frequently reported hazing
behaviors among college students involve alcohol consumption, humiliation, isolation, sleep deprivation, and sex acts, a recent Association for the Study of Higher Education report revealed. Jake would
come to experience nearly all of these.

College hazing began in the early 1800s as a way for sophomores
to needle freshmen. Fraternity hazing increased in the late 1860s
with the return of students who learned hazing practices when they
fought in the Civil War. Hazing "was conducted to impress the new
members with the honor being conferred upon them in their initiation into the brotherhood," historian Nicholas Syrett noted. "It was

also designed to recoup the masculinity and authority of the upper-classmen, who had been groveling before freshmen in their attempts to get them to pick their fraternity over others." Post–World War II, hazing grew more extreme and dangerous, and more likely to involve alcohol.

Twenty-first-century fraternity hazing is "even more brutal than before," said Susan Lipkins, a psychologist who runs InsideHazing .com. The media shows us only what Lipkins called "the tip of the iceberg" of fraternity hazing traditions, the more sensational incidents: Wilmington College Gamma Phi Betas either watched or participated as members blindfolded pledges, told them to strip, stuffed their mouths with Limburger cheese, and whipped them so violently that doctors had to remove a 19-year-old's injured testicle. Hofstra University Sigma Pis allegedly poured ghost pepper hot sauce on pledges' genitals and goaded pledges to vomit on one another. At the University of Tennessee, a Pi Kappa Alpha nearly died of alcohol poisoning because brothers were butt-chugging (funneling alcohol through a rubber tube inserted in their rectums). Washington and Lee University's Phi Kappa Psi used a stun gun on a pledge.

There's a little-known reason that hazing continues, despite laws criminalizing the behavior, more public fraternity crackdowns, and social media tools that make hazing easier to catch and prove. It's a reason that members of several fraternities confirmed to me. It's also why Sam (a pseudonym), an adult who was formerly one of the highest-ranking national officers of a fraternity whose hazing killed a member, continues to defend the practice.

In 2018, four members of the Baruch College chapter of Pi Delta Psi, all from Queens, New York, were convicted on felony charges of voluntary manslaughter in the death of freshman Michael Deng. The Pi Delta Psi fraternity, found guilty on a felony count of involuntary manslaughter, was fined and banned from Pennsylvania, where the incident took place, for 10 years. During a retreat in the

Poconos, fraternity brothers blindfolded Deng, forced him to walk across an icy path carrying a 30-pound backpack filled with sand, and repeatedly "speared" him, plowing headfirst into him and slamming him to the ground. Deng died from a resulting brain injury.

The national office of Deng's fraternity was quick to distance itself from the chapter with a statement claiming the brothers "violated the values and rules of our organization, including our strict no-hazing policy." But it turned out that the ritual that killed the freshman was a common fraternity tradition that was very much intertwined with the "values and rules" the national office publicly accused the chapter of violating. The problem, Sam claimed, was in the execution, not the concept.

All chapters of Pi Delta Psi, an Asian American fraternity, have a "standardized education," or pledge program, during which brothers learn Asian American cultural history, Sam said. Each pledge also had to keep a handwritten pledge book containing the fraternity's mission statement, a list of brothers and their backgrounds, and the pledge's reflections on the process. (At the time I interviewed Sam, most of these pledge practices were suspended.) While pledge books aren't uncommon among other fraternities, Pi Delta Psi expected pledges to memorize not only the information but also the page and line numbers where that information could be found.

Pi Delta Psi used pledge books, which many groups consider hazing, to give pledges a sense of early Chinese immigrants' experiences at the detention center on San Francisco's Angel Island. Sam explained that Angel Island officers repeatedly quizzed immigrants on minute details about family members living in the United States. "How many cobblestones were in front of their house? When was their neighbor's daughter born? The relatives of detained immigrants started sneaking books of answers into the detention center, which immigrants memorized cover to cover because they knew the smallest slipup could be reason for them to be sent back," he said. "The entire experience during our pledge process was designed to humble the new member and make him appreciate the progress of civil rights since that time."

The fraternity used similar reasoning to rationalize the initiation ritual that chapters called the Gauntlet, or Bamboo Ceiling, which was intended to reflect the discrimination experienced by past generations of Asian Americans. Sam said the ritual was supposed to go like this: To symbolize the immigrant's difficult attempt to reunite with his family in the United States, the pledge was blindfolded outside at night with only the voice of his Big Brother to guide him. As he tried to walk toward his Big, other brothers pushed him to the ground and held him down while shouting racial slurs at him and yelling at him to go back to his country. "The point is that you struggle to get back up to get to your Big Brother, like previous [Asian American] generations faced a lot of adversity, and to see if you have the resilience to overcome the adversity. Then, at the very end, when it looks like the pledge is completely physically and emotionally depleted, the other brothers help him up and carry him to his Big Brother to show that you can overcome but you have to ask for help."

At Baruch, Sam said, the chapter took the ritual too far. They did it on icy ground rather than grass, and they battered Deng instead of pushing him down. "The point is to get them tired, not to physically assault them," he said. One of the defendants told police that Deng was singled out for harsher treatment because he "wasn't going with the flow, which pissed off the brothers."

The Gauntlet was hazing, Sam admitted. And even though the ritual killed a member, Sam, who, as an adult national fraternity officer, had power and authority over more than 1,000 undergraduates, defended hazing. "Hazing works," he told me. "Hazing creates an unusually strong bond between people who weather tough times together, and the toughness also creates the illusion of reaching a worthwhile goal. It increases the value of the letters because you've undergone such a hard process of obtaining them."

Thus, one of the major reasons fraternity hazing persists: It appears that a number of the involved adults and alumni *want* it to. And it didn't help optics when the Fraternity and Sorority Political Action Committee (FSPAC)—which raises money for federal office candidates who "champion Greek issues," according to its website—reportedly tried to stall legislation intended to curb hazing. In 2013, media outlets reported that FSPAC had played a part in persuading US representative Frederica Wilson, a Florida Democrat who called herself the "Haze Buster," not to introduce her federal anti-hazing bill.

With this kind of pressure, it's no surprise that 95 percent of hazed students don't report the hazing. According to the Novak Institute on Hazing at the University of Kentucky, 37 percent of surveyed students said they did not report it because they didn't want to get the group in trouble, while 42 percent were afraid other group members might retaliate or ostracize them. The real surprise is that 25 percent of hazed students believed that coaches and advisors knew the hazing was happening and, worse, reported that alumni were physically present in at least a quarter of hazing incidents.

Some brothers told me that even as some fraternity-affiliated adults loudly condemn hazing in public, in private they tell students to do it anyway. A recent Maryland fraternity brother told me that alumni and chapter advisors are anti-hazing "on paper." But "even they secretly want hazing to continue. A lot of alumni say, 'You should haze.' They come back, tell us their ridiculous stories, and flex and sound cool. Then they get hammered with all the college kids and drive away."

Brothers described how some older members' attitudes help convince young pledges that they want to be hazed, or that the activities aren't technically hazing. Pledges might not know the difference; research shows that nine out of ten college students who are hazed don't actually believe they were hazed. A New York City freshman told me his chapter didn't haze and then described forced-drinking events that clearly constituted hazing.

Why might alumni and older members want hazing to continue? Many of them harbor a genuine belief that it is their responsibility to make their pledges into "better" men. They see hazing as necessary tough love, "designed to knock you down to build you up as a man," a southern sophomore explained. Others take comfort in the tradition; if the fraternity remains the same, the experience of being a member remains an unbroken line that continued under their watch and will continue, unchanging, into the future. They see themselves as stewards of the institution. Still others are convinced their life-long friendships with pledge brothers formed precisely because they faced adverse conditions together. They want new members to have these relationships, too.

A Virginia fraternity alum said his chapter's older members were "pro-hazing, pro-drinking, anti-change. This is understand-able. What they went through with their elders was objectively worse than what we went through, and yet they came through and were very good friends. The conclusion they drew from it, and the conclusion nearly all such groups draw, is that 'it worked, we came together, we're close now, and there's nothing wrong with it.'"

When he and other members of his class tried to reform their chapter's hazing practices, older members constantly pushed back. "It wears you down, it indoctrinates you. And some of us, myself included, were turning into what we'd tried to avoid becoming. When I was 19, I knew the emotional abuse was harmful, immoral, and should be abolished. When I was 21, I didn't have it in me to care anymore because I'd been called a whiny bitch for years."

• • •

Pat, a recent grad from Nevada, was his chapter's pledge master his senior year. "Hazing serves a point. Everything's supposed to be done for a reason. There's no reason to dump an ice bucket on a kid while he's sleeping," he said. That's easy to say but hard to justify. A northern brother told me that every hazing tradition "is attached to the morality" of a fraternity value, but then he couldn't remember the lesson he was supposed to have learned when he and his pledge brothers had to eat live goldfish.

Pat's strategy was to use hazing to, in his view, fix individuals' character flaws. When he saw a few pledges picking on another pledge, he made them walk around with their target all day (while Snapchatting him proof) to get to know the student better. He told freshmen he believed were "full of themselves" to dress in humiliating costumes, like girls' cheerleading uniforms. He ordered "loudmouth" pledges not to speak, and quiet pledges to get girls' numbers. He sent what he called the "bookish" pledges to mandatory gym hours with athletes and told the athletes to sit next to the bookish pledges in class. "Some quiet pledges needed to break out of their shell, and some people needed to be taught they weren't the best person in the world," he told me.

Pat learned these strategies from the older brothers who had hazed him. They demanded that he chug a beer in five seconds or he'd have to chug another. When he did, spiking the cup like a football, the pledge master ordered him to chug a mixture of whiskey, hot sauce, and tobacco "if you think you're so good at drinking." He did, and projectile-vomited. "I'm glad that happened to me. It taught me a lesson," Pat said. "I thought I was all that. I learned not to open my mouth and not to be a jerk. I learned to respect my superiors." Three years later, though, he was arrested for assaulting an adult.

Pat insisted that the word *hazing* gives what should be acceptable rituals a negative connotation. "A lot of hazing is essentially team building with alcohol," he said. "If you called it brotherhood building or character building, people would see it differently."

Pledges endure the mistreatment for many reasons. Jake convinced himself that if older brothers had participated in a hazing activity, then it must be okay. And perhaps more students are willing to be hazed, and hazed hard, because the stakes of acceptance seem higher than in the years before social media. The "I'm in, you're out" dichotomy has never been as stark as it is now. Many kids believe that, as the recent Maryland alum told me, "Hazing is a necessary evil everyone goes through because they want so badly to be part of the culture. There's a big fear of missing out. Now that everything's showcased—you see on Facebook everyone's at parties and you're not—there's a big pressure to be included."

There's another, more basic human instinct that could help explain why hazing continues, why otherwise nice people participate in it, and why it's so hard to curtail: Hazing can be viewed as a means of group survival. People generally want to believe they are decent citizens who make good decisions. So when they do something stupid or cruel, they feel uncomfortable afterward when they try to reconcile their behavior with their image of themselves. Social psychologists call this tension or anxiety "cognitive dissonance." Cognitive dissonance theory suggests that because we want our behavior to be consistent with our beliefs, we try to minimize that discomfort. One way to do that is to change our beliefs so that the behavior makes sense to us.

In 1959, researchers decided to test how cognitive dissonance applies to groups. They hypothesized that people who undergo a humiliating initiation to get into a group will rationalize their behavior afterward by concluding that the group must be worth the pain of getting in, or else they wouldn't have degraded themselves. To get into a group that held discussions on the psychology of sex, the researchers had college women read embarrassing or obscene words such as *fuck, cock,* and *screw*—remember, this was the 1950s—and sexually graphic passages. The group discussion they participated in afterward was designed to be "one of the most worthless and uninteresting discussions imaginable" about secondary sex behavior in animals. The researchers found that the initiates who read the most embarrassing material were most likely to believe the group was valuable. In the 1960s, different researchers took the experiment further. Instead of asking students to read sexual material, they gave them electric shocks, ranging from weak to powerful. Sure enough, the more painful the shocks, the more a student later convinced herself of the value of a similarly worthless group.

This is what happens during and after hazing, social psychologists say. Pledges convince themselves that their fraternity membership was worth the suffering by coming up with rationales ("This fraternity is awesome"; "Our pledge class bonded"; "Everyone else had to do it"). By the time they've been initiated, former hazees are persuaded that membership justifies not only the hazing they endured but also the hazing they might inflict on the next pledges. Hazing leads "future society members to find the group more attractive and worthwhile," Robert Cialdini wrote in his excellent book *Influence.* "The more effort that goes into a commitment, the greater is its ability to influence the attitudes of the person who made it. . . . As long as it is the case that people like and believe in what they have struggled to get, these groups will continue to arrange effortful and troublesome initiation rites. The loyalty and dedication of those who emerge will increase to a great degree the chances of group cohesiveness and survival."

For alumni, if the hazing continues, the unchanging tradition psychologically validates that their own experiences were acceptable. "Hazing has become the central tenet of fraternal culture, I don't deny that," Sam said. "It's just human nature. Something will be worth more to you if you invest more time and effort into it. If we're just given something, no matter how valuable it actually is, we're going to value it less if it's just handed to us."

This may be why hazing rituals have names such as the Gauntlet. For 2017 Penn State pledge Timothy Piazza, who died following this tradition, the Gauntlet was an obstacle course of drinking stations where pledges had to quickly consume various kinds of alcohol. Many brothers want pledges to feel that they are completing a quest to get into the club, that not just anyone is worthy, that the letters of the fraternity must be earned, that membership is an exclusive privilege reserved only for those who work for it.

One of the problems with this mentality is the idea that by joining something larger than they are, these young students believe they must subordinate themselves to it. In some cases, they are made to feel that they should prioritize the image of the fraternity over the well-being of a brother. On too many occasions, fraternity members have tried to cover up or ignore a pledge's injury, presumably because they wanted to protect the fraternity. In 2016, for example, Towson University Tau Kappa Epsilons made a 19-year-old pledge eat cat food and drink what was apparently vinegar and pickle juice, burning his esophagus and causing him to vomit blood. They reportedly bullied him into delaying medical treatment so the fraternity wouldn't "get into trouble." He was eventually hospitalized with significant damage to his esophagus, tongue, intestinal lining, and stomach.

At Penn State, Piazza's turn through the Gauntlet, a Beta Theta Pi chapter hazing tradition, led him to drink what prosecutors called a "life-threatening" amount of alcohol: 18 drinks in 82 minutes. His subsequent drunken falls injured his brain and ruptured his spleen. Rather than getting him the medical attention he needed, fraternity brothers left him lying there for 12 hours—and a brother directed the pledge master to "make sure the pledges keep quiet about last night."

When Michael Deng lay dying after the Pi Delta Psi Gauntlet, fraternity brothers waited two hours to take him to the hospital. The fraternity's 28-year-old national president reportedly instructed the brothers to dispose of any fraternity items in the rental house. One of the defendants testified that the fraternity encouraged pledges to lie to police. He also said the fraternity had a "special email address" for brothers to inform fraternity leaders if a pledge had suffered a hazing injury, so the organization could come up with an excuse.

Even if some adults who run a fraternity's national headquarters truly do want hazing to stop, they likely aren't deploying the manpower necessary to enforce their own rules. So impressionable kids are pledging allegiance to a group that is mainly supervised by other impressionable kids. The Baruch College Pi Delta Psi chapter president testified that he "did not have the authority" to stop the Gauntlet ritual that killed Deng, but that another brother, the "pledge educator," did.

Piazza's mother told the *Today* show that she wasn't concerned when Piazza said he wanted to join a fraternity because she had read that Beta Theta Pi was a "non-hazing, non-alcohol fraternity." But between 2010 and the time Piazza pledged, major hazing incidents occurred in at least 23 Beta chapters across the country—and those are just the instances in which chapters were caught and the media found out about them. That means that about 16 percent of Beta Theta Pi's approximately 144 chapters (as of 2017, the year Piazza pledged) were caught hazing.

Then again, fraternities could argue the flip side: 84 percent of Beta chapters did not conduct major hazing (or were not caught). Sam explained a national officer perspective: "It's very difficult to have complete oversight even if you have a seasoned National Board.

Accidents and perversion do happen. Is that worth it in the end? If 70 to 80 percent of the process is going right, you're positively impacting people's lives, you're producing leaders, is the good that you do as an organization worth the minority of instances where there's humiliation, mission creep, mental or physical harm coming to these very young college students, even death? And if the answer is no, then how much do we have to minimize risk to be worth it? Those are the fundamental questions I ask myself that I don't know the answers to. Those answers will produce the answer to whether Greek life can justify its own existence."

One of the most common fraternity hazing techniques is "planned failure." Planned failure involves "near-impossible tasks where failure is punished with hazing," according to a 2016 article by University of California–Santa Barbara professor Aldo Cimino. Even in some chapters that don't haze, brothers try to scare pledges into worrying that they will fail to be good enough to be initiated.

Some chapters set up pledges to fail because they want them to believe that their activity—5:45 A.M. jogs, calisthenics, a buffet of gross food—isn't so much hazing as a punishment tailored to their individual pledge class because they made a mistake. The pledges don't know they would have had to complete these tasks anyway. They don't know the brothers often manufacture reasons, as Daniel did when he barged into the basement and yelled at Jake's pledge class, "You guys don't know how badly you fucked up! You have just opened the gates of hell!"

Members also might use this technique to avoid personal responsibility for the hazing. "If hazees believe that they can avoid some hazing, but continually fail to meet the conditions for doing so, they may blame themselves or 'the rules,' rather than the hazers. This is especially so if the rules of hazing are seen as pre-dating the hazers, who are themselves bound by tradition," Cimino wrote.

And that's the crux of the issue: tradition. The perceived weight of tradition is an authority unto itself. If the boys believe that the good of the group overrides the comfort of the individual, they might feel more invested in showing respect for the traditions that govern the group. "The things we did were traditions that came down. They told us, 'It happened to us,' so we did it to pledges below us, and the people above us did it to us because it happened to them," said the Maryland alum. "Hazing only exists because it always existed. It proves that tradition is like the worst thing that's ever happened. People are sold on it. This is the way it's always been, so that has to be the way it is now."

Yet many fraternity chapters, such as Oliver's, do not haze. Brothers who told me their chapter runs only nonhazing pledge activities or non-humiliating team-building exercises believe their brotherly bonds are just as strong as or stronger than the bonds within chapters that haze.

Some of the nonhazing pledge activities brothers described include taking weekly classes about fraternity history and traditions; organizing a community service project; completing assignments related to setting goals for themselves in college and beyond; taking classes on how to write a résumé; and learning etiquette. "We learned how to be a gentleman, how to be appropriate around women. I thought it was amazing that finally someone was teaching me proper etiquette. Like if you're walking down the street with a woman, you walk between them and traffic, to protect them from danger. Wait until the woman sits before you do. How to introduce someone. I thought that stuff was fun," a New Jersey junior said. "We were shown what was good to wear, where your tie should line up, where to put a tie clip, how to match things, cuff links. Interesting things improving people's behavior that I'll never forget."

A Pennsylvania chapter requires its pledges to join at least one other campus organization. A New York chapter has its pledges cook and serve a three-course dinner for brothers' girlfriends. A Virginia chapter puts pledges in charge of a major annual philanthropy event, which "involved us dividing up tasks based on our strengths, meeting with local business owners, and actually running the event," a brother said. "While some of these assignments were stressful, they emphasized the importance of teamwork. We were never allowed to leave someone behind or let someone do all the work. It really pulled us together as a family, and we learned a lot about each other's strengths and weaknesses."

An upstate New York chapter consisting mostly of engineering students combines education and team-building projects. Pledges have weekly quizzes and discussions about assigned reading from the fraternity's education guide (about leadership, ethics, etc.). They plan a fun residential community event for students who live nearby, a community service event (such as a park cleanup), and a brotherhood event (usually nonalcoholic, such as a campus-wide game of Capture the Flag).

The pledges also participate in strictly nonalcoholic one-to-one class bonding events with older classes of brothers to get to know them better; shadow brothers to learn how they handle their duties, like manning the door at a party; and handcraft a gift for the brotherhood. Usually the gift involves building furniture from scratch or buying furniture and painting it. Handmade gifts have included a bench, large coffee table, TV stand, and foldable beer pong table. "Our secret to success was a strict adherence to our belief that all people are worthy of respect, including candidates. It seems impossible to respect someone and want them to become your brother and at the same time pressure them to do things that are against their health or better judgment," a recent grad said. "Coming into a fraternity where it feels like everyone is on your side and wants to see you be successful is a powerful thing. It creates strong relationships from the get-go and perpetuates a positive environment. Alumni felt the same way; they always praised us for continuing the mission of the chapter."

When Ben founded his South Carolina chapter, on a campus where other fraternities hazed, he filled the pledge period with what he called "shared experiences." He regularly sent the pledges to study hall together, told them to attend a "pledge breakfast" once or twice a week, and put them in charge of organizing tailgates, a major affair. "That can be an adverse situation sometimes because they have to come together and delegate responsibilities," he said. "I found I didn't have to get them into line, put 10 bottles of liquor in front of them, and say, 'You have to drink this' because we don't know what else to do."

Ben assigned pledges these nonhazing tasks because he believed the process taught them to work together, rely on one another, and hold themselves and their pledge brothers accountable, "which in turn begins to build a healthy foundation for trust, friendship, and ultimately brotherhood," he said. "They learn to work with the fraternity brothers, which is 'managing up,' in a sense," pitching the fraternity treasurer for event funds and approaching brothers to access tents, banners, and music equipment.

Brothers and pledges together went on weekend excursions to the mountains and day trips to Six Flags. "We had 12 brothers drive the pledges somewhere to do social activities as a group," Ben said. "We focused on having shared experiences any way we could get them. A lot of that comes from having a fraternity house where they can come over after class or just be around each other. There's not a super formula to it. It doesn't take a lot for people to become friends. That was the premise I began with when thinking of ways to bring 50 fraternity brothers and 20 pledges together, and it worked."

CHAPTER 4

Why Are Students Drinking?

FOR HOMECOMING WEEK, Zeta Kappa was matched with Beta Sigma. Jake quickly learned that this meant his chapter would be getting drunk with Beta Sigs for the next six nights. Beta Sig was at the bottom of the bottom tier, but because there were more fraternities on campus than sororities, the middle-tier Zeta Kappas considered it a win to be paired with any sorority. Neither MZN nor Omega Phi had scored a match. Still, some of the Z-Kaps made "Beta Siggy Piggy" jokes, mocking the handful of overweight sisters and calling even the average-weight girls "whales." Jake didn't participate. "It's a douchey thing to say, even behind closed doors, but looks are unfortunately how most guys rank sororities," he told me.

The brothers told the pledges each to buy a 52-ounce thermos to carry alcohol on the bus rides, which were an important time to get drunk in case the evening's destination checked IDs. What was the point of pregaming at the house if you lost your buzz on the ride to the actual event? (While the chapter had two or three sober monitors to watch 200 people at their house parties, they didn't always assign monitors for off-site socials.) Because Jake was too intimidated to risk buying alcohol at the local gas station the brothers frequented, Ty was happy to fill Jake's thermos; he had a fake ID. Jake was gradually developing friendships with several pledges—Sebastian, the good-looking Canadian; Eric, the goof with the cool eyes; Logan, the redheaded future leader—but Ty, who was genuine, kind, and didn't try to be cool, was his favorite. Jake was coming to rely on Ty's unflappability to help bolster him through the pledge process.

Jake soon put the thermos to use. On the bus to the club for the first night of Homecoming Week, brothers intermittently yelled, "Drink!"—and everybody did. Several guys continued drinking until they puked or passed out. Jake didn't drink enough to black out, but he did experience his first "brownout," as another brother called it: Without losing consciousness, he "started to forget things."

Now the pressure to drink came from pledges as well as brothers. "I gotta rant about this: how much drunk people always want you to be drunk with them even though you don't want to get to that level," Jake told me later. "It was really emphasized on the bus ride. Some of the pledges who always overdo it forced me to take a drink from my thermos or else they wouldn't leave me alone." One of the most frequent perpetrators was Bryce, who had skipped multiple pledge meetings and an EP but attended every social function.

Jake and Ty watched as Bryce guzzled straight whiskey and repeatedly hit on a sister who already had a boyfriend. "Give up your boyfriend. Spend the night with me," he tried. She rebuffed him again and again.

Jake also felt constant pressure to get together with girls: to talk to them, dance with them, hook up with them. When a pledge was spotted making out with a girl, a brother inevitably would post a picture to the chapter's private Facebook page. Comments would fly about her looks (sometimes with a number rating) and whether she was slutty. **Hey, I fucked her once** wasn't an unusual comment. The brothers also posted pictures of "whales" for the guys to make fun of. The freshmen learned to follow the brothers' lead, doing the same on the pledges' Facebook pages. ("The way you see the upperclassmen act, it changes how you act. It continues that cycle," Jake told me.)

Jake thought this behavior was "creepy," but he nevertheless worried that he wasn't living up to Zeta Kappa standards. While he was getting better at talking to girls, he noticed that at every event, several other pledges were "able to really get with" sorority sisters, either on the dance floor or in darker corners. Meanwhile, brothers made fun of the pledges who weren't hooking up. At the club, Jake and several pledges stood around chatting on the perimeter of the dance floor. A brother posted pictures of them on Facebook, tagged Quinn, Logan, and others individually, and commented, **Nice sausage fest happening in the corner.**

Later that night, Jake, Ty, Quinn, Wes, and a few other pledges went to a diner to talk about their "successes and failures with girls." (Only Ty had significant experience in this arena.) The guys decided they were at a disadvantage because Beta Sig had just had its Big/Little Night, which meant the freshman girls were often attached to their newly assigned Big Sister. Even so, the boys resolved to "make the best out of this week."

"We're all competing too much against each other," Quinn told the guys, sounding awfully sure of himself even though he had admitted to a few pledges that he had yet to kiss a girl. "This is how it's supposed to work, guys, okay? We have to pair up. One talks to the Big and one talks to the Little. You're supposed to work on them both equally."

"Shut up, Quinn," the pledges said.

Out of the others' earshot, though, Jake told Ty, "I've heard other guys say what Quinn said. It's really supposed to work. We'll stick together this week and help each other out, right?" Ty agreed.

But it was hard to have game when they were exhausted. Throughout the week, the pledges got home between three and four in the morning, sleeping only a few hours before dragging themselves to class or to the house. The pledges got just two hours of sleep before Thursday's 5:45 A.M. jog. Jake felt guilty for awakening his dorm roommate every time he opened the door. Although they were on good terms, they weren't more than acquaintances.

On the second-to-last night of Homecoming, Jake and Ty strategized. They would try to dance with girls in pairs rather than in the usual larger, amorphous group. In the hotel ballroom, they spotted a Big/Little Sister pair dancing apart from the crowd. When Jake and Ty made moves as if to join them, the girls were friendly (and, it turned out, extremely drunk). As they got into the music, the sisters even insisted, weirdly enough, that all four of them hold hands while they danced. Jake couldn't believe it: Quinn's strategy had actually worked—that is, until the Big said she had to go, leaving Jake and Ty both holding hands with the Little.

For a while, Jake and Ty awkwardly danced with her, playing what to Jake felt like a "subconscious tug-of-war." Eventually, when the girl leaned toward Jake, Ty let go and meandered off. *That was really cool of him,* Jake thought. He felt great. When the sorority pledge wanted to spin him around, he let her, laughing. When the music slowed, they pulled each other close. Jake decided she was too drunk for him to make a move, but he ended the night on a high. Sure, several other pledges and brothers were making out with girls. But Jake was content that a girl had simply chosen to dance with him. "That was such an accomplishment for me when I won her over!" he told me later. "That meant either (a) she was really, really drunk or, hopefully, (b) I'm a legit good dancer and she was actually having a great time!"

After she left, Jake found Ty and thanked him. "Hey, man, I'm really sorry about that," Jake said. "Next time we're both into the same girl, I'll back off."

"Don't worry about it. It's totally fine," Ty assured him. He also told Jake a rumor he'd heard from Quinn: At the next pledge meeting, Zeta Kappa supposedly planned to drop a few pledges who hadn't been pulling their weight. Jake was slightly worried. He wasn't bonding with the brothers like Quinn was, and he'd left some parties early, and even skipped one, because he often didn't want to drink. Ty calmed him down, as he'd already done multiple times when Jake got anxious. Somehow, Ty was able to shrug off these strange pledging experiences as if they were nothing unusual. Jake was already starting to think of Ty as his "rock." At Jake's request, Ty agreed to test him on the pledge book before the meeting.

Ω Ω Ω

The Thursday after the busted pregame, PhiEp held another house party. Because Tuesday's party had gone smoothly, Oliver assumed the previous week's incidents were two unfortunate flukes and that the chapter could move on. He needed to put the mishaps behind him so he could focus on strengthening the chapter, pulling up members' grades and increasing their involvement, before the Most Outstanding Chapter Award slipped out of reach. Some of the brothers weren't taking their responsibilities seriously enough for his taste. He wanted them to attend more meetings and events and improve their commitment to the development of the new pledge class.

Tonight's party was going fine. There were only about 30 brothers and 40 guests in the bar room; it was still early. The first influx of guests was happy, and the party had been properly registered— Oliver had double-checked personally. He went upstairs to study in the library. He had been more of a partier when he was a freshman. At Big/Little Reveal, the night when the freshmen learned who their Big Brothers were, he didn't stop at one shot of the "family" drink (tequila with a dash of Tabasco). He was so excited to join a family, and the celebration was so much fun, that he downed three shots back-to-back before moving on to beer. (No one in the chapter was forced to drink, not even at Big/Little Reveal. If someone didn't want to drink, no problem. If someone got too drunk, the brothers usually tried to cut him off, get him some water, and send him to bed.)

Oliver was in a completely different place now. These days, he didn't party much as he sorted out how to balance academics, his presidency, and at least some fun. Being a fraternity president was like having a full-time job. He remained clearheaded most of the time because he thought he should keep a vigilant eye on his brothers. If something went wrong, he believed, "it's on me." Oliver was surprised that even in a house of well-meaning guys, there had been two police write-ups already.

One brother had already come to him for help. Like Oliver's high school friend Christopher, Patrick, a curly-haired sophomore, didn't always make wise choices, but what he lacked in judgment, he made up for with a big heart. Recently, Patrick had asked Oliver to be his "accountability buddy," an idea he'd gotten from two brothers who graduated in the spring. Patrick thought he was partying too often, drinking too much, and sleeping too late. He was missing classes and having trouble finding time to do his homework. "I want to make some lifestyle changes, get in better shape, eat better, do better in school," he told Oliver. "I'm slacking off on a lot of those things." Oliver helped Patrick set weekly and quarterly goals. Every Sunday, they met to assess Patrick's progress.

Other brothers had asked Oliver to teach them self-defense moves because of his martial arts background. He was happy to work with them. He had even informally led a martial arts class in the basement with half a dozen PhiEps.

About an hour into the party, Oliver received a text from the night's sober exec: Can you come downstairs please?

When Oliver got downstairs, the guests were leaving the house. The exec grabbed him and pointed out the window. Two city cops lingered outside.

While campus police were relatively lenient and accustomed to dealing with college kids, the city police who conducted random patrols could be hard-core. Tonight, the exec told Oliver, they had announced without preamble, "You need to shut this down now."

"We have our registration permit, and everything's going well here. Do you want to do a walk-through?" the exec had asked them.

"No. It's past 10:00 P.M., the noise ordinance is in effect, and you need to shut the party down or we'll write you up," the officer said.

PhiEp's noise level was not unreasonable, and it was just 10:02. The exec had turned off the music and told the crowd the party was over.

Many fraternity brothers believe they constantly have to combat stigmas and stereotypes from various corners of their lives. But Oliver thought the city police, specifically, had a "convoluted understanding" of fraternities. "A lot of them have the idea that we're a bunch of douchebags who don't care about anything but partying and are bound to cause a ruckus. But we're not like that," Oliver told me later.

The previous year, PhiEp seniors had hosted a party at a satellite house. When a group of non-Greek guys tried to come in, the brothers at the front table refused them. One of them punched a brother at the table. Three others beat up a brother at the front gate so badly that he had to go to the hospital. When the trespassers finally left, the PhiEps called the city police. But the police seemed concerned only that the PhiEps had thrown a party in the first place, and they ignored the assault that required one of the brothers to get stitches. Oliver had been disappointed in the police ever since.

Now he was nervous. Because of these officers, he would be in trouble with the police, the IFC, and the alumni, even though his chapter hadn't done anything wrong. *They're going to be upset and probably lose faith in my leadership,* he thought. He called Trey. "How can the city police just do that?" he asked him.

"They don't go by the same rules. It's best to just do whatever they want, because they can actually get you into serious trouble," Trey advised.

At the monthly Alumni Board meeting the following week, the alumni laid into Oliver for the chapter's three violations in 10 days. Outraged, they told Oliver the chapter had never had so many back-to-back complaints. They said Oliver needed to work it out or the board would step in.

Oliver quietly listened to what they had to say, ready to accept responsibility, as he believed a leader should. The board members were men over 50, except for Nick, a twentysomething who had refounded the chapter several years ago and served as its president after the alumni had shut it down for nearly a decade. (Oliver told me, "Our Alumni Board felt the fraternity had lost its values and people were conforming to stereotypical ideas of frat boys.")

Oliver considered himself a good guy, and he and his chapter had good intentions. *Forget about winning the Most Outstanding Chapter Award,* he thought. The alumni had the power to strip him of his presidency, refuse to allow future sophomores to run for president, or, worst-case scenario, shut the chapter down again.

Two days after the board meeting, Nick texted Oliver: Hey, I'm in the neighborhood. Mind if I stop by so we can talk for a bit?

In Oliver's room, after some chitchat, Nick turned serious. "All right, let's talk about the past two weeks. Every single president sometime during their term has had a proving ground. I had mine, Trey had his, which was also a lot of noise complaints. Now this is yours. So this is the moment where you can either get the board on your side and earn their respect and show you were the right choice to be president—or you can not do that and kind of fail. This is the time you either rise or fall."

Oliver was both inspired and stressed. It felt as if everything he had worked for had come down to this moment. He staunchly believed that "you are responsible for your own fate." Now he had to do whatever was necessary to regain the alumni's trust or he wouldn't be able to achieve any of his goals for the rest of his presidency.

"How should I address this situation?" he asked Nick.

"Communication is key. Overcommunicate as much as you can. If there's an issue, the board wants to hear from you immediately, understand what's going on, and know you're handling it. Otherwise, they worry and assume you're not on top of it."

For the next few hours, Nick helped Oliver craft a two-page letter to the board that detailed the chapter's party protocol and risk-management strategies. He explained the chapter's sober brother policy. He described how brothers were tasked not only with monitoring guest lists but also, as Oliver told me, "looking out for risky situations involving girls or overconsumption. This all relies on accountability. We all receive the drug/alcohol and sexual assault programming, and we all know what to look for and how to throw a safe party. On top of that, it's the general value of character that makes these things possible. You have to make sure these guys have their priorities right and aren't just in college to party or get with a girl for one night. Those tend to be the guys that give fraternities a bad name."

Oliver's letter explained that the chapter did an excellent job of managing risk, but that it had gotten in trouble because of "various unpreventable external factors that arose." He described each of the three incidents and what the brothers would do to prevent them from happening again.

Oliver hoped the move could save his presidency and the chapter, and that the local media wouldn't hear about their issues. He could envision the headline: PHI EPSILON COMMITS THREE VIOLATIONS IN 10 DAYS. Even though the violations had been small—technicalities, really—the situation would sound so much worse than it was.

Ω Ω Ω

On the last night of Homecoming Week, the Z-Kaps and Beta Sigs piled into buses headed to a bar for the Heaven and Hell Mixer. Most of the girls wore skimpy devil getups. Jake wore all white and a laurel wreath crown.

Tonight's bus was the noisiest of the week. The girls belted out karaoke songs as brothers walked the aisles giving out drinks. Jake hadn't planned to drink, but when an older brother specifically came up from the back of the bus to offer him a pull, he drank. The tequila hit him quickly. When the sophomore girl sitting alone across the aisle from him engaged him in conversation, he tried to keep up, but he was dizzy and drunk. From the seat next to Jake, Sebastian watched, amused.

"What's my name?" the Beta Sig sister asked.

Jake hesitated.

"I told you my name on Tuesday! How could you forget it?"

"I-I'm sorry," Jake said. He had probably been too sloshed to remember.

"Yeah, it's too late for that. What's my name?"

Jake felt as if he were walking in a minefield. He guessed repeatedly until he finally got it: Madison.

"Yo, you should go sit next to her and talk to her, eh?" Sebastian said.

"I dunno, man, I dunno if she's asking for anything," Jake said.

"Come sit with me!" Madison said.

As soon as Jake sat down, she grabbed his wreath and put it on her head. "This looks so much better on me, doesn't it?" she slurred.

"Yeah, it definitely does," Jake said.

She did something to her hair. "Does my hair look better braided or unbraided?"

"Oh . . . well, it looks fine either way," Jake said.

"You're only saying that because you're a guy," she said, frowning.

Aaaah, can't process. Too wasted, Jake thought. *Am I messing up really bad? What is happening here?* He realized she was flirting with him, but he dismissed her interest because she was at least as drunk as he was.

"Okay, what's the thing you fear the most?" she asked.

"Uh, spiders?" Jake ventured.

"Are you afraid of girls?"

Jake did not know what to say to that.

"I know you're not afraid of girls, but play along. Are you afraid of girls?" she repeated.

"Uh, yeah, yeah, I'm afraid of girls."

"Oh yeah? What scares you about girls, huh?"

Jake was baffled. He wasn't afraid of girls. "Uhh, their long hair?"

"I don't think that's really why you're scared of girls. Try again."

"Uhh, okay. Uhh, their legs because they don't have hair on their legs?" Jake said, then inwardly kicked himself for being stupid.

"Girls get hair on their legs. They just shave it. I just shaved my legs today," Madison said. She draped a leg over Jake's lap and moved his hand to her thigh. "Touch it!" she said.

Jake couldn't tell whether she was toying with him. He caressed her thigh, as she wanted him to. Because she didn't ask him to kiss her, he didn't make any further moves.

"Are you ticklish?" she asked, and didn't wait for an answer before tickling him. They wrestled that way for a few minutes more.

As the bus pulled into the parking lot, Madison asked him to hold her purse while she zoomed to the back of the bus to talk to her sisters. When she returned, she seemed surprised to see that Jake had her purse.

"Uh, you asked me to hold on to it for you," Jake explained.

"I don't remember that at all," she said.

As she got off the bus, Jake reflected on what had just happened. *Maybe it's best that I didn't try anything with her. She must have been really drunk.* He doubted she would have hit on him if she'd been sober; she was mainly friends with older brothers, and he was just a pledge.

At the bar, Jake checked the pledges' Facebook page. A brother had taken a picture of him and Madison with their hands on each other, tagged Jake, and written, **Jake's trying to get it on w Madison Mills. Does this make her body count six this week?** A string of comments followed: **Nerf dart rape!** and **Nerf dart motherfucking rape.** And then: **Pledge Jake: Do it.**

Jake had mixed feelings about the post. Certainly, he wasn't going to obey a command to get with a girl who was too drunk to consent. But he was surprised to find that he was proud they thought he was getting somewhere with a girl, even if he had touched only her thigh. He believed his chapter had gained some respect for him.

At the bar, though, he lost respect for Bryce. Bryce was standing next to him as they watched the DJ, a good-looking twentysomething girl. "I'm going to fuck her tonight," Bryce told him. "You watch. I'm going to go into that booth and I'm going to fuck her."

"Okay, man, whatever," Jake said. Bryce had been getting on everyone's nerves lately. Before last night's ballroom party, he had texted the group to ask if anyone could cover his pledge chores for him so he could make the early bus to the hotel. **Do it your fucking self. We've done enough chores for you,** Eric answered.

As they maneuvered toward the bar, a group of girls passed them going in the opposite direction. "Whoa, Jake. Slow down so I can get a longer view of this ass!" Bryce said.

"You know what, man, I'm just going to walk around by myself," Jake said, and turned away.

At a house party two nights later, he nursed a couple of beers while chatting with fellow pledges. He was feeling pretty good about the low-key event until a brother ordered him to drink from a two-story funnel snaking down the back of the house. "Pledge Jake! Chug!" Jake reluctantly chugged. Twenty minutes later, Tanner, a brother who had already tormented several pledges since rush, grabbed Jake and dragged him into a circle with alumni who were shotgunning 16-ounce beers. Jake got through three-quarters of the can before feeling sick and excusing himself to sit on a couch in the Great Room.

He was there for only a minute, trying to will himself to recover, when another brother spotted him. "Pledge Jake! Get the fuck up and drink!" The brother held out a bottle of vodka.

There was no way Jake was going to take a pull of vodka when he had just shotgunned most of a 16-ounce beer. "Nah, not now, maybe later," he said.

"Big fat pussy," the brother called him, then informed the other brothers, "Pledge Jake is a big fat pussy!" Shouts of "Pussy!" reverberated throughout the room.

Embarrassed, Jake left the house as soon as he could, upset about the mistreatment and wondering again if he should drop the fraternity. He didn't want to hang around people who were "just going to be forcing me to drink all the time," and he questioned whether he could ultimately fit in with the group. "I left early because I knew by staying, I was just going to continue being hazed pretty badly," he told me later, still angry. "Why is there such a forceful insistence on drinking, even when you clearly tell the brother you don't want to? Why is it that at a frat party, if you're not drinking, you're a pussy who doesn't like to have fun? I'm there to socialize, talk to some girls, and I was planning on just nursing a beer or two since Homecoming Week has trashed my liver. Only a few brothers get like this, but it's those who feel they need to haze the pledges that really piss me off the most. It's really my biggest complaint about Greek life so far: just how much drinking is emphasized in the fraternity experience. It honestly sucks that I can't go to a party and willfully remain sober when there's so much peer pressure to get hammered and to drink more than you feel comfortable with."

Why Fraternity Alcohol Interventions Don't Work

Drinking is not just a Greek issue; college alcohol abuse has been considered a major public health concern in this country for decades. But the statistics from about 100 empirical studies are clear: Fraternity members drink more, and more frequently, than any other students on campus. They are more likely to be diagnosed with alcohol use disorders, and they have more alcohol-related consequences. An expert told journalist Caitlin Flanagan that, outside the family, fraternities "are the single largest provider of alcohol to underage drinkers in the country." And multiple studies have found that the more involved a student is in his fraternity, the more likely he is to engage in risky drinking behavior.

Drinking is one of the oldest American college traditions, and many schools have had the alcohol-themed songs to prove it. In 1639, the first president of Harvard College lost his job because his wife, who supervised the campus brewery, let the students run out of beer. By the 1940s, college drinking was considered "a symbol of good fellowship." Faculty members often attended student-hosted "beer parties," and fraternities frequently served wine at dinner to teach members "to appreciate proper wines with food."

In the mid-1980s, when the minimum legal drinking age was raised to 21, faculty members and other adults were less likely to attend undergraduate parties, potentially lessening students' exposure to models of responsible drinking. As students focused on not getting caught, rather than adjust how much alcohol they drank, they changed where they drank it. Although schools were now responsible for policing underage drinking on campus, "collegiate life was far too drenched in drink to be derailed by such a little thing," *American Hookup* author Lisa Wade wrote. "College drinking didn't slow down during Prohibition, and it didn't slow down in the 1980s."

Currently, college students—whether or not they are Greek—drink more often in fraternity houses and at Greek parties than in any other location on or around campus, including bars, sports events, and non-Greek parties. And students reportedly drink more intensely than in years past. One study found that 77 percent of freshmen "drink to get drunk."

Why would college students do this to themselves? From a developmental perspective, they are at a crossroads. On their own for the first time in their lives, they are trying to establish their adult identity and fit in with a new community in a new environment. They may be scared, vulnerable, and uncertain. They might drink to do what they see others doing, or because they believe the "liquid cour-age" will make them more sociable, as Jake did when he drank to be able to "talk to girls." (Men are more likely than women to drink as a social lubricant.) "I am terrible with girls sober. I'm awkward," a Texas senior told me. "The guys joke about this. They say God couldn't have graced someone with better looks but a terrible per-sonality when it comes to girls. I get nervous. I ask myself what do I say to this chick, do I talk about cars, do I talk about hockey? So for me, it's a way to open up and try to be chattier."

For boys in particular, drinking is a socially acceptable way "to satisfy their [emotional] dependency needs while they maintain a social image of independence, even as it masks those needs" to man-age their feelings and develop coping strategies, researchers report. Of course, there is a cost: Male college students have the highest rates of alcohol-related problems among any demographic.

In the years after the drinking age shifted, rather than focus on enforcing the new law, many college administrations reportedly looked the other way, either quietly tolerant of student drinking or in denial that alcohol abuse remained a campus problem. Decades later, it still is. Consider how simple colleges make it for students to party, with easy majors and no-Friday-class schedules available for those who'd rather drink than think. "It's societal in that we're told this is how you're supposed to behave in college. When you see col-lege depicted in movies and pop culture, everyone has a Solo cup in their hands. Those cues make you think there's unlimited alcohol here, so I should be able to drink an unlimited amount," said a New England fraternity brother who also mentioned the pressure on stu-dents to make the college years the best four years of their lives. "You binge-drink to impress people. Alcohol lets you do crazier things. College is a unique time where you're allowed to be wild without anyone really chastising you about it."

While some schools have enacted more vigilant student drinking policies, underage students continue to believe that it's okay, or even expected, to drink in college. This self-reinforcing misperception is key to understanding college student drinking. Late adolescents, psychologists have found, experience an unusually powerful pressure to conform to peer norms. So when college students misperceive that everyone else is drinking more than they are—a common mistake, according to several studies—they increase their own consumption. The rise of social media has exacerbated the problem, as students are more inclined to post pictures showing off the parties they attend rather than the solitude of the weekend nights they stay in, adding to the sense that everyone else is out drinking. These comparisons happen at a school level, too. "Students sometimes aspire to be this weird, idealized fantasy image that they perceive other schools to be, even if it's untrue," former national fraternity leadership consultant Nathan Holic said. At some schools, he said, drinking is part of a "competitive spirit: 'No, Illinois does *not* drink harder than us! This is Indiana!' So I don't think this is something that's unique to fraternities or that fraternities popularized."

Not all college students drink, or drink to excess, of course, and researchers have pinpointed who's doing what. Black students drink less than students of any other race. The students who are drinking to get drunk are "the most privileged subset of undergraduates, and those who would (unwisely) emulate them . . . [,] the children of white, college-educated parents, young people whose free time is probably spent not working to help support themselves, but rather participating in certain activities, most notably Greek life and athletics," *The Atlantic* observed.

To be sure, there's something different going on with the predominantly white Greek groups. After drinking, these fraternity brothers are twice as likely as other students to have sex with someone without getting consent, and fraternity and sorority members are one and a half times more likely to forget what they did or where they were. An American Psychological Association study found that intervention programs that work to reduce drinking among college students do not work on fraternity and sorority members. In some cases, researchers discovered that fraternity members *increased* their alcohol consumption following such a program. At least one study found that even when a fraternity house is designated a "dry" house, its members drink no less than members of "wet" houses.

The most evident reason that drinking is such a persistent part of Greek culture is that it's easy. When the chapter owns a house or brothers welcome members at a private off-campus residence, students have a place to drink away from the eyes of responsible adults and law enforcement. Research shows that chapters with a house binge-drink more frequently than chapters without one. Whether or not fraternity brothers have a house, their group likely includes members over 21 who can provide them with alcohol (and, studies show, guys who are more likely than non-Greeks to own fake IDs).

Kirk, the transfer student, pointed out that brothers might feel that they've prepaid for the alcohol anyway. When he visits his first chapter, "I'll go to happy hour with alumni who are 24, 25, 26. We'll have two or three drinks and chat. No one's getting shitfaced. Then, Saturday night, I'll go to the college with the actives and there's so much free alcohol. You think, *If I'm paying [hundreds of dollars] at the beginning of the semester for social dues, which are only used to buy alcohol, I should get my money's worth.*" While not all chapters allocate social dues specifically toward alcohol, the fees might fund events at which alcohol is served. Social fees can be steep. At Louisiana State University, social dues range from four to five hundred dollars per person a semester. At other schools, social dues can reach nearly a thousand dollars a semester.

Greek drinking can't be fully attributed to access, though. Researchers have found that fraternity and sorority members are more likely than other students to believe that partying and drinking are important; it's okay to drink to feel more comfortable around others; drinking makes it easier to meet new people; and at group functions, people who drink have more fun than people who don't. They are much more likely than non-Greeks to say they drink to cure hangovers, to forget about grades, to cope with girlfriend/boyfriend issues, to celebrate special occasions, because they like the taste, or because it seems like "the thing to do." They often see drinking not as a problem but as a solution. A Maryland senior said, "At the end of the week, we'd all drink together to patch up our dramas. If you had a problem with someone, you'd get a drink with them. One brother slept with another guy's girlfriend. The judicial punishment was 'Go to the bar and get drinks.' Two hours later they were fine."

Drinking has become "a quintessential fraternity activity," a New York senior said, that in plenty of chapters is assumed to be the norm. Fraternity members drink more if they believe their peers are drinking, or if they think their peers will approve of their drinking. They are, experts say, "an extreme on a continuum of college men's drinking, dramatizing what may be going on to a lesser extent in traditional student life among a range of men."

In several cases, as in Jake's fraternity, pledges are socialized to these extreme norms right away. This behavior has deep roots in fraternity culture. A 1979 study described the socialization process linked with fraternity membership "as a kind of education in which the subject is drinking and the classroom is the fraternity house." Because brothers drink whenever they want to, but control their pledges' consumption of alcohol, drinking becomes a privilege that symbolizes full membership in the group. New members then might continue to drink to gain their brothers' approval. When I asked Jake why he took a pull of tequila on that bus ride even though he didn't want to drink, he said, "You just want to appease the brothers. If they like the drink they offer, you want to show them you like it, too."

College students arrive on campus at the height of a developmental stage where they yearn to belong. Fraternities offer something to belong to. Thus, the stakes may seem higher for a pledge, who thinks he has to prove his worth to be initiated officially as a true member of the chapter. Research shows that pledges who believe that drinking will help them become more involved in a fraternity social activity consume more alcohol than pledges who don't make that association.

That might explain why pledges are so willing to participate in forced-drinking activities. They don't realize the danger. But it looms large. In 2012, Pi Kappa Alpha brothers sent Northern Illinois University freshman David Bogenberger and his pledge brothers from room to room in the Pike house to answer questions and take shots of alcohol. (This pledge activity was the kind of forced-drinking hazing that had infuriated Jake.) Bogenberger reportedly was pressured to drink so much alcohol that his heart stopped and he died. In September 2017, Louisiana State University freshman Maxwell Gruver died of "acute alcohol intoxication with aspiration," according to his autopsy, after Phi Delta Thetas reportedly ordered pledges to recite the Greek alphabet and answer questions about their fraternity—and forced them to chug hard alcohol if they answered incorrectly. Two months later, Florida State University Pi Kappa Phi pledge Andrew Coffey and Texas State University Phi Kappa Psi pledge Matthew Ellis also died because of drinking.

Remarkably, the spate of deaths—which hazing expert Hank Nuwer said is neither an unusual pattern nor an unprecedented number for a calendar year—did not necessarily change the behavior of chapters that conducted similar activities. "We aren't holding back because a lot of things we see as tradition. There's a certain template that goes into the activities we do, and if we follow that and have responsible brothers willing to take pledges to the hospital if they get to that point, then that's why we continue to do it," a Mississippi sophomore told me in December 2017. "We're more worried about other fraternities on our campus because the school will suspend everyone if anyone does anything, not just us. We see ourselves as a lot more responsible and a lot less intense with hazing than other fraternities, but we still haze. We always say at rush, 'We're a non-hazing fraternity,' and I'm so used to saying that, but ha."

Like the pledges who drink to gain brothers' approval, a fraternity chapter collectively can come to view drinking as a tool to prove its worth in the larger Greek community. Because one of the characteristics some student bodies use to rate fraternity chapters is how "party-hard" they are, the tiers come into play here, too. Researchers found that members of fraternity and sorority chapters that are known for drinking believe their houses are more popular, and their members more attractive, more sexually active, and wealthier, than chapters whose members drink less than they do. Fraternity brothers may be more likely than other college students to get hammered in order to look cool or boost self-confidence with girls, because they're ranked by it. You can see how Greeks' logic can get skewed. "There's a lot of peer pressure to go to the bars. But there's also a lot of social pressure," the Maryland senior said. "We have all these social events with sororities, and you're going to want to go, especially if it's a higher-tier sorority. Even if you have a test in two days, you're going to want to meet these girls. It's good for the fraternity. And then you're nervous, and you need to have two or three beers before you can start talking."

If college drinking is such a long and proud tradition, what has changed? One difference is that today's students aren't just pounding beers. They're bingeing on hard alcohol, which is more potent, hits more quickly, and is easier to hide. And they're often downing as much as they can *before* a party or other event so that, as one brother said, "It hits me by the time I get there."

Pregaming has effectively become a tradition for many fraternity chapters, brothers told me. They pregame to prime themselves for social functions or because the event venue won't serve teenagers. A study of undergrads at 14 universities found that students who attended fraternity/sorority parties consumed more drinks before the event than did students who attended parties or functions at residences, bars/restaurants, and other campus events. This style of fast-paced drinking, said Joseph LaBrie, a psychology professor who studied preparty blackouts, "makes self-regulation appreciably more difficult and negative consequences more likely. Prepartying has been found to predict numerous consequences among college students such as academic neglect, hangovers, passing out, and fighting."

Returning to the idea that the fraternity is a classroom, what is it trying to teach? Because a long-standing mission of fraternities is to make each member "a better man," in some chapters "older brothers believe a man should know his way around how to handle beer, liquor, and wine, especially if he wants to learn how to eventually drink responsibly or know his limit," said the Mississippi sophomore, who didn't drink before college. "Forced drinking ultimately opened me up to what drinks I like or don't like, and how to properly take shots and chug beer."

The sophomore's justification may give us an important clue to why drinking is such a staple of Greek life: Drinking is strongly linked to masculinity. It is a cultural symbol of manliness (see, for example, almost any beer commercial in the history of always). More than two-thirds of male college students consider consumption of large amounts of alcohol without vomiting or other adverse reactions to be a demonstration of masculinity. Even in the 1800s, fraternities encouraged drinking because breaking college rules was a display of masculinity.

Guys who can't or don't drink up may be viewed as weak or feminine ("Pledge Jake is a big fat pussy!"). Drinking games usually

assess how quickly a player can drink, how much he can drink, and/
or how well he can hold his alcohol. "Men who are able to display all
these attributes are deemed manly," researchers have noted. The
Texas senior compared drinking behaviors to "maxing out on the
bench press. You want to max out more than your friends. You want
to drink even more than your friends, which avalanches into this
terrible drinking problem that a lot of fraternities get a bad rep for,
but rightfully so," he said. "They're doing it because their buddies
are doing it, and then they're drinking just to drink. And it's stupid,
but you're perceived as a badass if you take a shot of vodka before
class." (Incidentally, Michigan scholars have found that a major reason college women drink heavily is to impress male students by
"drinking like a guy," which probably contributes to high drinking
rates among sorority women.)

Because drinking is considered macho, many men already feel
societal pressure to drink to prove they are "real men." Think about
how much more intense that pressure could be within an all-male
group of impressionable, perhaps insecure students whose mission
is to turn boys into men. It's arguable that brothers are trying to
educate younger members in how to drink, pushing them early into
a rite of passage that, by law, only adult men can engage in but, by
community standards, college boys are expected to perform. Forced
drinking may be a deeply misguided way for fraternities not only to
gauge whether pledges are "man enough" to join their ranks but
also to help them get there.

Therefore, fraternities that define themselves by stereotypically
masculine attributes, such as Jake's fraternity, might naturally encourage heavier drinking than fraternities such as Oliver's, which do
not define their group that way. A junior in Iowa credits his mid-tier
chapter, which has two gay brothers and is one of few chapters on
campus not currently on probation, for teaching him how to drink
responsibly. As a non-Greek freshman, homesick, lost, and "not tran-

sitioning well," he said he was "almost killed" by drinking. "I did it to fit in. I was at an extremely low point in my life. I never drank in high school, and I thought it was so cool to get blacked out and act stupid to impress people."

Once he joined a fraternity, however, older brothers modeled responsible drinking, and his perspective changed. "I looked up to them because they got their schoolwork done and still had a good time on weekends without blacking out," he said. When we spoke, he hadn't blacked out since joining the fraternity.

Studies show that the more a boy is concerned about appearing manly, the more likely he is to drink heavily. Further, men who embrace traditional constructs of masculinity, as fraternity members tend to do, are more inclined to believe alcohol will make them more aggressive, courageous, or more likely to take risks—all qualities associated with masculinity. So boys who are more desperate to fit into a fraternity with hypermasculine standards are more likely to drink heavily to play the part. That's why alcohol interventions that work on other students don't work on Greeks. These programs often focus on managing drinking with strategies to moderate consumption. But for fraternity brothers, drinking isn't a simple activity. It is not only a means to an end—a strategy to hook up, make friends, gain approval, and win contests—but also an end in itself, proof positive of manliness. Intervention programs might teach boys how to reduce the risk of alcohol abuse but fail to offer a replacement for alcohol's rewards.

Will fraternity leaders? In September 2018, the NIC announced that its member organizations have until September 2019 to implement a ban on drinks above 15 percent ABV unless a licensed third party sells them. Brothers told me they don't expect the move will stop members from keeping bottles in their rooms or curb long-entrenched drinking traditions.

Some schools already have similar measures in place. At one such university, the rule "encourages more use of hard alcohol because when people are told they can't do something, they're more likely to do it anyways and be under the radar," a midwestern brother said. Instead, he said, the NIC should "properly educate fraternities on alcohol use. Students are never taught about how to drink responsibly. We currently have no education system through IFC. Chapters have to take it upon themselves to bring in guest speakers."

Other members worried that older brothers who model responsible drinking and/or help maintain safe protocols will move out of the house, leaving younger students unregulated. A North Dakota senior suggested that the NIC could create a nationwide medical amnesty policy so that if someone needs help, students can call the police or paramedics without consequence to the fraternity. His school already has this in place for students. "I've been at parties where police walked right through the crowd and they're tunnel-vision going to the person who needs help; they bring them out, and that's the end of it," he said. "It's hammered into our head that it's okay to ask for help from law enforcement without the risks. If someone's having an emergency, it's a lot better for them to get help from paramedics than for people to cover it up."

Another solution would be for the NIC to focus on changing fraternity culture before or while it changes the rules. Studies have shown that social-norms campaigns, which reduce students' misperceptions by giving them accurate information about healthy norms and actual student behavior, effectively reduce heavy drinking and alcohol-related negative consequences. The NIC could also reframe what it means to be Greek. If students weren't so worried about their tier, they wouldn't believe their opposite-gender interactions carry such high stakes that they require intense liquid courage. If guys are exposed to a broader variety of ways to express masculinity, they won't be as likely to try to prove themselves mostly by drinking too much. "People drink because of that sense of expectations," a Michigan brother said. "Fraternity events are almost all centered around interacting with sororities and the way you represent yourself. Drinking lowers the walls. Guys think the more they drink, the looser they'll be, the funnier they'll be, the more able they'll be to talk to someone. It takes time for that confidence to build, so you keep drinking more—and then it turns into binge drinking."

And because at his school, like many others across the country, the campus store even sells flasks, the students are given yet another reason to think that drinking is okay.

Ω Ω Ω

The morning after he shotgunned the 16-ounce beer and chugged who-knew-what from the funnel, Jake was sick. Part hungover and part sleep-deprived, he slept most of the day, setting an alarm to wake him for the pledge meeting. But he slept through the alarm and woke up at 7:10 P.M. The meeting was supposed to have begun at 7:00. He had a spotless attendance record at Zeta Kappa meetings. He posted on the chapter Facebook page that he was too sick to make it to the meeting. Then he reconsidered.

As much as Jake had debated quitting the night before, he didn't want to lose his friendships with his pledge class. He knew that if he were no longer in the fraternity—like Isaiah, like Jamal—his pledge brothers wouldn't hang out with him again. He decided to continue pledging. "The rest of the guys all seem to be going through the same stuff as me," he told me. "The fact that none of them are dropping pushes me to do better and to tolerate more when it comes to hazing and everything."

Tonight was the night the chapter would supposedly drop pledges. *I need to show I'm dedicated to the fraternity,* he thought. Despite a throbbing headache, he threw on his frattire and hurried to the house. In the basement, the other pledges were still waiting to be summoned to the meeting. Relieved that the brothers didn't know he was late, Jake practiced the Greek alphabet with Logan. Rumor had it that during Hell Week, the final week of pledging before next month's initiation, the pledges would have to recite the entire alphabet in six seconds—the amount of time it would take for a match they'd be holding to burn down to their fingers.

Before the meeting began, Greg passed out paper. He told the freshmen to rank the top seven brothers they viewed "as a role model or mentor." Guessing the purpose of this exercise (requesting Big Brother assignments), Jake panicked. Five minutes was not enough time to think. At the five-minute mark, he had listed only Greg, the pledge master; Steven, the liberal junior; and Andy, the chapter president. He forced himself to put down four more names.

At the meeting, Z told the boys to choose a partner and rent a tent together for a pledge retreat later that month. (Jake was worried. "I've really gotta clear my weekend now," he told me, though he didn't want to go. "I feel like this is one of those things where if you don't have a damn good excuse, like you had to go home because your whole family died, you have to be there.")

Z finished his speech. "Pledge Rob! Stand up and recite the creed," he commanded. Rob stammered through the first half of it, making several errors. Z interrupted him, "No. Pledge Matthew! Stand up and recite the creed." Matthew tried to say it too quickly and transposed words. Jake and Logan made eye contact, each hoping Z would call on them because by now they knew the creed cold. "No!" Z said. He addressed the group. "How can you expect to become a brother if you don't even know the fucking creed? You need to know this! Get the fuck out of here. Meeting adjourned."

Assuming the rumor about dropping pledges hadn't been true, the pledges exhaled and left the house. Ten minutes later, Daniel posted on the pledges' Facebook page, **Pledges: you will report to the** house at exactly 12:30 A.M. Not 12:29, not 12:31. Wear comfortable clothing and bring a pillowcase.

At 12:25, all the pledges but Quinn were lined up outside. Jake and Logan organized them in alphabetical order. The pledges silently ran into the house at exactly 12:30, with Jake and Logan holding the double doors. In the darkened Great Room, the pledges stood in line, bowing their heads, staring at the floor. Jake was just thinking that it felt like a scene from a military movie when the door opened and Quinn ran in late, out of breath. "Shit, man, you've got balls," someone whispered, and the pledges snickered.

The pledges stood still. The house was silent. After about half an hour, they heard footsteps and a door close. Following another long wait, Greg and Z finally walked to the front of the room.

"You know I would defend each of you. But sometimes I just can't," Greg said. He took off his baseball cap and wiped his eyes. "You started off as 43 and now you're down to 37. You either get through this stronger together or die weak."

Z took over. "Your work here is going to grow exponentially over these next few weeks. No one in this brotherhood became a brother without a lot of work. Everyone has made sacrifices. If you don't want to be here, you know where the doors are," Z said. "Go home. And please remove Bryce from your group text." Jake looked up. The brothers must have taken Bryce away after the pledges had run into the house.

The pledges filed out of the house, glad the pillowcases were a red herring. When they were outside, Jake said, "Um, is anyone actually upset about this?" His pledge brothers gave a unanimous no.

Eric laughed, his mismatched eyes crinkling. "Shit, I'm glad they told us to come in clothes we don't care about, because when I realized they were kicking out Bryce, I got nut all up in my pants."

CHAPTER 5

Girls and Group Identity: How Chapters Can Influence Guys' Attitudes

SOME OF THE FRESHMEN were uncomfortable, and Oliver knew it. "Hey, don't worry," he told them. "We're here to help you." It was the first day of rehearsals for Serenade, a two-night event during which the freshmen danced and lip-synched in front of every sorority house that had requested their presence.

PhiEp was happy to hang out with any sorority; State U had about a dozen more fraternities than sororities. Usually they ended up mixing with five sororities in particular. Three were top tier, two were middle tier, and four of the five were "low-key, fun girls who aren't really caught up in mainstream sorority bullshit," as Oliver described them. While sorority sisters cared more about their rank than most of the fraternities did, State U Greeks were relatively easygoing about tiers. Oliver thought that top-tier sororities deigned to socialize with PhiEp because "we're those guys who don't give a damn about the rankings. That attitude is something girls find attractive, and they come over more." For Serenade, PhiEp had scored invites from sororities in every tier. They would perform at seven houses on Monday and six on Tuesday, the most performances ever requested of the chapter, to the brothers' knowledge. Perhaps the PhiEps's rank had risen, but they didn't know—or care.

One of the reasons Oliver had chosen to rush PhiEp was that the brothers were reputed to be gentlemen. A brother had told him during his initial tour of the house, "The Apple Pie Boys is one of our nicknames because we're not typical fraternity boys. We treat women really well, and that's something we pride ourselves on. We're the only fraternity here that walks girls home every night." Oliver had found that characterization to be true. He told me, "At other fraternities you walk your girlfriend home. But with us, if random people are alone, we'll walk them home. It's a very little thing, but it grabbed me. It's the little things no one sees you do that make the biggest difference in your character."

Oliver wanted Serenade to go well, particularly because the alumni had responded positively to his letter about the recent write-ups. They told him they appreciated the update, and they commended his strategies for handling future situations. Oliver had micromanaged every party since. He "started to handle things quicker, better, more efficiently," working out specific risk-management policies to prevent or address uncommon scenarios (such as the uninvited pregame guests). He pushed himself to think ahead, and then to think even further ahead than that. "Because I got a positive response from the alumni, I matured a little bit, like I was growing up, doing something right. It gave me a confidence boost," Oliver told me. There had been no other issues.

"When I was a freshman," Oliver told the pledges now, "I was super nervous about dancing because I was not an outgoing, dancey person in high school. When I was going through rehearsals, I was like *Damn, I have to dance in front of a bunch of people?* I had never done that before and was super uncomfortable about it. But it was so much fun."

Now Oliver was one of the choreographers, along with four of his best buddies. They had spent hours devising a new 8.5-minute routine to a mashup of nine songs. For a full week of daily rehearsals, Oliver and his friends would teach the pledges the moves, pull individuals aside to work with them one-on-one, encourage the uncomfortable guys to loosen up, and give motivational pep talks or strict lectures urging them to work harder.

During their serenades, some of the more stereotypical State U chapters danced suggestively and/or sang explicit lyrics. Some of them apparently got their pledges borderline blackout drunk before performing. "They get gross, and it gets super uncomfortable," Oliver told me. PhiEps didn't operate like that. The point of their performance, usually the longest on Greek Row, was to make fun of themselves. Their routine wasn't sexual. It was funny, like the brothers. "We're not trying to act super weird around girls because that's not what we do. We just want to be us, do our thing, and people seem to like and respect that." This year, the PhiEps even had a fog machine.

Oliver continued his pep talk to the pledges. "Look, we wouldn't be doing this if we didn't feel strongly about it. We love Serenade. It's so much fun, and it will boost your confidence super sky-high. A lot of brothers are here to help you out. It's not about your dance technique; it's about having a good time. You'll look like you know what you're doing because it's choreographed, but these are not insane *Step Up* moves. You're supposed to look goofy," he said. "You'll see. Monday and Tuesday are two of the best nights in college. If you get into it, you'll not only dance good; you'll have way more fun."

Then he changed his tone to emphasize that the fraternity was counting on them to work hard. (He explained later, "My style is I'm a hard-ass, more or less. So I was pushing them to do well, pushing mental toughness.") He would continue to be hard on them for the rest of the week, yelling at them to pay attention during the three-hour rehearsals.

On the first night of Serenade, the pledges were assembled in their required jokey outfits: black shirts, tight jeans shorts, high white socks, and white Converse or Vans. After a senior delivered a pump-up speech, Oliver chimed in. "Hey, everyone, you know I've been a dick to you all week, but I'm super proud of how hard you guys have worked and how far you've come. You look super good, and everyone is going to be super stoked to see this." After a preperformance cheer, they broke the huddle and walked to the first sorority house of the night, where sisters clustered on the patio, stairs, and balcony.

As Oliver had expected, the PhiEp pledges came through. They were synchronized, even if the moves were limited to fist bumps, jumping, and crouching in formation. As Oliver described it, "Everyone was super pumped because they were really excited to impress their freshman girl counterparts."

The girls were cheering even before the performance ended. When the music stopped, that was the guys' cue to approach the girls, introduce themselves, and try to get some sorority sisters' numbers. The pledges had been instructed to memorize the words to every song so that, during the performance, they could look directly into the eyes of a girl in the audience as they lip-synched. "you go with whoever's in your line of sight," Oliver told me. Afterward, "you go up to someone you were staring at uncomfortably for 8.5 minutes. Guys meet dates and girlfriends this way." By the end of Tuesday night, all 28 pledges had multiple girls' phone numbers.

After the last performance, three of the pledges separately thanked Oliver. One was a freshman who had hurt his ankle during rehearsal. Oliver told him the performance wasn't worth aggravating the injury and put him in charge of the fog machine instead. "I appreciate you looking out for me. I know I can be kinda reckless, so thanks for keeping me in check," the pledge said. Another freshman told Oliver, "You're a great president because you know when to be stern and when to be kind and caring."

"Thank you so much for putting in the time to teach us all this stuff. It's been so awesome and so much fun," a third pledge said.

"Sure, man. It's just as fun for me as it is for you guys," Oliver replied.

Then the pledge said something Oliver had never expected to hear. "Well, you're a great leader and a great man, and I want to be just like you." He walked away, rejoining his pledge class, leaving Oliver speechless.

Oliver still didn't consider himself to be "the fraternity-president type." But the presidency, it turned out, required many of the same skills he would have needed had he been the pledge trainer he had aspired to be. He tried hard to balance discipline with compassion, adapting a leadership style that led his men both to take him seriously and to trust him because they knew that "at the end of the day, I care about them. So it was nice to have this impact while being the president and kind of being a big brother to all these guys."

Ω Ω Ω

As the semester wore on, Zeta Kappa assigned the pledges additional chores and expanded their hazing activities to include hours of monotonous tasks. Jake got into the habit of skipping certain classes because he either was too tired from EP sleepovers and other late-night activities or he felt obligated to spend that time fulfilling his chapter duties. Jake and Ty agreed that each week of pledging felt like an entire month. But they were enjoying their opportunities to get to know the brothers—and to meet sorority sisters.

By week seven, because several pledges were now having sex with sorority girls, Jake thought he should buy condoms, too, just in case. He was driving to the store when Greg posted on Facebook a list of items that pledges were to bring to that night's EP: 10 one-dollar bills, a pillowcase, and a cucumber. The pledges flooded their group text: **What the hell are those for?**

Ty, who had rented the tent he and Jake would share at the pledge retreat, texted to ask if Jake could pick up a cucumber for him, too. And that was how Jake found himself dying of embarrassment at a self-checkout register beeping "invalid item, invalid item," drawing a store employee to help him buy a pack of condoms and the only cucumbers he could find: in his estimation, at least a foot and a half long.

At the house, Jake was distressed to see the other pledges' much shorter cucumbers. As they laughed their heads off at the giant cucumber he handed Ty, Jake tried to play it off. "Haha, hey, I'm more of an endurance sort of guy," he said, without knowing what he was trying to say.

When the pledges were gathered in the informal chapter room for EP, Z walked in. Immediately, every pledge bowed his head. (Jake told me, "We're so subservient to him by now, it's not even fucking funny.")

"Okay, get out pens and paper because you're going to take notes on what you need to get for Hell Week and your pledge retreat," Z said. He listed the items in a monotone: "For your retreat, you already know about the tents. Bring a sleeping bag and your pledge book. For Hell Week, you will need the following materials. Four black T-shirts. One Zeta Kappa T-shirt—get it from older brothers. A pair of tighty whiteys. One pillowcase—and it has to be dark, not a fucking white pillowcase you can see out of. A Ping-Pong paddle. A coloring book and a pencil. A bag of sugar. A large bag of peppermints. A bottle of nice alcohol—it has to be good. Four boxes of matches. A banana. Your homework and whatever supplies you need to complete it. A Ziploc bag that contains your phone, wallet, and keys. Your Big Brother paddle and class paddle. All right. That's it for me." Z left the room.

During the EP session, Greg talked about the third core value, trust, and emphasized the importance of loyalty. After his speech, he asked the pledges to line up in alphabetical order and led them upstairs, where several brothers stood in the bedroom doorways. Each brother took one pledge individually into his room. A senior Jake didn't know well closed the door behind them. "As you know, during this EP we're on the subject of trust," the brother said casually. "So I wanted to ask you—and be truthful—do you believe there's anyone in your class who isn't trustworthy or doesn't deserve to be in your class anymore?" he asked.

"Well, the only person I can think of was Bryce, but the brothers have since removed him," Jake said.

"Okay. Thank you very much for your answer," the brother said, and dropped Jake off in the informal chapter room. Once the pledges were gathered again, the brothers strode into the room looking furious.

Greg, his baseball cap askew, was so angry he was shaking. His nose twitched. "Oh my fucking God, I am so fucking angry at you all. Do you not fucking know what the value was that we talked about? It was fucking trust. That's about loyalty! Several of you ratted out your fellow pledges! You wanted them to be fucking dropped! Do you fucking realize how bad you fucked up? I'm so fucking pissed I can't even shout." He shook his head in disbelief. "You're supposed to be together as a class, not ratting each other out. We all thought you fucking learned that by now!"

The pledges looked at one another. *Ahh shit, that was a test,* Jake thought. He was upset with himself for mentioning a name.

Greg looked disgusted. "That's it. Everyone get in line again and put your goddamn pillowcases on. Bring your cucumbers."

Greg shut them alone in the basement. Jake, feeling awful, instantly confessed: "I said, 'Bryce.'"

The pledges brushed it off. "Don't sweat it." "You're all right."

"I'm going to admit I mentioned someone else's name," Logan said.

"Me, too," said another pledge.

"Who?" the pledges asked.

"I'm not going to fucking tell!" Logan said.

"Wow, you guys really fucked up by saying someone's name," Quinn said, self-righteous.

"Shut *up*, Quinn!" the pledges said in unison.

Greg barged through the door. "We're all really fucking angry at you guys right now. Get your cucumbers out and get rid of them. I don't want to see them again the next time I enter this room."

"How do you want us to get rid of them?" someone asked.

"I don't fucking care." Greg slammed the door.

"He doesn't want us to eat these, does he?" a pledge asked.

Jake hated cucumbers. He suggested that maybe the pledges could hide them somewhere. "Nah, man. We all gotta eat them," a pledge said. They held a quick vote and started to eat. Jake felt sick. For 20 minutes, the room was silent save the sound of reluctant gnawing.

Wes and Ty finished early and offered to help eat the other pledges' cucumbers. Ty finished what was left of Jake's. When the cucumbers were gone, the bloated pledges lay uncomfortably around the room.

Greg returned. "Hm, it smells like cucumbers in here," he said, calm now. "I need you to give me the 10 singles we told you to bring and then line up in this order." He seemed to call out names randomly. "Now put on your pillowcases."

He led them back to the informal chapter room. Through the pillowcases, they could hear Greg and Z reading something that sounded ritualistic. "As part of your journey toward membership in Zeta Kappa, it is proper for an initiated brother to serve as your individual guide, mentor, and role model," Greg said.

Jake's spirits soared. *Holy shit, it's Big/Little Reveal! What a turn-around!* This was why he had joined a fraternity, wasn't it? For the brotherhood. He was eager to see his official Big Brother. *Is it Greg? Andy? Steven?*

"Turn to your right," Greg said. "Big Brothers, take off their pillowcases."

As someone raised his pillowcase, Jake waited nervously. Then his heart dropped. None of the brothers from his list stood in front of him. He was standing in front of Victor, a quiet, well-mannered junior whom he had met only once because he was rarely at the house. Meanwhile, the pledge next to him was celebrating with Greg. *The brothers on my list didn't want me,* Jake thought, dejected. But he quickly put on a happy face for Victor's sake. "Hell yeah! This is great!" he said to Victor.

"Huhhuh, yeah. I'm really excited," Victor said quietly. He had an unusual way of speaking, slowly and punctuating his words with an awkward laugh.

As they walked upstairs together, Victor said, "I know some of these things don't really work out the way they should, but huhhuh, I hope you aren't disappointed by this or anything."

Jake faked it. "Are you kidding, man? This is great, this is great!"

When they walked into a bedroom, several brothers cheered. Jake was surprised to see Andy and Ty with his Big Brother, another junior whose relaxed, agreeable personality matched Ty's. "Welcome to the Blackbeard family!" Andy said. He explained that he was Jake and Ty's Grand-Big (their Big Brothers' Big). He introduced the other juniors and sophomores in the room who hadn't been assigned a Little this fall, and an alum who was considered the family patriarch. Blackbeard was known for its campus leadership, Andy explained. He told them the family motto ("Just a BJ"), the family sport (volleyball), the family beer (Pabst Blue Ribbon), and the family liquor (Southern Comfort).

"Which brings us to what we have for you two tonight," Andy said, and pointed to a full 32-ounce bottle of SoCo on his shelf. "Let's get the shots going to Jake and Ty. You have to start drinking now because we've got buses coming soon for Lucky Strike."

"That's awesome!" Jake said. Lucky Strike, a bowling and entertainment complex, was one of his favorite places. Jake and Ty began downing shots.

"You and Ty better finish that bottle," Andy said. "That's what I did, that's what Victor did, that's what every guy here did. It's family tradition to finish the bottle."

Victor made Jake a mixture of Coke and SoCo that was easier to swallow than straight liquor. Jake took a few gulps per shot.

"No, you're doing it all wrong!" said one of the sophomores, whom Jake supposed was now his fraternity uncle. "You have to put it up to your lips and throw it to the back of your mouth. Just down that shit." He helped Jake tip the glass. The liquor burned. Jake shivered. "Okay, you're getting better at it." Jake tried it on his own, but half the shot missed his mouth.

Victor and the juniors took some pulls from the bottle to assist the freshmen. Before the bottle was emptied, a brother called out from the hallway, summoning first brothers and then pledges to the basement. "Come on, guys, time for Lucky Strike!"

Jake and Ty drunkenly staggered downstairs. On the way, the pledges gossiped about their families: who was in the most powerful family, who was in Blue Steel, which was known to have brothers who were good with girls. Quinn was in Grey Goose, the family of class fuckups.

In the middle of the room, two air mattresses covered in trash bags were surrounded by a circle of empty chairs. Behind those chairs was another row where the Big Brothers were drinking and laughing. Greg told the pledges to turn off their phones and sit in front of their Bigs. Victor handed Jake a drink. "Huhhuh, this is going to be really fun. You're going to really enjoy this," Victor said. "Let me ask: Do you like girls?"

"Hell yeah, I like girls," Jake said. He had barely finished the sentence when two strippers wearing costumes with ties and top hats sashayed into the room, to the brothers' boisterous cheers. One woman gave Logan a lap dance while the other threw Wes onto a mattress and brushed his freckles with her breasts.

"Kinkier!" a brother shouted. The lap dancer stripped down to a thong and pulled Jake onto a mattress.

"Nerf dart rape! Nerf dart rape!" the Z-Kaps chanted. Jake, on his back, watched the room spin.

The stripper reached into a bag, pulled out a large plastic penis, and grinded on Jake. He was too drunk to feel anything, which was a relief, because he didn't have to worry about sporting wood in front of his entire fraternity. The stripper took off Jake's shirt, continuing to gyrate.

"Nerf dart rape! Nerf dart rape!"

The stripper moaned. "Ohh yeah, I'm gonna come. I'm gonna come!" She pressed the plastic penis, which sprayed shaving cream all over Jake's face and chest. As the brothers burst out laughing, the stripper rubbed the shaving cream, hard, onto Jake's chest and, inexplicably, slapped him several times on the chest and face. It hurt like hell. *This isn't fun. This isn't sexy,* Jake thought. He wished the chapter had gone to Lucky Strike instead. When the stripper slapped him on the stomach, which was already bloated from the SoCo and cucumber, he was glad he was too drunk to cry.

Back in his seat, Jake watched one stripper make Matthew deep-throat Eric's belt while the other woman took off Ty's pants and boxers. One pledge threw up on the floor. Jake listed to his side, also nauseated. Victor lifted him up and led him upstairs to the Great Room, where he collapsed on a couch.

"Are you all right?" Victor asked.

"Yahmgoodmgood," Jake slurred. The room was empty and quiet, to his relief. With some water and rest, he thought, perhaps he could rally.

Instead, Victor brought out the bottle of Southern Comfort. "Huhhuh, we're almost done with this bottle," he said. He poured some into his own cup and emptied the rest of the bottle into Jake's.

Jake obediently drank until he could barely see. "Mission accomplished," Victor said, shaking the empty bottle. It was 2:00 A.M. "Do you want a ride home?"

In Victor's car, Jake desperately tried to stay composed as every motion made him want to retch. The moment he closed his dorm's entrance door behind him, he threw up into the nearest trash can.

When he woke up in the morning, he was still drunk. And he never wanted to see another cucumber again.

That evening, Victor invited Jake to work out with him at the gym. "You should try your best to stick this out, because once you get to the other side, you're going to learn a lot more about the fraternity's secrets," Victor said. While spotting Jake, Victor explained that when he was a freshman, Andy had also made him finish the bottle on Big/Little Night. "It's good bonding," he said. "Huhhuh, I hope you're enjoying the hazing so far and the games we make, because it's always a good bonding experience with your pledge class."

"Yeah!" Jake said, thinking, *Hell no*.

"That's what I enjoyed most about my pledge semester, how it really bonded us. I'm totally for hazing as long as it's not stupid shit that has no purpose behind it."

"Right!" Jake said, thinking, *I'm still bruised from the stripper beating the shit out of me*.

"How Do I Get the High Fives?": Why Good Boys Sometimes Do Bad Things

When parents send their sons to college, they likely believe they have raised good boys. And most of them probably have. Certainly, some students bring sexist and/or racist behavior with them from high school, but it's probably safe to say that, on the day of their high school graduations, it wouldn't occur to the majority of them to participate in activities like these:

- University of Southern California, Kappa Sigma: Members distributed a "gullet report," establishing a rating system for women (using numbers and racist code names) and requesting hookup reports: "I want raw data on who fucks and who doesn't. . . . The gullet report will strengthen brotherhood and help pin-point sorostitutes more inclined to put-out. . . . Note: I will refer to females as 'targets.' They aren't actual people like us men. . . . Loop n' Doop: A target that is very easy to take down. All she takes is a good amount of liquor (loop) and she will be good to go for you to fuck her (doop)."
- North Carolina State University, Pi Kappa Phi: A pledge book included lines such as "It will be short and painful, just like when I rape you"; "You can only trust a nig*** as far as you can throw them"; "Man that tree is so perfect for a lynching"; and "If she's hot enough, she doesn't need a pulse."
- University of Central Florida, Sigma Nu: At least one member was recorded chanting "Rape" and commenting, "Let's rape some bitches" and "We're gonna rape 'em, who cares."
- University of Richmond, Kappa Alpha: In a party invitation, a brother mass-mailed: "Tonight's the type of night that makes fathers afraid to send their daughters away to school. Let's get

it. . . . We're looking forward to watching that lodge virginity be gobbled up for all."
- University of California at San Diego, Sigma Alpha Epsilon: Pledges were told to get topless photos of women with RUSH ΣAE written on their chests—"rush boobs"—for an October event.

No matter who initiated these activities, the good boys in each chapter didn't stop them from happening. Objectification of women and tolerance of racism are massive problems in fraternity culture at large. But not in every chapter and not by every brother. Parents need to know what can happen to their good boys and why. And if students first understand why it happens, they can prepare themselves to intervene or refuse to participate. Why are these behaviors coming from (historically white) fraternities rather than from other college groups? How do boys like Jake, who entered college without strong prejudice, slide into a quiet acceptance of behaviors that are misogynistic (chanting "Nerf dart rape" at Jake and the stripper) or racist (using nicknames such as "Black Sam" and "Curry Dick")? And why are some chapters, like Oliver's, refreshingly different?

The answers can be at least partly explained by three psychological phenomena associated with group membership: groupthink, group polarization, and conformity.

Groupthink

Groupthink occurs when individuals unquestioningly internalize a group's norms, prioritizing consensus over critical evaluation and individual responsibility. Yale research psychologist Irving Janis identified several relevant manifestations of groupthink: irrational and dehumanizing actions directed against out-groups (in this case, women, racial minorities, and GDIs/non-Greeks); an illusion of invulnerability; ignorance of the ethical or moral consequences of decisions; and strong pressure on members who express doubts about the group's shared illusions. "Victims of groupthink," Janis wrote, "avoid deviating from what appears to be group consensus; they keep silent about their misgivings and even minimize to themselves the importance of their doubts." Rather than protest Zeta Kappa's hazing, drinking, and treatment of women, Jake gradually began to rationalize, and then defend, his chapter's behavior.

Groupthink causes individuals to feel less personal responsibility for the consequences of the group's choices. They believe they can take a riskier stance because if the group is unsuccessful, the responsibility is shared. More subtly, groupthink can be an extension of the brain's inclination to take shortcuts. "The human brain takes in information from other people and incorporates it with the information coming from its own senses," neuroscientist Gregory Berns has said. "Many times, the group's opinion trumps the individual's before he even becomes aware of it."

This process affects groups of any age. But 18-year-old students often have neither the cognitive development to be able to extricate themselves easily from the influence of a group nor the awareness that they are mentally programmed to be so vulnerable to its whims. Greek groups can be particularly prone to groupthink because of their emphasis on group cohesion and high levels of pressure to conform and comply. Several studies have found evidence of groupthink among Greeks in which "independent thought is devalued and group like-mindedness is paramount," leading members to exhibit significantly lower levels of open-mindedness than non-Greeks.

Part of group identity can involve defining oneself in relation to the group and against the out-group, and feeling an accompanying sense of superiority over outsiders. For the chosen brothers to be "in" historically white fraternities, other students—often nonwhite, always women—have to be out. And in defining the "others," as Janis observed, groups tend to dehumanize them.

This sense of entitlement over out-groups may help to explain the prevalence of sexism and racism in many chapters. Fraternity members display more degrading and objectifying images of women in their rooms (including sexist artifacts such as inflatable dolls) than other college men, consume pornography at significantly higher rates, and are more likely to refer to women's bodies with degrading sexual language. *Journal of Criminal Justice and Behavior* researchers speculated that "these ideals likely are reinforced though groupthink and are passed on from older members to new pledges."

This is not unlike the way Jake's pledge brothers learned from older members that rating and mocking women on their group Facebook page was acceptable behavior. Or how, on the first night of pledging at one Tufts University fraternity, brothers demonstrated their group values by forcing new pledge brothers to watch two naked women have sex with each other. When one pledge asked to leave, his request was denied. As he wrote in a 2015 op-ed for the university's newspaper, "I stood there watching 18-year-old boys perform oral sex on these women. I watched as they were told to see who could bring one of the women to orgasm first. I watched on the outside, often turning my eyes away, horrified and disgusted, standing next to seniors in the fraternity enraptured by the scene, standing next to Tufts alumni who had returned to this off-campus basement to watch this 'tradition.' . . . I dropped the fraternity the next morning and was warned that I could not tell anyone what I had witnessed the previous night." Later that year, Indiana University's Alpha Tau Omega chapter reportedly held a hazing event in which a member was required to give oral sex to a woman on a mattress while a naked woman watched and half the brotherhood cheered him on.

Because Oliver's fraternity defined itself as being both offbeat and kind to women, members' rooms were more likely to display movie posters than demeaning images of women. BGLO fraternity members, too, generally objectify women less often than white fraternity members, according to Rashawn Ray, a University of Maryland sociology professor. It's possible that BGLO brothers are more inclined to treat women as equals because, unlike the IFC, their Greek council typically consists of both fraternity and sorority members; they could be governed by (or govern alongside) the women. For this reason, it will be interesting to monitor the trajectory of Lambda Phi Epsilon, the largest Asian American fraternity, which recently appointed two women as International Board officers.

Another potential reason for BGLOs' better treatment of women is that at predominantly white colleges, black fraternity members feel more accountable. "Black fraternity men, and many black students, cannot overcome the reputational constraints of the small black student population. . . . White fraternity men can be anonymous, while black fraternity men perceive themselves to be constantly visible and therefore continuously held accountable for their treatment of women," Ray wrote in the *Journal of African American Studies*.

BGLO members told me that while this accountability is common among other school organizations consisting mostly of black males, fraternities stress the point from the start. "When I was pledging, one of the first things the older members told us was 'You will be a Kappa man whether you're wearing letters or not. From this point forward, you hold yourself to higher standards. You can't do or say the same things you may have before joining the fraternity. You will be recognized as a member of this fraternity, and you represent all of us,' " a Tennessee BGLO senior said. "I told the younger members of our chapter the same thing. Our population is smaller and therefore eyes are always on us." ·

In Ray's work, most black fraternity men, compared to white fraternity men and black men who were not in fraternities, were observed treating women respectfully. Researchers also observed them speaking out against other men who talked disrespectfully to women. A Georgia BGLO member said that while campus visibility plays a major role in brothers' treatment of women, so do their backgrounds. "Because a lot of my brothers were raised by single moms, they take respecting women to a very high standard. They don't want anyone disrespecting their mothers or their sisters, so they do the same to other women," he said.

Group Polarization

Group polarization is a tendency for groups to form judgments that are more extreme than their members' personal opinions. For example, juries whose individual members sway toward guilt as a group are more likely to recommend a harsher sentence than would each member alone. Experts have theorized that polarization happens for three reasons: Individual members are exposed to the group's rationale during discussions, may feel pressure to conform to the group's opinion, and/or take an even more extreme position than the group average to try to get the rest of the group to like them more.

Studies have found that group polarization can, for example, make students feel more negatively about their school, extremize students' evaluations of faculty, and lead already prejudiced high school students to adopt even more racist attitudes.

Group polarization is more common in homogenous groups— and many historically white fraternities are highly homogenous. Chapters usually accept mostly white, mostly middle- to upper-middle-class, often similar-minded boys, who are paired for social events with mostly white, mostly middle- to upper-middle-class, often similar-minded girls. If students are "not the right fit," they usually aren't allowed in. Jake told me once that a benefit to fraternities is that "the culture each one attracts will naturally help you find someone who's a lot like yourself."

"That minimizes diversity, though," I replied.

"It definitely does, and that's a big problem in fraternities. That's kind of why you'll see not too many minorities rushing fraternities. I don't think a lot of chapters are flat-out racist. It's more the subtle idea that fraternities want guys who are a lot like themselves, so not much changes."

Also, fraternities historically have been spaces in which white men have enjoyed privilege. The fear of losing some of that privilege can lead to racist or sexist activities. Some fraternities go out of their way to choose racist party themes. An invitation to Duke University's annual Kappa Sigma "Asia Prime" party read, "Herro Nice Duke Peopre. We look forward to having Mi, Yu, You, and Yo Friends over for some sake. . . . Chank you." Baylor University Kappa Sigmas threw a "Cinco de Drinko" party, at which students dressed as maids and construction workers; a bartender was in brownface. During California Polytechnic State University at San Luis Obispo's multicultural weekend, Lambda Chi Alphas threw a party at which they dressed as gangster stereotypes, and at least one member was in blackface. Arizona State University's Tau Kappa Epsilon chapter marked Martin Luther King Jr. Day with a party at which brothers dressed as racial stereotypes, drank from watermelon cups, and mocked African Americans. They hashtagged their party #blackoutformlk.

Many fraternities excluded minorities from the start. In the Civil War, nearly every member of Sigma Alpha Epsilon, which was founded at the University of Alabama in 1856, fought for the Confederacy. In 2015, SAE's continued racism was exposed when members were recorded singing, "There will never be a nigg** SAE." They had learned the song on a national leadership cruise sponsored by the fraternity; the chant was reportedly well known nationally among SAE leaders. Meanwhile, the SAE national office's official website touted the fraternity's Confederate roots as late as December 2014.

Group polarization also can lead fraternity members to adopt even more sexist attitudes—or push one another to more disturbing displays of aggressive machismo. Recall how the Facebook comment thread escalated when brothers goaded Jake to hook up with Madison, devolving from "Nerf dart rape!" to "Nerf dart motherfucking rape" to "Pledge Jake: Do it." When Lehigh University researchers asked fraternity men if they treated female students with respect, the most common response was "On an individual basis, yes, but when you have a group of men together, no." The respondents told the researchers that when they were grouped with other men, they sensed a pressure to be disrespectful toward women.

Kirk unknowingly echoed the same idea. At his first chapter, "None of the guys are individually misogynistic. But when you get all of them together, yeah, they're going to objectify women," he told me. "We'll be talking about sex, and one of them will say that a girl's only good for giving head. No one would ever say that in [my current chapter]. If someone said half the shit people at [my first chapter] say, other brothers would call them out for saying sexist shit. At [my first chapter], people don't get called out for anything."

The chapter has the power to prevent prejudice from seeping into brothers' attitudes. In a New England house of "nice Jewish boys," when a new pledge drank on Bid Night, he said "bigoted things we'd never seen from him in the rush process," the chapter president at the time told me. The president called a meeting the next morning, and the brotherhood unanimously voted to revoke the pledge's bid. "If we see something happening, we try to stop it. No one who enters our house should be made to feel uncomfortable for any reason."

Conformity

While groupthink is an irrational way of making decisions, discouraging creativity in order to promote sameness of thought within the group, conformity involves an individual changing his actions to comply with social standards. As students spend more time with one another, in the course of their interactions they often behave more alike. Groups devise their own normative standards for members' appearance and behavior: Sperrys, not Vans. Polos, not cargos. Hotties, not whales. When people internalize these standards, they may succumb to further pressure to conform.

In the mid-twentieth century, psychologists found that when asked to judge an ambiguous test, such as an optical illusion, individuals usually parroted the opinions of the other people in the room. In 1950, social psychologist Solomon Asch decided to test whether participants would conform to group norms even if others in the room gave an obviously incorrect answer. Asch hypothesized that people wouldn't bother to conform to the group opinion when the answer was clear.

Asch was wrong—and his results stunned academia. For the experiment, he brought college students, one by one, into a room with seven other participants. He presented a picture of one line and a separate picture of three lines labeled 1, 2, and 3. One of the three lines was the same length as the line in the first picture, while the other two differed by as much as several inches. Asch then had each person call out the number of the line he believed to be the same length as the first. Unbeknownst to the college student, who was the last to be called on, the other participants were in on the experiment, and Asch had instructed them to give an incorrect answer on 12 out of 18 trials. At least once, even when the lines were obviously different, three out of four college students repeated the group's wrong answer.

New research using brain-imaging technology suggests a biological explanation for the variation in people's tendency to conform. Neuroscientists monitoring brain images during conformity experiments like Asch's have found that participants aren't necessarily imitating the majority merely to fit in. Instead, participants' visual perception seems to change to align with the answers of the rest of the group.

In 2005, neuroscientist Gregory Berns conducted a similar experiment, this time using MRIs to measure participants' brain activity. Berns observed that deferring to the group took some of the pressure off the decision-making part of the brain. He saw increased activity in the amygdala when his test subjects did not conform to group opinion. Amygdala activity can lead to a rise in blood pressure and heart rate, sweating, and rapid breathing. "Lots of things trigger the amygdala, but fear is, by far, the most effective," Berns wrote in *Iconoclast*. "Its activation during nonconformity underscored the unpleasant nature of standing alone—even when the individual had no recollection of it. In many people the brain would rather avoid activating the fear system and just change perception to conform with the social norm."

Researchers in the Netherlands discovered that when a person learns that his opinion differs from group norms, his brain emits an error signal. The signal is produced by the same area of the brain engaged when someone faces financial loss or social exclusion. That signal triggers a process that can impel the person to conform to the group, changing his opinion even when the group view is wrong (as in the Asch experiment).

The Dutch experiment is particularly relevant here because it rated looks. The scientists took MRIs of volunteers' brains as they evaluated the attractiveness of a series of faces. After they rated a face, they were told the "group" rating, a fictional number manipulated by the scientists. Thirty minutes after the experiment, the scientists unexpectedly asked the participants to rate the faces again. The participants who conformed the most to the group ratings were those whose brains had emitted the strongest error signals when they learned that rating. The researchers concluded that a person's tendency to conform is partly based on his brain's response to social conflict; the strength of the error signal determines the threshold that triggers conformity. "Deviation from the group opinion is regarded by the brain as a punishment," the study's lead author said. "The present study explains why we often automatically adjust our opinion in line with the majority opinion. Social conformity is . . . reinforced by the neural error-monitoring activity which signals what is probably the most fundamental social mistake: that of being too different from others."

Imagine, then, the pressure during adolescence, the life stage in which the pull toward conformity is strongest. Compared to adults, younger college students are more likely to worry about what other people think of them. They experience more self-doubt, are less confident in their belief system, and are more interested in making friends. They are vulnerable to the influence of older fraternity brothers, whom they want to like and accept them, because their brains register deviation from the community norm as a true threat. And their behavior is reinforced by the chapter, which rewards or punishes members according to group standards.

When fraternity brothers praise or laugh with a member who

degrades or objectifies women, researchers say, "the peer group has reinforced such behavior as good, and it is likely the case that men in the fraternity will continue to engage in it. Similarly, if such acts are not punished or go unchecked by campus administration, men learn that they can get away with this behavior." Kirk told me that fraternity culture inherently objectifies women because "a high-tier sorority is a prize. That's how a lot of the guys at [my first chapter] see women," he said. "The seniors hook up and get high fives. You want those high fives. How do I get the high fives? I hook up with this girl. It's not really about the girls, it's about the praise of your brothers, about your brothers knowing you hooked up with this girl."

He recalled a recent conversation during which a brother revealed he was sleeping with a sorority sister. "She's a normal girl, mid-tier sorority, nice, average girl. We didn't know he was sleeping with her. So one guy asked rhetorically, 'Are you really fucking her if none of us know about it?'"

In any group, the pressure to conform can cause members to ignore the potential dangers or the immorality of certain activities or attitudes, which can potentially lead to high-risk behavior as students try to keep up with one another. Psychologists have found that adolescent groups with high levels of conformity experience more negative behavior, with group members and toward outsiders, than do groups with lower levels.

The kids who insist most stridently on conformity are typically the most influential students at school. Researchers say that even in late adolescence, popular cliques are more conformist than other groups. So it makes sense for many reasons when fraternity brothers, usually seen as high status on campus, are more conformist than other college men. This stage in cognitive development creates a perfect storm that draws boys to fraternities at a time in their lives when they are especially vulnerable to groupthink, group polarization, and conformity.

The innate fear of not conforming may be elevated in fraternities because of hierarchies, threats of hazing, or the idea that the chapter can arbitrarily choose to drop a member. Even the *Journal of the Association of Fraternity/Sorority Advisors* reported, "Upon entry, members whose values are incongruent with the norms and value set of the organization tend to leave, either voluntarily or involuntarily. As these 'different' members exit, the remaining membership tends to be similar to one another." This is what happened when Isaiah left (or was made to leave) Zeta Kappa and when Jamal dropped out because he couldn't afford the initiation fee, reducing the diversity of the chapter.

Given the Dutch experiment, it's easier to understand how conformity can change the way a fraternity brother views "others"; how he might gradually come to think a girl whom he previously found attractive is now a "whale"; and how he might be subconsciously persuaded to view women not as people but as "targets."

Even if a boy enters a fraternity with no hint of sexism or racism, it's possible that, in certain chapters, his views might shift to square with group attitudes without his realizing what's happening. A *Journal of American College Health* study found that, compared to non-Greek men, students who joined a fraternity between their first and second years of college "showed increases in their perceptions of peer approval of forced sex and peer pressure to have sex, as well as increased high-risk drinking and number of sexual partners compared with men who did not join a fraternity." These increases predicted the likelihood that the students would use coercion, make unwanted sexual contact, rape, or attempt to rape a year later.

But there is hope. As we've seen, peer culture can have an enormous effect on teens. If students believe their social circle *disapproves* of sexual assault, as in Oliver's chapter, they are less likely to commit sexual assault. If students believe they are accountable, as did the BGLO members mentioned earlier, they are less inclined to shirk personal responsibility. Many of the fraternity brothers I interviewed whose chapters did not tend to objectify women have at least one thing in common: Like Oliver's chapter, they have an appreciation of diversity and of differences in perspective.

It turns out that diversity may be a key to reforming fraternities: chapter scholarship funds to recruit and assist lower-income members; recruitment policies that favor nice guys over jerks; Advisory Board and staff roles given to women and other nonmembers. Diverse groups, studies have shown, do not polarize. In diverse groups, individual viewpoints matter and are influential. "Diversity helps because it actually adds perspectives that would otherwise be absent, and because it takes away, or at least weakens, some of the destructive characteristics of group decision-making," James Surowiecki wrote in *The Wisdom of Crowds*. "If you're careful to keep the group diverse, and careful to prevent people from influencing one another too much, the individual mistakes people make will be irrelevant. And their collective judgment will be wise."

Ω Ω Ω

Jake had a squirrely feeling in his stomach as he got out of the car at the edge of the woods. It had been a three-hour drive to the middle of nowhere. Now he and Ty watched as the brothers searched through the brush for the hidden trail that was supposed to lead them to their campsite. They could see late-autumn snow on the mountaintops in the distance. They had lost cell reception on the drive.

Eric tried to defuse the tension. He wore short bike shorts, a punishment from the brothers for some minor infraction. "Yo, Jake, time me to see how long it takes me to get one of my balls out the bottom of these things."

Finally, Z, decked out in full camping gear, motioned to the group. Their heads bowed to avoid looking at him, the pledges followed him through the woods into a clearing with a fire pit. Z told the pledges to set up their tents quickly because they needed every minute of the next three hours before sunset to chop wood for the fire.

Some of the Big Brothers helped the pledges chop down an enormous dead tree. As a sophomore taught him how to wield an axe, Jake thought, *I kind of feel like a man.* In groups of 10, the pledges, aching and dirt-streaked, carried heavy sections of the tree to the fire pit. Because they were not allowed to wear gloves, their hands were blistered and bloodied.

At dusk, the brothers started a blazing campfire. Z instructed each student to share one thing he wanted the chapter to know about him. Most of the pledges offered a version of how grateful they were to be there and how they looked forward to getting to know the older brothers. Sam earnestly said he was thankful "to know the meaning of brotherhood now, after all the stuff we've been through."

The brothers focused on different matters. "We have the potential to become a top-tier fraternity," an impassioned sophomore said. "But we have to create more relationships with sororities and get more involved." The last brother to speak was Daniel, the chapter VP. He made fun of Sam's comment. "You don't know the meaning of brotherhood yet," he said, laughing at the pledges. "None of you do. But that's a good thing. Because it shows that you guys are in for a lot, if you get through Hell Week."

That wasn't the first time Jake had heard a brother use the caveat. "*If* you make it through" was a frequent disclaimer. "*If* you can become a brother." As if Hell Week were so grueling that after the 11 prior weeks of pledging, a pledge could either drop or be dropped, just like that. Jake dreaded Hell Week—especially because the pledges would have to sleep at the house. For now, though, a more urgent fear overtook him. While he was enjoying bonding with his chapter via hard work instead of hazing, he didn't think that was all that the brothers had in store for the pledge retreat.

Z stood up. The pledges averted their eyes. "And that concludes our Confession Ceremony. Pledges, go to bed."

In their tent, Jake and Ty tried to guess what would happen tonight. "I don't think they're going to do much to us," Ty ventured. "I think we're going to try getting some sleep."

"No, man, that isn't how this game works!" Jake said. He insisted they quiz each other on their pledge books for an hour before they bundled up and tried to sleep.

As he nodded off, Ty whispered, "Please don't wake us up, please don't wake us up."

At 1:00 A.M., the brothers woke them up. "Get the fuck up! Get up and line up!" they shouted, pounding on the tents. Freezing and half-asleep, the pledges dragged themselves outside, shivering in their jeans and sweaters.

"Look at the ground!" Daniel yelled.

Greg told the pledges to place their hands on the shoulders of the pledge in front of them. "Bow your heads, don't look up, and follow me," he said. He blinked a flashlight on and off and jogged into the woods. For about half an hour, the pledges struggled to keep up, tripping over fallen branches in the darkness, scrabbling to maintain contact with one another so that no one would get lost as they traveled deeper into the woods.

In a clearing, Greg told the group to stop and line up next to a decrepit once-white shack. Flashlights clicked on, illuminating six tombstones. Brothers stood behind the graves. From the door of the shack, Z spoke: "The gates of death are the portals of life. The acorn dies and the oak is born. From the chrysalis rises the butterfly. So it is with man. Pledges, eventually you must die for your fraternity."

The light clicked off. Each pledge again placed his hands on his neighbor's shoulders. This time, following Greg, they had to run, clinging to each other's sweaters. A few times, Jake lost his grip on the pledge in front of him, but he managed to catch up with the group.

After what seemed like an hour, Greg told the pledges to stop. Flashlights revealed the brothers standing across from them. They were nowhere near the campsite. *Oh shit, we aren't done,* Jake thought.

Z spoke. The pledges' heads dipped. "All right, you guys. We stopped you out here for a little trivia game, as we call it, to see if you know your fucking pledge books by now. I'd better not be fucking disappointed." Even though Jake had expected this, he was petrified.

Daniel shone a flashlight in Quinn's eyes. "When was this chapter founded?" Quinn couldn't remember. Daniel asked two more pledges the same question. Jake couldn't believe they didn't know the answer. Daniel was furious. "Does anyone fucking know?" he bellowed.

Jake and several other pledges called out the correct answer. "Correct. I really fucking hope you guys know the creed by now," Daniel said. He pointed to Matthew. "Creed, go."

Matthew messed up. "WRONG!" Daniel said, and shone the flashlight on JB. "Creed, go."

JB made it about halfway through, then forgot a few words. "WRONG! This is so fucking embarrassing! How do you not know the creed by now?" The other brothers booed, shaking their heads. "We do this at every fucking meeting! The fact that you don't know the creed is a fucking disgrace to this fraternity!" Daniel strode to the other side of the line. "You at least must know the Greek alphabet. Do you fucking know the alphabet?"

"I don't know it," the freshman said.

"WRONG!" Daniel focused the light on someone else. "Say the

fucking alphabet." The pledge said it correctly. "Fine." Daniel directed the light at Jake. "The alphabet. Say it!"

Jake knew the Greek alphabet backward and forward. He could say the whole thing in six seconds. Now, though, he was anxious and under tremendous pressure, cold, tired, and out of breath. He said the words quickly, trying to stay composed. The light was hurting his eyes. He choked, missing *psi*.

"WRONG!" Daniel yelled. "What the fuck is wrong with you?" Jake flushed, ashamed, berating himself for screwing up. He was chagrined both because he *knew* this stuff—he had prepared for this like an AP exam—and because he hated to disappoint people. Only six pledges got the alphabet right.

Daniel yelled again. "You're not going to make it through Hell Week! None of you are going to make it through Hell Week if you don't know this shit. You're either going to live together as a class or you're going to die together, and goddamn, you guys are going to fucking die together!"

For the first time ever, Z raised his voice. He was so intimidating that he made Daniel seem like Santa Claus. "IT'S BEEN NINE FUCKING WEEKS! YOU'RE SUPPOSED TO KNOW YOUR PLEDGE BOOKS BY NOW! WE DO HALF THIS SHIT AT EVERY FUCKING MEETING. I HAVE QUIZZED ALL OF YOU AND YOU STILL DON'T KNOW YOUR SHIT! YOUR TIME'S RUNNING OUT, BOYS. HELL'S COMING. HELL'S FUCKING COMING."

When we spoke the next day, Jake was operating on little sleep. The brothers had permitted the pledges to return to their tents for three more hours before waking them at dawn to return to campus. Jake hadn't been able to nap because he had to do his pledge chores, study hours, and gym hours. But he defended the brothers for hazing the pledges. "We were all doing a bad job," he rationalized. "Me and the other pledges concluded that this was a fair warning for what it would be like and the type of questions they're going to ask us and the type of pressure we'll be under during Hell Week. So the retreat was really a tough-love sort of situation where they're preparing us to know our shit."

Hell Week was 14 days away.

As they waited to be summoned to the second-to-last pledge meeting before Hell Week, the pledges frantically studied their pledge books in the basement. The pledge retreat had spooked them; they worried about how intense Hell Week would be. Greg and Daniel came into the room as the pledges were rehearsing the creed. "It seems like you guys are starting to learn your pledge books. Keep up the good work," Greg said. "But we're actually here to talk to you about the travel exec who's going to be here Wednesday to Friday."

For a few days every year, Zeta Kappa sent a national representative to check on every chapter, Greg explained. The travel executive was tasked with making sure every brother was following national rules, including the hazing ban. For those days, the pledges would get a reprieve: no mandatory study hours, gym hours, or chores—they would have to complete them later in the week—no 5:45 A.M. jog, and the EP sleepover had been moved to Friday night. "This guy is coming to see if we're following the constitution of Zeta Kappa verbatim," Greg said. "Which means we are asking you to forget about every single fun or interesting thing that has happened to you over the last several weeks. None of it has happened."

Daniel jumped in. "Yeah, guys, um, listen. They can shut chapters down. So it's really important we stay in the clear, and for us to do that, it will require none of you to tell him what has been going on during your pledge semester. Nothing 'fun,' at least."

"So the cucumbers, they were never a thing?" Eric asked.

"Nope, never happened," Greg said.

"What about the strippers, eh?" Sebastian asked. "Were the strippers ever a thing?"

"No, you guys actually went to Lucky Strike that night," Greg replied.

"Yeah, and those overnight rituals you have during EP?" Daniel said. "Those never happen. You never stay over at EP. There was no retreat, either."

This was the first time the pledges felt empowered to talk about hazing with the brothers even if they didn't use the word. By naming the hazing activities, the pledges were letting the officers know that they knew that what the brothers had done to them was somehow wrong. And interestingly, Jake thought, the officers were indirectly acknowledging that they knew it, too.

"What about the jogs? Are they a thing?" another pledge asked.

"Nope, you definitely don't have to jog early in the morning," Greg said. "Also, is Z a scary guy?" The pledges hesitated and then shook their heads. "Good," Greg said. "He's a cool guy. He's approachable. And if he comes up to you while you're talking to the TE, you're allowed to say hi and you're allowed to talk to him, like every one of us."

"What about pledge chores?" someone asked.

"Pledge chores don't happen," Daniel said. "And you're not fucking pledges. You're new members. Do not use the word *pledge*."

"What about our pins?" a pledge asked.

"You're not forced to wear them at all this week," Daniel answered. "In fact, keep them in your pockets at all times but don't show them around."

Greg raised a finger. "Remember: Each and every one of you remained sober during Homecoming Week. Also, don't mention 'getting signatures' from brothers. You just interview them," he said. "Listen, this guy just graduated in May. He's going to seem friendly and try to be cool with you, but you've got to watch out because we've had TEs in the past corner pledges and get a confession from them. If you give him anything, anything at all, it could potentially ruin our chapter."

An hour before the TE was to arrive, all pledges and brothers were summoned to the house, where Andy, the chapter president, reiterated the message: "Don't tell him anything. Be as vague as possible. Don't say a word."

This is a test to see if we're going to allow them to get away with all the hazing, Jake thought. *Are we going to stay loyal to our chapter?*

When Jake told me about this discussion, I asked what he thought he would do. "When we first started talking [before college], I would've told you that I would definitely rat them out. Hell, yeah. This is my chance to prove hazing goes on and happens right under Nationals' noses!" he said. "But now I'm completely subservient. Because I'm so close to the end, so close to actually becoming a brother. If I were to rat them out, I'd be blamed by everyone. It's really changed me because I'm just passively letting all this happen to us even though I now have the best chance to straight-up talk about it with someone. It's such a weird feeling. I feel like I'm going back on my own beliefs on hazing and the pledging process."

"What makes the fraternity so appealing that you want to stay?" I asked.

"I want to finish the job I started. I've come so far over these last several weeks. I never knew if I was going to make it through rush—and I did. I never knew if I'd find a group of brothers whom I most connect with out of all the fraternity brothers on campus—and I have. I never thought I'd meet so many great people in my pledge class—and I have. I don't want to lose that. I've changed in terms of how social I've become, how much more extroverted. It would all go to waste if I were to confess anything. It's a test to see if we're going to remain loyal to one another. Everyone's in agreement. No one's going to say a word. I trust them. As tempting as it may sound and as ridiculous as the hazing has been, I don't think any one of us will betray the brothers."

Meanwhile, Hell Week loomed. The officers had explained that they'd confiscate the pledges' phones and laptops; the freshmen weren't allowed to be in contact with anyone outside Z-Kap for the entire week. They couldn't talk to their girlfriends. They couldn't even talk to their parents.

Victor and another brother told Jake that their class had lost several pledge brothers during Hell Week because if pledges didn't know every detail in the pledge book, the chapter dropped them. Victor also warned him, "Every brother will be a dick to the pledges except for your Big and Greg."

"Why?" Jake asked.

"You'll find out at a later date. Everything that goes on during Hell Week is for a good reason."

Jake was unhappy with this explanation. "Our lives are going to be hell anyway because of the hazing, but what good does it do if the brothers are dicks for a week? What does that accomplish?" he asked me. "I'm expecting some sort of great revelation as soon as I become initiated that makes me like"—he spoke in falsetto—"'It's all clear to me now!' But I really don't see how that's going to happen. It's impossible to think of what good can come out of all this. How can you justify it?"

I asked him how he was feeling about Hell Week. "I am so fucking nervous, to tell you the truth," he said. "I have no idea what they're going to do to us. This week feels like the calm before the storm."

Jake didn't tell the national representative a thing.

Ω Ω Ω

The Phi Epsilon alumni were pleased with the new pledge class. The freshmen had enjoyed their pledge retreat, which they planned on their own, and the Homecoming tailgate they hosted had been a success. Many of the freshmen were stressed out because they had to manage these events while also studying for classes and maintaining their social life, but that was routine for pledges at this time of year.

At first, because he was focused on the freshmen, Oliver didn't notice the apathy among some upperclassmen that had gradually crept into the house. Certain juniors weren't fulfilling their responsibilities: throwing away old food, cleaning out the fridge, sweeping the floor, picking up clutter in the library. Oliver could understand why some students dismissed these tasks as insignificant; he figured this happened in every fraternity. "Freshman year, you're pumped up to give back and work hard, but after that, it kind of dies down," he said. "But that moment where you have to question, 'I could take the easy road and not take out the trash or I could take out the trash right now even though it's a pain'—small things like that make a big difference in the long run. Those little details got lost along the way. The guys in the class above us stopped caring."

For a while, Oliver let the indifference slide, attributing it to the inevitable clash among classes or a refusal of brothers with seniority to be governed by a younger student. It took a major mistake for Oliver to notice that these seemingly minor oversights were indicative of a larger problem.

For the past few years, the State U PhiEps had run Carnival, a philanthropic event that raised funds for a children's hospital. The four-hour festival, which included carnival games, snacks, smoothies, and music, was intended to raise awareness of the campaign, much of which relied on online donations. In three years, the chapter's efforts had raised more than fifty thousand dollars. Last year's Carnival had been the most successful yet, packing the quad with students and locals.

In addition to Carnival, some PhiEps did Relay for Life, a team fundraising event for which members took turns walking around a track overnight to raise money for the American Cancer Society. And occasionally, alumni or members of the campus community contacted the fraternity to ask for assistance with assorted tasks ("My relative is moving. Do you have two guys willing to help out?").

Oliver assumed the two philanthropy chairs, both sophomores, would get the brothers as enthusiastic about the fundraiser as they had been in past years. About three weeks before Carnival, Chef started asking Oliver questions about the event. Chef, who worked in the kitchen every weekday from 9:00 to 6:00, was the only near-constant adult in the house. A mother in her early 50s, she was "easily the best chef in the Greek system," Oliver said, on a campus where other fraternities were unhappy with cooks whose standard fare was deep-fried corn dogs and sandwiches.

Even better, Chef, whose two grown sons had been Greek at other schools, genuinely cared about the brothers. She cooked each brother his birthday dinner of choice. PhiEps often visited the kitchen to chat with her. Some of them considered her an in-house therapist. Oliver had confided in her about his presidency, classes, friends, and dating life. (He'd had occasional hookups but no serious girlfriends in college, and he was okay with that.) She taught Oliver how to cook several dishes and to play cribbage; they played nearly every day. Many of the brothers thought of her as a second mom, their "mom away from home."

Oliver credited Chef with helping him run the house. From the start of his tenure as president, she had taught him important lessons. The first week he was in office, she bought him a planner to keep him organized. She guided him through business and management decisions and showed him how to be more efficient. She also was quick to tell him if she thought an issue had to be addressed, such as guys not doing their chores. "She does a lot for the community we have. I wouldn't be even remotely as successful a president without her," Oliver told me. "She consistently provides insights of an adult that I couldn't get anywhere else."

Actually, the State U PhiEps had several adults looking out for them, which was likely a major reason the chapter was a relatively healthy one. The Alumni Board met at the house once a month. Older alums stopped by unannounced about every other week, and young alums visited at least once a week to see how the brothers were doing. Past presidents like Trey were frequently in touch with the current officers. The alumni's presence gave the brothers a sense of continuity—and of their responsibility to keep the fraternity in good standing, to make prior generations proud.

"Has the bouncy house been ordered yet?" Chef asked Oliver now. "How do you want to handle catering?"

"Oh, wow, I haven't heard about any of this stuff, I'm sorry," Oliver said. "I'll check with the philanthropy chairs." He had no experience with this kind of planning and was unfamiliar with the necessary logistics. His doubts crept in again: *Me being so young, it's hurting the cause a little right now.*

The philanthropy chairs hadn't even reserved the space on the quad. "Ohh, yeah, we should probably do that," one of them said.

"Okay, well, this needed to happen a while ago, and I thought you were on top of it. We have a deadline to meet. Get it done," Oliver said, frustrated.

"Sorry, man."

Oliver sighed. "Do you want me to help?"

"Nah, we'll take care of it now," they promised.

Over the next three weeks, Oliver repeatedly offered his assistance, but the philanthropy chairs insisted they had their own vision for the fundraiser. Oliver backed off, believing it was important for brothers to feel a sense of ownership of their event.

There was a slight drizzle the morning of Carnival, but rain hadn't significantly dwindled attendance in years past. Oliver and about 10 other brothers woke up early to set up the tents and organize the catering. By 2:30 P.M., half an hour before the Carnival start time, there were still fewer than 15 brothers helping to set up on the quad. Usually the entire chapter was on site. Oliver called as many brothers as he could, but the few PhiEps he reached weren't enough to draw a crowd. Only about 30 guests showed up, the worst attendance by far in the history of the chapter's philanthropy. Not even the alumni were there. The philanthropy chairs had forgotten to notify them.

Oliver was embarrassed and angry. On one hand, he "clearly should have been more involved in the event because the philanthropy chairs had planned it so poorly. It felt like I can't just delegate tasks to someone, like I can't let anyone do anything on their own." On the other hand, he couldn't help wondering whether the sophomores had made such a mess of the event because he was their leader. This year's fundraising total was the lowest in chapter history, only about a third of the previous year's totals.

Oliver concluded that he should have stepped in because the philanthropy chair, who didn't have many responsibilities, was not a particularly respected position in the house. The two this year didn't have the energy or motivational skills to psych up the brothers for success. Oliver could see now that the apathy that had been slowly seeping throughout the chapter was, he said, "like a poison. And it spreads very easily." Several juniors were purposely dodging their house responsibilities and, worse, the time they should have been spending with the chapter's younger members. Oliver understood that students were busy and wanted to be out and about. He wasn't the type of officer to insist that brothers' lives be fraternity-centric, but the brotherhood lost strength if the brothers didn't value it, and the younger members would follow the older brothers' example.

Really, he blamed himself. Apathy was "the enemy," Oliver believed, and he hadn't defeated it. He remembered a video he'd seen once in which a man's dog was misbehaving in public. An onlooker saw the man becoming frustrated with the dog and remarked something like, "Why are you punishing the dog? You should be punishing yourself. If you had taught the dog better, he wouldn't be doing that." That's how Oliver felt. "I could have done a better job of leading the charge," he told me, miserable. He knew he had let his fraternity down.

CHAPTER 6

Looking Out for One Another— and "Helping the Fraternity Out"

ON A NOVEMBER AFTERNOON, Jake was studying when he got a text from Sebastian: Yo Eta Phi's having their semiformal Saturday and my friend requested a "cute nice boy." Jake texted back, Hey I fit one of those two requirements! Sebastian, who was going to the semi with another sister, responded, She's not the prettiest girl but it's going to be a fun event. Jake was undeterred by his pledge brother's assessment of her looks. Sebastian, who was experienced with girls, was a harsher judge than Jake. Once, when Jake told Sebastian he had a crush on Beth, Sebastian rated her Facebook profile picture "a solid 7." Jake was pleased because a Sebastian 7 meant, for Jake, at least a 9.

Excited to go to his first sorority function, Jake contacted the sorority sister, Kayleigh, right away. Over the next few days, they frequently texted to get to know each other and to plan their outfits. They mostly discussed the challenges of managing pledging and classes simultaneously. They decided that rushing was harder in sororities, but pledging was more difficult in fraternities. They were both looking forward to, in her words, "forgetting about our problems for just one night."

At the next EP session, Greg and Chase, the social chair, gave the pledges a new, unexpected assignment. "You're going to write a 500-word essay, due at the next EP, about a scene from an interracial porn," Chase said.

"The essay has to make me want to jerk off," Greg said. "Oh, and none of you can use the same video."

The next day, after another sleepless overnight at the house—more overnight rituals, more hazing—Jake searched for porn online. He scrolled several pages down to find out-of-the-way videos his pledge brothers wouldn't use. He settled on one about a black boss and a white employee, hoping that because the black guy was the boss, the assignment would seem less racist. Jake glanced behind him to make sure his roommate, who was studying on the other side of the room, couldn't see his screen, then discreetly placed his laptop on his lap. (He explained later: "I was trying my best not to get a boner but to analyze the video as if it were an AP Lit project. And then I 'overachievered' and wrote a 1,000-word summary of the scene in great detail using vocab that would make the SAT proud.")

Soon after Jake submitted the essay, Greg posted on the chapter Facebook page, Nice work, Logan. And Jake, you're a goddamn Shakespeare.

When Jake arrived at the house for chores, several brothers begged to see his essay. "I've got to see this essay *now*," one insisted.

"In due time, in due time," Greg said.

As the pledges selected their videos, they posted links in their group text so that no one would accidentally use the same one. Eric trolled the pledges by posting random porn links on Facebook, too. Once, Jake checked the pledge Facebook page during class only to find his screen dominated by a close-up of an anus.

He later learned that he had been out-overachievered. Logan had written a 1,500-word, MLA-formatted essay with in-text citations and a "Works Cited" page.

The evening of the Eta Phi semiformal, Jake met up with Sebastian, who filled their thermoses. (Jake told me the 90-minute bus ride would be "just enough time to get really drunk.") At the house, several brothers congratulated Jake. They seemed proud of him. "Nice job getting this hookup," one brother said. "Just grab her by the pussy," said another.

Jake told me he was "proud of myself, of how far I've come in the last several weeks. I mean, I never would've pictured myself already going to a major Greek event and getting this involved with Greek life, even before I'm initiated!"

Let's just have as much fun as possible tonight, Kayleigh texted him. Jake hoped she was implying a hookup, even if they had little in common. She was nothing like Beth, for sure. Jake and Beth's friendship had developed as they talked in class and occasionally texted. They shared the same taste in movies and books and a love of old TV shows. Beth was intellectual, like Jake, and he admired her creativity and her sense of humor; one of her hobbies was writing plays. But while he thought she was beautiful, because she was non-Greek he saw her only as a friend. "I really do like her, but I don't know that we could have a relationship," he said. "At fraternity parties I couldn't hook up with girls. Parties would be just to mingle and drink if I were with someone. Then I wouldn't be able to really help the fraternity out by getting the girls."

When I asked him what he meant by "help the fraternity out," Jake explained, "The fraternity would look better if I was more available. You're better able to throw a big party if guys are willing to socialize." Part of "being social" in his fraternity, he said, meant that guys were willing to hook up.

Tonight, Jake knew his chapter expected him to get together with Kayleigh. "I feel like my chances are better than they've ever been," he said. "She asked for the date. It's like all the work of proposing was taken into her own hands. Now it's just up to me not to screw up. It's on a silver platter for me."

At the club, Kayleigh was enthusiastic and fun, though initially she seemed hesitant to make physical contact while they danced. But the more she had to drink, the closer she got to Jake—at one point, grinding on him so explicitly that he realized, surprised, *This girl definitely wants it!* During a break, he checked his phone. Eric had posted a screenshot of his texts with a guy in another fraternity.

Eric: **Jake is at the Eta semi w Kayleigh.**

Eric's friend: **Good for him. She's a fucking animal!**

All Jake's pledge brothers knew exactly where he was, whom he was with, and what could happen. The comment thread made clear that his pledge class had expectations and were proud of him already. **Jake you're definitely in for sure. This girl will do anything.** And then, during one of the last dances of the night, Kayleigh whispered to Jake, "I'm going to make the bus ride home magical for you."

As the bus pulled out of the parking lot, Jake and Kayleigh waited for the overhead lights to shut off. Squirming with anticipation, they drunkenly cursed the lights. "As soon as those lights turn off, I'm going to be all over you," Kayleigh said.

No girl had ever said anything like that to Jake, who was simultaneously bewildered and horny. After 15 minutes, when it was clear the lights would stay on, the pair decided to move to the back of the bus, which was darker and quieter. They made out with abandon. Kayleigh was the third girl Jake had ever kissed. She put his hands on her breasts. "Do you want me to give you a handy?" she asked. "But I'm not going to try to make you come because I don't want you to make a mess."

"Uh, okay," Jake said. He had never been to third base before. He was still incredulous that he was barely into college and already hooking up with a sorority sister.

"Don't worry, I know what I'm doing," Kayleigh said, and then yanked him, too hard, and yanked again. At first, Jake didn't say anything, because he was both grateful that a girl had her hand on his penis and distracted by wondering what he was supposed to do with his own hand, which was currently making new discoveries in her underwear.

When he could no longer ignore the pain, he whispered, "Um, so you stroke it, don't pull it. We're not that strong." He gently showed her what to do. She took his hand and did the same on herself, guiding him through which movements to use and where to use them. *This is a lot further down than I thought,* Jake mused. *I'm getting educated!*

The next day, Jake saw Kayleigh at the library, where they exchanged awkward but friendly hellos. Neither of them expected to hang out again. "We were both really drunk, and now that I'm looking back on it, I don't think it was a very natural sort of thing. I feel like we were both in it just to hook up," Jake told me.

But it made for a good story. Back at the house, the pledges swarmed Jake to hear how far he'd gotten. He shared that he had "a really fun bus ride, got to third base," and then told them about the dick yanking, "to make it funny."

"Why make it funny?" I asked him.

"I think that story was good because it implies I got some action while also being something to laugh at," he said.

"At you or her?" I asked.

"Kind of both."

"Don't Drink the Punch": Mixers, Matches, Rape, and the Sorority POV

Two fraternities, two drastically different outlooks. In Oliver's chapter, which didn't care about its tier, brothers saw girls as people. In Jake's chapter, which prioritized moving up through the middle tier, girls were potential conquests. Kayleigh became a sexualized expectation, and then a narrative. She was someone to get with to "help the fraternity out," as if Jake could improve Zeta Kappa's image by copping a feel.

When boys first join fraternities, they are no more likely than non-Greeks to have committed sexual assault. But studies have found that fraternity brothers are three times more likely to commit rape than other students. Kinsey Institute researchers went so far as to conclude that "fraternity culture, marked by hooking up, sexual competition among brothers, and collective disrespect for women[,] make[s] fraternity rape a virtual inevitability." And after a Georgia Tech Phi Kappa Tau's email instructed brothers about "luring your rapebait" by weakening a girl's defenses with alcohol, sexual assault prevention expert John Foubert remarked, "The 'rapebait' email could have been sent from almost any fraternity at almost any American college."

After conducting the research and reporting for this book, I disagree that fraternity rape is inevitable. It is not true that "almost any fraternity" could have sent the "rapebait" email. At Oliver's chapter, an email like that would have gotten its writer expelled from the group. Fraternities differ both among and within campuses, and just as a few brutes can alter a group's ethos, so can a few good men. One study found that on measures of sexual aggression, hostility toward women, drinking frequency, and drinking intensity, members of low-risk fraternities did not differ significantly from students who were not fraternity members.

Several brothers I spoke with bemoaned the public's tendency to assume that all fraternity brothers are—their word—*rapey* because of what they like to call "a few bad apples." But while it may be unfair to assign blame to all fraternities for the crimes of some, the problem is obviously bigger than a few bad apples. Certain chapters across the country have become "known" on campus to be rapey, with repeated alleged offenses over a period of years. For the most part, this information is passed along through a whisper network; the fraternities and brothers involved rarely get in trouble, because the assaults are not officially reported.

Unfortunately, the apples may come from rotten trees. In recent years, even fraternity chapter presidents (at Cornell, Baylor, Temple, and Utah State) have been charged with sexual assault or sexual abuse. As police told a local news station regarding the Utah State case, it is the president's responsibility to ensure that no brothers commit these types of violations. Brothers told me that some adult Greek leaders minimize the seriousness of these issues, addressing them by telling members to watch a video or attend informational sessions about sexual assault rather than changing aspects of the culture that encourage brothers to objectify women.

Some of this intransigence, we might charitably think, is because those leaders simply don't know what to do. But in some cases, the leadership doesn't just fail to address the problem; it actively exacerbates it. In 2016, the NIC and the National Panhellenic Conference—the umbrella groups for national historically white fraternities and sororities—reportedly lobbied Congress to make it more difficult for students accused of sexual assault to get in trouble. The Safe Campus Act would restrict colleges from investigating sexual assaults unless the alleged victim reported the crime to the police and "until the completion of the criminal investigation and any subsequent trial." The bill did not impose similar restrictions on investigations of students accused of physical violence or theft.

Every advocacy group that works with sexual assault victims opposed the bill. The criminal justice process could take years, forcing the victim to continue attending school with her/his accused rapist. Kirsten Gillibrand, US senator from New York, told the *Huffington Post*, "This proposal is completely backwards. We should be making universities more accountable for providing a safe campus, not less."

In January 2016, when a Brown University chapter disaffiliated from its national organization (a rare move for a house), a student officer said the major point of contention was Nationals' disregard for the issue of campus sexual assault. "We believed in order for us to function as morally upstanding members of the Brown community, especially if we were going to play a part in fighting the scourge of sex assaults on campuses, we needed to disaffiliate from an organization providing money for laws [through the NIC] to make it more difficult to prosecute sex assault on campus," the officer told me. "Also, at conventions, representatives made light of the issue, saying you could get in trouble for as little as shaking a girl's hand. It was a toxic culture that Nationals vehemently denies, but you could feel it in the way they dismissed our claims."

Because of the NIC's "counterproductive tactics," the national office of Lambda Chi Alpha boldly disaffiliated from the group. Eventually, after vocal backlash from outsiders and members, the NIC and NPC withdrew support for the bill. But they continued to support the Fair Campus Act, an almost identical bill that excludes the law-enforcement mandate. And the fact remains that adult officers of fraternities and sororities spent hundreds of thousands of dollars and months of resources, even hiring former Senate majority leader Trent Lott, to make campus rape tougher to prosecute. As in the past, Greek leaders attempted to use their power to avoid accountability, one of the characteristics that make good fraternities worth joining.

There's no denying that the organizations are powerful. When a University of Oregon study found that nearly one in two UO sorority sisters are victims of nonconsensual sexual contact, an "alarmingly high" rate compared to non-Greek women, the university's reaction was unexpected. UO psychology professor Jennifer Freyd, who authored the study, said, "When we saw the magnitude of the rates, we were just blown away."

But despite her findings and a task force chairwoman's conclusion that "fraternities are dangerous places for women," UO announced plans to expand the campus Greek system. "There is high demand among students for increased opportunities in fraternity and sorority life," a UO spokesperson told me. "We have worked on a number of ways to address the concerns around sexual violence. This is nothing new. The issues around sexual violence on campus have been around for 30 years."

Freyd was stunned by the school's response. "We didn't set out to 'get' fraternities. We measured different variables, and this popped right out. I thought the university would be as alarmed as we were, that they wouldn't knowingly expose people to such a thing. But they were completely resistant to halting the expansion. That's when I began to understand the power of the Greek system."

Absent from most media coverage of fraternity sexual assaults is an examination of the nuances of the system that is contributing to campus rape culture. But it's crucial—and fairer to fraternity brothers, many of whom deplore this behavior—to investigate what it is about the fraternity experience that might, as John Foubert and his research team concluded, cause students to be more likely to commit sexual assault.

Multiple studies have shown that sexual victimization happens more frequently during fraternity parties and following fraternity events; on college campuses, more than a third of reported rapes occur in a fraternity house. Police say it's easier to commit sexual assault at parties in large multi-floor fraternity houses than in crowded apartments or dorms.

It's also possible that fraternity rates of sexual assault are higher than non-Greek rates partly because of access and opportunity. The Greek system is known for throwing major parties, and fraternities are in control of these parties. Members determine who can come in, who gets alcohol, and how much they get. Fraternity members see more girls on their turf than non-Greek guys do, sometimes hundreds in a night, girls who are often drinking and steps away from bedrooms in a situation in which casual hookups aren't an unusual goal for either gender. The low-risk fraternities mentioned earlier created environments that minimized opportunity without putting the burden on women to change their behavior.

It's well documented that sorority members are sexually assaulted at much higher rates than nonmember students. One study reported that sorority sisters are four times more likely to be sexually assaulted than non-Greeks. The National Institute for Justice has concluded that sorority membership is one of the most common factors that increases sexual assault risk (alcohol is another).

I was surprised when a smart young fraternity alum, now a law school student, told me the following: "Fraternities are accused of sexual assault a lot. You hear crazy statistics. It's ridiculous. If they were honestly true, sororities aren't partnering to do any event if they think there's a chance of that happening."

Wrong. Many sororities do partner with "rapey" fraternities, so the behavior continues. And here's why.

When Erin, a senior at a southeastern university, was a freshman, a fraternity recorded her drunk pledge sister having sex with a brother at a mixer and passed the video around the chapter, she said. The victim didn't discuss the incident with her sisters; Erin never learned whether the sex was consensual. But even if the freshman was raped, her sorority sisters were angry at her for damaging relations with a high-ranking fraternity on campus. They complained behind her back because the fraternity wouldn't mix with them anymore. "I was like, 'I can't believe she would do this to us,' blaming it on her. We still wanted to hang out with them because they were a cool, cute fraternity," Erin recalled. "Now I can't believe I thought those words. The sororities inflict values on us, and it's really con-fusing, so we take it out on each other so we can keep partying."

Why would a sorority turn on a sister who may have been raped? Because of the tier system, many sorority chapters vie for the atten-tions of the highest-ranked fraternity houses they can attract, which are often considered to have the best or the most parties. Because alcohol is officially prohibited at national historically white sorority houses, national leaders don't allow chapters to host mixed-gender parties with alcohol. The rule is intended to decrease sororities' in-surance premiums, but it has the added negative effect of making sorority sisters think they must go to fraternity houses to party.

Greek life commonly involves an out-of-date courting system in which fraternities try to convince their preferred sororities, or vice versa, to pair with them for Greek Week, Homecoming activities, mixers, and other events. As a result, Greek life puts a dangerous emphasis on coupling, and many chapters feel obligated to pander to the opposite gender to score invitations. "There's not much em-powerment for sorority women because we have to do things to make sure the guys like us," a North Carolina sorority sister said. "We have to please them and dress a certain way so they'll invite us to parties."

The pressure can go both ways, depending on the campus. "For Homecoming, it's going to be considered a defeat if we get a sorority lower than the sorority we were paired with last time," a Mississippi brother said. "It's all up to the sororities to pick. All we can do is warm up to their girls, go to all their philanthropies and events, make sure we're where they can see, and get an in with their sisters or hopefully with their execs. It's a reflection on your tier, who your Homecoming pair is. There's lots of pressure in our chapter—and it's something we need to stress even more."

At a Missouri school, sororities have made videos persuading the brothers to partner with them for Homecoming or Greek Week.

Reese, a recent sorority graduate, told me, "These videos said, 'We're hot girls, we're party girls, we're down for any kind of partying that you want.' We'd sexually advertise ourselves rather than saying we're smart girls, confident, achievers. We'd show girls drinking at pool parties in their bikinis."

The sisters portrayed themselves this way because "the fraternities like to pair with sororities with attractive girls who they think they can hook up with easier. So the sorority encouraged us to 'go out and drink and see what happens.' It felt like, 'If you hook up with them they'll like you, and that's what we want.' That was the message the sorority sent," Reese said. "They required us to go to all these fraternity events to 'support sororities,' but it was really about establishing relationships so girls could find hookups. It felt like hazing. If you said you didn't want to go, they'd say, 'Do you not want to hang out with your sisters?' If I didn't go, I wouldn't be 'bonding with the sisters.'"

Some adult Greek leaders try to silence members who speak out about these issues. When Erin wrote a newspaper article about her sorority's confusing messages about sexual violence, the sorority's regional director removed her from her chapter officer position. "They shamed me for writing it. The advisor said, 'This is going to follow you for the rest of your life,'" Erin said. "They said speaking up was 'bad for recruitment.'"

Sororities again silenced members who were upset about a controversial fundraiser. Sigma Chi fraternity chapters, which raise money for an alum's cancer foundation, run a signature philanthropic event called Derby Days. The series of campus competitions can culminate in a performance in which sorority sisters dance and participate in a Q&A. In front of an audience of hundreds, sisters participating in the 2016 University of Mississippi Derby Days Q&A were asked questions such as "Which Sigma Chi would you go down on?" "What type of sausage would you prefer: linked or Sigma Chi?" and "So you're telling me your nickname's not BJ?" At least five sororities reportedly instructed their sisters to stay quiet about the event. When a sister voiced her opinion about Derby Days on social media, her sorority reportedly terminated her membership.

During the 2015 Derby Days at the University of Illinois at Urbana–Champaign, banners hung on the Sigma Chi fraternity house, apparently created by the sororities. A Tri Delta banner pronounced, "We never stop at third base," with a picture of a Barbie-figured woman playing, as *Jezebel* aptly phrased it, "dick-baseball in heels." A Kappa Kappa Gamma banner featuring a curvy woman in a Number 69 baseball jersey (also holding what appears to be a dick bat) read, ΚΚΓ <3 SΣx (Sigma Chi) and "It's always a home run when a Kappa grabs the bat."

William & Mary graduate Meghan McCarthy wrote of her Derby Days experience, "The event seemed to confirm so many negative stereotypes about women and men. That women valued, above all else, being seen as sexually desirable to these men. And that men wanted and encouraged the women to perform as objects for their entertainment." When McCarthy and a sister asked their sorority to boycott Derby Days, the sorority's response was "That would be political suicide." McCarthy wrote in *The Atlantic*, "I was taken aback by the fact that these women would openly acknowledge what I thought we were too old to admit in college: These men were popular. And that made them powerful. And if we rocked the boat, we could be shunned."

Many brothers told me that fraternity members also feel pressured to attend parties. The kinds of parties Greeks throw can be problematic. Mixers—usually parties for one fraternity and one sorority—are often themed events. Past parties have advertised themes such as "Colonial Bros and Nava-Hos"; "ABC (Anything but Clothes)," where sisters wear bubble wrap, duct tape, or lingerie; and

"Champagne and Shackles," at which dates are handcuffed to each other until they finish a bottle of champagne.

At parties at a North Carolina school, new sorority members were expected to help fraternities recruit brothers by dressing provocatively and getting the boys drunk, said a recent graduate. Five days after her pledge class joined the sorority, "the sophomores said, 'This is what you do, where you go, what you wear.' We were told to dress as some sort of prize to these men. I saw gross things: someone's dress off completely, people going off into rooms together. It was definitely not a safe environment," she said. "They had this mentality of *We have to impress these guys to increase the reputation of our chapter.* Our entire initiation was wrapped up in how promiscuous you could be in that setting."

Some sorority members told me about fraternities that are "known" to slip roofies into the drinks they foist on girls, but the sisters stay quiet. When Charlotte, a Tennessee sister, suggested her sorority report an offending fraternity's behavior to the university, her sisters said, "Our sorority's going to look really lame if we report it, so leave it alone." Rather than avoid interacting with men who promote this culture, some sororities send members into their parties. Instead of saying, "Don't go," they say, "Don't drink the punch." The women choose to party at high-risk fraternities because if they party at low-tiered houses, they fear their rank will drop. Much as drinking can be conflated with learning how to be a fraternity man, perhaps the women's equivalent in some traditionalist sororities is successfully walking the tightrope between sexual attractiveness and sexual availability. While each member is answerable to the sorority for her sexual behavior, the onus is on the individual to stay safe.

All 250 to 300 of Reese's sisters drank frequently, she said, even with fraternities "known" to spike girls' drinks, and even though they heard about other sorority members who were sexually assaulted at fraternity parties. "We still wanted to match with them because they offered leverage for Greek Week or Homecoming events," Reese said. "If the guys could raise a lot of money for Greek Week, we could create a really awesome set for Skit." (Skit is one of several judged events in a fraternity-sorority team competition to become Greek Week or Homecoming champion.)

A Maryland graduate said his school's Greek system sent mixed signals, too. It held mandatory meetings about sexual assault, but matched fraternity chapters with sororities and said the groups had to attend together. At the same time, he said, many students join fraternities and sororities to drink and hook up in the first place. "Does rape culture exist? Yeah. And the majority of us are just as disgusted about it as everyone else. But a lot of people get blacked out and hook up with girls and neither or one doesn't remember what happened. Most of those stories don't have hard feelings. I've heard many girls laughing about waking up to somebody and not having met them. That happens and they'll start dating and they think it's an okay thing. Then it happens with another girl who is mortified by it. At the end of the day, it's just a group of hormone-filled teenagers. All the problems you imagine are going to exist will exist."

Sexual assault is overrepresented in the Greek system partly because, as it functions on many campuses, the system pushes teenagers of both genders to pair up. Interaction with fraternity brothers is a membership requirement for many sororities. Several chapters use a system in which sisters must accumulate a total number of points each semester to be able to attend the formal or to be in good standing. Many sisters told me that attendance at mixers and other fraternity events is one of the expected ways to obtain these points, in addition to participating in charity events or earning high grades. An Indiana chapter even doubles the points for party attendance if the sisters are trying to secure an escort for a major party week.

Lacey, a senior there, told me she pushed sisters to attend fraternity parties. "If only 10 of your girls show up, you insult the fraternity, and then why would they ask you back?" When not enough of her sisters attended one party, the fraternity canceled every future party the chapters had planned together.

It's important to remember that Greek culture can also sexualize and objectify fraternity brothers. A Missouri sorority has held a fundraiser that requires sisters to recruit brothers from every fraternity to dance in scanty Speedos. And some guys feel social pressure to hook up. Brothers told me about fraternities that hazed new members if they didn't get enough girls' phone numbers or if they didn't bring enough girls home. "So you're an 18-year-old impressionable kid thinking, *If I don't hook up with girls a lot, the brothers won't like me.* And then after you drink alcohol you have situations that turn really bad," the Maryland graduate said.

A Michigan junior said the pressure on his campus to hook up comes from certain sorority members. "When a friend in a sorority wants to pair me with her Little or someone in their 'family,' saying no can turn nasty pretty quickly. The pressure to hook up stems from the potential uncomfortableness that might manifest in the refusal of a hookup. The friend is offended, as well as the sister she intends to set up," which reflects poorly on both the brother and his chapter, he said. "Girls will say, 'He's such a dick,' or 'He didn't want to hook up with [name]; don't talk to him,' and it spreads like wildfire across a small Greek community. Fraternities are measured by their sorority relations, so appeasing them is a priority."

On more than one occasion, he said, a brother has declined to sleep with a sorority sister who had sex with other brothers. In some cases, he said, the sister "acts as if the entire fraternity has wronged her," turning her sorority against the chapter. The sorority then shuns the fraternity, refusing to cohost events or canceling scheduled functions. "It usually lasts until our groups are forced to be paired for a Greek event mandated by the university. Then everyone has to get their shit together."

While many fraternity members don't feel any sexual pressure from brothers, in chapters that prioritize status, members may feel compelled to push one another to attend mixers and/or to hook up. And they're doing so in an environment in which alcohol is plentiful and groupthink can skew boys' attitudes about women. According to a *Criminal Justice and Behavior* study, "Fraternity men were significantly more likely to receive informational support from their friends to use adverse and abusive tactics to gain sexual access. In addition, fraternity men reported receiving significantly greater levels of peer pressure from their friends to have sex . . . which, in turn, increased the likelihood of sexual assault."

But certain sorority sisters keep going back. When Lacey was a freshman, her chapter's upperclassmen pushed new members to attend a mixer hosted by a fraternity "known" to sexually assault women. A brother slipped something into a pledge sister's drink, Lacey said. Even though the sister was raped, the sorority continued to partner with the fraternity. Two years later, Lacey said she was raped by a different fraternity member, who was subsequently suspended by their university following an investigation. But she didn't want her sorority to stop pairing with the rapist's fraternity. "The relationship keeps going because nobody wants to cut a chapter off," she said. "Most fraternities wouldn't pair with us because we're a bottom sorority; top-tier fraternities only pair with top-tier sororities. We do not pair outside our tiers. If you're only pairing with five or six fraternities, cutting one out would cut out a lot of your social schedule."

That's the major reason many college women make excuses for "rapey" fraternities and keep returning to the scenes of the crimes. It's why Erin turned on a sister who might have been raped. "Girls blame other girls because we're obsessed with the rankings," Erin said. "Sorority rankings are very much defined by the guys who want to mix with them."

The Greek system can be an insular bubble in which students can easily forget that their lives won't always remain Greek-centric, that there is a wide world beyond the confines of Greek Row. Much as an adult who has a workplace run-in or hears something unsavory about a colleague might keep her head down and her mouth shut so as not to jeopardize her job, many sorority sisters feel similarly trapped. If they speak out, these 18-, 19-, 20-year-olds fear they'll be abandoned by the tight-knit community they've worked so hard to get into and the friends in whom they've invested the majority of their time at college. As they inflate the importance of the rankings, they forget to prioritize their selves.

Both sorority sisters and fraternity brothers are caught up in a cycle of peer and systemic pressure that rewards them for coupling up and partying hard. "We're pressured to get as many girls to the parties as possible. There are discussions about not going because it's dangerous, but some people argue, 'If we didn't get hurt this time, it's not a problem,' or 'It's a good fraternity and the roofieing is just made up.' But we know it's not, because girls are getting roofied," said Charlotte. "So we keep having mixers with fraternities that roofie girls." And the behavior doesn't stop, rewarding high-tier fraternities, even if they're "rapey," at the expense of both the sorority sisters and the lower-tier fraternity gentlemen who treat women right.

Ω Ω Ω

Oliver knew he had to address the Carnival fiasco at the next chapter meeting. He told me, "I'm pretty passionate about PhiEp. I want this place to be the best it can be. When it comes to things like this, I'm going to be blunt and not pull my punches. No one wants to be the bad guy. I'll do it because that's what needs to happen, but you don't get any joy from that."

By this point in his presidency, Oliver was used to speaking in front of the brotherhood. But that didn't mean he was comfortable giving his peers a reality check. They knew him to be calm and composed, so when he spoke at the meeting, obviously frustrated, the chapter took notice. "We're here for a reason. We're here to give the freshmen the same experience we all got. You need to be able to sacrifice a little bit so you can help the bigger cause," he said. "The attitude that a lot of you have right now, not really caring, is fucking pathetic. And saying you *want* to do something is one thing, but having the ability and conviction to do it is another. So stop being weak-willed and actually carry through on what we need to do."

When Oliver finished, he was relieved to see people nodding and snapping their fingers in agreement. At the next chapter meeting, Diego backed Oliver up with a speech about complacency. "We need to fucking step up!" Diego said. "For those of you who know the guy who started this fundraiser, what do you think he'd think if he came back now? Would he be pleased with this event? No! When you put on an event like Carnival, fucking think about who you're representing, who this is for, and fucking think about something other than yourself!" Oliver felt validated. Maybe the voice of a respected senior would persuade the brothers that this was a real problem, not just Oliver's opinion.

Oliver slightly modified his leadership style because of Carnival. He began to have private conversations with his closest friends in every pledge class, asking them to act as advocates for his plans. He still hesitated to confide in them about personal matters, but he earnestly shared his ideas. Each time he planned to suggest something to the chapter, he would first speak with these proponents, who could then motivate their friends to support it. He took extra time to talk to his advocates privately so they would trust his judgment. He hoped they would become so accustomed to supporting his ideas that they would come to do it automatically.

But there was still too much tension in the house. Disagreements on the direction of the chapter had escalated. Brothers were keeping to their own small groups rather than socializing with PhiEps in other pledge classes. Some of the juniors were skipping meetings, and surprisingly, so were some of the freshmen. Now that their pledge period had ended, some of these new brothers complained that they weren't included in the decision-making processes. There was nothing specific they wanted to do; as they told Oliver, "We just feel we're in the shadows." From Oliver's perspective, these freshmen often raised trivial matters at meetings. Rather than allow their irrelevant ramblings to waste meeting time, an officer inevitably would cut them off.

Knowing he needed to do more to pull the house together, Oliver called Trey for advice. "Come up with something lighthearted and fun to make the mood nice," Trey suggested. "That's why I started dodgeball during Work Week."

And that's why Oliver started Prank War. Without warning, he texted several brothers: I'm starting a Prank War. No destruction of property and nothing harmful. Anything else is fair game. He launched the battle by deodorant-bombing a junior's bedroom, dispersing an entire bottle of Axe spray and shutting the door. For the next week, brothers zip-tied various items together (a table to a bed, an Xbox controller to a ceiling pipe), removed bedroom doors, and so forth. One morning, Oliver got out of the shower to find that Felix, a quiet, mellow junior, had taken his towel, Vaselined his bedroom door-knob, locked the door, and hidden the keys, leaving Oliver to careen around the house naked to hunt for them.

By the time Prank War ended, it had accomplished Oliver's goal: to disrupt the apathy, primarily among the junior class, and to get the brothers involved in something fun together. He was pleased that his chapter had enjoyed "a lighthearted, fun thing that wasn't a party and gave us more depth because it encouraged the idea that you don't need to drink to have fun." The political disagreements dissipated, meeting attendance improved, chores resumed, and risk management ran flawlessly. For a time, Oliver believed the Most Outstanding Chapter award was still within reach. So when Trey told him that holding a literary event could help win extra points with headquarters, Oliver was game. At the next chapter meeting, without prodding, nearly a dozen brothers volunteered to participate in a literary open mic night.

Three weeks later, 60 guests from several sororities and a few fraternities sat in rows of chairs on the PhiEp lawn. Many students drank boxed wine out of glassware. Some brought cheese. They watched a variety of PhiEp performances, including a song, a trumpet duet, a piano performance, a poetry recitation, and a funny reading of a *Fifty Shades of Grey* excerpt. A senior wrote and performed a hilarious play he had written specifically for the occasion. One of Oliver's good friends acted out and recited comedically by memory the entire final planet Mustafar scene from *Star Wars: Episode III*. It was one of Oliver's favorite nights of the year.

Ω Ω Ω

Shortly before Thanksgiving, Jake and Beth made a deal to review each other's Psych 100 projects. Occasionally, they ran through their edits on the phone. A few days before Hell Week, Jake suggested they go over their work in person.

When Beth came over to Jake's dorm, she noticed Jake's duffel bag on the floor, surrounded by the unusual array of items Z had told the pledges to bring. "Whoa, why are you packing all those matches?" she asked. "What's the bag of sugar for?" He promised he would tell her what he could after he survived the week. All he knew right now was that he would be permitted to leave the house only for classes.

"How are you going to eat?" she asked.

"I heard they're going to provide very small rations of food at the house," Jake said. He thought of something and reached into his refrigerator for the espresso shots he drank every day. "Actually, do you think you might be able to store these for me and bring them to class?"

"Of course."

He also handed her some emergency cash to hold for him and a container of Ibuprofen "in case I'm massively hungover."

After she left, Jake thought about their exchange. She was kinder about his request than his high school girlfriend had been about anything, and Beth was just a friend. Or maybe Jake wanted more. Here was the kind of naturally developing relationship he had hoped for in college, wasn't it? They had met by chance instead of through what he called the "formulaic" setups of Greek life. Jake vowed to ask her out after Hell Week.

For the last party before Hell Week, the Zeta Kappas hosted a cartoon-themed club mixer with Alpha Rho. Jake, having debated at length whether to go with a Clone Wars or Pokémon costume, dressed in a Pikachu onesie; he was the most dressed-up guy in the chapter. Zeta Kappa held the pregame in its house, where brothers had set up beer pong tables in the basement and kegs in the bedrooms. The guys started drinking before the sorority sisters arrived, chatting mostly about the members who were attending the Theta Epsilon semiformal. One of the pledges had agreed to a blind date with a Theta Ep before he checked her out on Facebook. The brothers now laughed, saying he'd gotten paired with a whale. Tonight's joke was that he was "out harpooning."

Most of the 100-plus Alpha Rhos wore sexy outfits with a cartoonish top—*SpongeBob* camis, *Angry Birds* crop tops. The girls squealed over Jake's onesie, asking him to take selfies with them. As Jake chatted with the girls, Tanner came over with a large bottle of Captain Morgan. He interrupted Jake, put the bottle to his lips, and ordered, "Pull until I say stop." Jake pulled for more than 10 seconds. Tanner gave him a nod of approval. Jake thought the stunt "made me look pretty impressive with the girls."

When Jake spotted the only other person at the pregame wearing a onesie—a Tigger—he zoomed over to introduce himself. He was pleasantly surprised to find that she was Laura, the girl with the mini-golf shirt whom he had almost gotten together with at his first fraternity mixer. He easily started a conversation with her, impressed she knew enough about *Star Wars* to carry on a discussion about it. She was the only sorority sister he had met who had seen all the movies.

As they talked, Laura moved closer to him. Older brothers interrupted them a few more times, encouraging Jake to drink until he was at least as drunk as Laura. Behind Laura, several brothers gave Jake nods of respect. Daniel held two fingers in a V to his mouth and waggled his tongue. *Everyone's thinking I'm getting with this girl, but I'm only trying to chat with her,* Jake thought. He was torn. He desperately wanted to earn the brothers' approval, and getting with another sorority girl would go a long way. But after the strange evening with Kayleigh, he had come to a realization. "I'm the type of person who prefers one partner who I develop a long-term relationship with, as opposed to hooking up with a different girl at every social. To me, it really doesn't mean much to drunkenly make out with a person. There isn't any real affection there. It's mostly fueled by seeking pleasure after drinking a lot of alcohol," he told me. "This semester I've tried to save myself for the fraternity, but I think I'm going to just seek a relationship with one person."

Jake didn't want to jeopardize even the remotest possibility of a relationship with Beth, and he liked Laura too much to hook up with her one night and ditch her the next. He reminded himself not to get so drunk that he forgot about Beth.

As they waited outside for the buses that would take them to the club, an Alpha Rho sober sister pulled Laura aside. Jake looked away but heard every word. "Laura, you're very intoxicated right now. You should either not drink anymore tonight or go home. You can barely even walk."

Laura protested, "No, please let me stay! I'm with this really cute guy tonight."

Jake was surprised and flattered. *That's me! She's with me! I'm the really cute guy*, he thought. *Aw, man, tonight's going to be hard.*

The sober sister relented. Jake and Laura shared her flask on the party bus, where colored ambient lights illuminated the stripper poles in the middle of the aisle. A few Alpha Rhos and drunk Z-Kaps gyrated on the poles. Several pairs of Z-Kaps and Alpha Rhos made out during the ride. Laura rubbed against Jake, her intentions obvious. *I'm not going to put my hands on her,* he told himself. *No, no, I'm not going to acknowledge her moves.*

At the club, when Jake and Laura danced, she slid her body up and down his. He tried to figure out how to explain that he liked her but couldn't hook up. As the crowd began to disperse, he offered to pay for a Lyft back to campus. The brothers noticed them leaving together and gave Jake knowing looks.

In the car, Laura leaned on him. He chose his words carefully. "This has been such a fun night and you seem really laid back. Thank you for making this such a great time," he said. "But there's a girl in my personal life I've been meaning to ask out and I was wondering if I should do that because I was hoping it works out, and hopefully she says yes if I ask."

She took it well. "Oh, yeah, definitely ask her if you like her," she said.

For the rest of the ride, they talked about their weeks of rushing and pledging. Both of them had been forced to drink, they discovered. Both had been hazed. When he dropped her off at her dorm, they hugged in their onesies. "The Zeta Kappas assume I got with her that night," Jake told me later. "I didn't confirm or deny. So in terms of the brothers' respect for me, it went up anyway."

Ω Ω Ω

At about 1:00 A.M., after a PhiEp house party had ended, Oliver was playing a video game in his room when Beau, who had been his bunkmate in the sleeping porch, came in. "Hey, Javier is having a rough time right now. Would you go talk to him?"

Javier was a junior who'd had problems controlling his drinking sophomore year to the point where his personality changed drastically when he partied. After the chapter prohibited him from drinking for two months, he had toned down the behavior. But lately he'd been drinking too much again, and now he had punched a hole in a wall in his room. Beau had come to get Oliver while another sophomore stayed with Javier. On their way to Javier's room, on the other side of the house, Beau told Oliver that Javier was "half-crying, half-raging" and "freaking out about the future."

Javier was sitting on his bed, his swollen hand bruised purple and covered in white plaster dust. Behind him, the hole in the drywall, which was lightweight to begin with, exposed a broken plank. Oliver asked Beau to get wet paper towels from the bathroom.

"Hey, what's up, man, how's it going?" Oliver asked Javier.

"I'm stuck," Javier moaned, still drunk. "I'm just stuck. Nothing's moving forward."

"Well, yeah, dude, that's completely normal. Nothing to beat yourself up about. That's how people feel when they're our age," Oliver said.

"But I'm stuck in the same place. I don't know where to go or what I want to do," Javier said. "That's how I feel!"

Beau reentered the room and handed the wet paper towels to Javier, who dabbed at his hand.

"Yeah, who really knows what they want to do at this age?" the other sophomore in the room said. "There's a whole life ahead of us."

For an hour, Oliver and the sophomores did their best to soothe Javier until he could go to sleep and sober up.

The next evening, Oliver called a meeting of the Judicial Board to discuss Javier's case. "We're seeing a relapse of his sophomore-year habit. I think it would be a good idea to get him away from booze. He had a sober period last year. Maybe we should do that again. What do you guys think?" Oliver asked, then stepped back so that Felix, the most senior J-Board officer, could run the meeting.

A few members of the eight-man board wanted to discuss disaffiliating Javier. "This is getting to the point of ridiculous behavior. He should have learned his lesson a while ago," one said.

"Maybe this is just a one-night thing," said a brother who didn't know Javier well.

"No," said Geoff, the VP, "it's not a one-night thing. That's not possible with him."

After the board voted, one of the brothers found Javier and brought him to Felix's room, where Oliver and the board sat in a half circle on the bed and a couch. "Hey, man," Oliver began. "We're going to talk about last night and everything that happened. I'm going to let the J-Board facilitate this discussion."

"Do you remember what happened last night?" Felix asked Javier.

"Yeah, a good portion of it," Javier admitted.

"What was going on?" Felix asked.

"I made mistakes like I did a while ago. I was way too drunk. I shouldn't get that way," Javier said. "Whatever you guys want to do, I'll pretty much be game for."

Felix nodded. "We're going to put you on a six-week sober probationary period," he said.

"Yeah, that sounds good to me," Javier agreed.

"You're going to have to pay for the damage you caused, too," Felix said.

Javier was fine with that. Everyone in PhiEp knew they were expected to pay for their own mistakes.

Another Tuesday night, another house party. In the bar room, Oliver watched as one of his brothers, who was obviously tanked, made out with a sorority sister who seemed equally drunk. Because the girl was leaning away from the brother, Oliver guessed she wasn't sure what she wanted. *They probably shouldn't be making decisions if they're that drunk,* he thought. When the girl took a break to chat with her friends by the door, Oliver overheard her say, "I don't know if I want to hook up with him. I might stay, I might not."

Immediately, Oliver pulled his brother aside. "Hey, man, you need to not be hooking up with that girl. She's kind of not sure what she wants, and if that's the case, there's not any room for you to be doing this. So don't—or you're going to answer to me."

"Why do you think that?" the brother asked.

Oliver told him what he had overheard.

"Oh. Okay," the brother said, and lumbered off to the other side of the room.

Usually, it was that easy to intervene; Oliver had done it several times. When he believed there was even the smallest chance that a potential hookup was "in a gray area," as he put it, he didn't hesitate to cock-block. If a girl looked uncertain with a brother, Oliver would "walk up and interject myself in the conversation, coming across as a total dick, and completely swoop in on the girl, like, 'Do you want to grab a drink?' or 'Do you want me to show you where the bathroom is?' If they're uncomfortable, they're going to say yes," Oliver told me. Then he would get the girl settled in another area of the room.

Oliver's chapter made it a priority to try to avert situations that could lead to sexual assault. The State U fraternity presidents' retreat, an overnight camping trip, also had focused mainly on how to prevent sexual assault. The chapter presidents had resolved to make sure their chapters took the issue seriously.

State U's IFC required chapters to have a sexual assault presentation and a drug-and-alcohol-abuse presentation each year. Oliver's chapter believed it took these programs more seriously than some of the other chapters. For sexual assault education, Oliver's chapter brought in an organization that spent an hour and a half explaining how sexual assault happens and how to prevent it. This year, Oliver had scheduled the presentation for the fall, before the party season peaked. (He also brought in campus police officers to deliver a talk about safety, robberies, and emergencies.) Separately, Oliver had developed his own three-step process to discuss Greek community incidents at chapter meetings: Explain what happened, parse what might have "made the situation go wrong," and discuss how to prevent that kind of incident from happening in his own chapter.

Earlier in the year, rumors had spread that a sexual assault charge was being leveled at the fraternity house across the street. At the next chapter meeting, Oliver told the guys what he knew, which was only that girls on campus said that at a house party, what was supposed to be a casual hookup had reportedly escalated into nonconsensual sex. "Look, you know how we should treat women. Everyone knows how we're supposed to carry ourselves," Oliver had said. "We shouldn't be pressuring girls to drink a lot more, shouldn't be focusing on hooking up or getting laid that night when that's not the important thing. That's what gives rise to the idea that fraternities are the ones you see in the news. We don't do things like that, obviously. Always remember if someone looks too drunk and she says yes, that is not consent. That's not the appropriate move, especially if you're more sober than she is. And you need to be looking out not only for yourself but your guests as well."

Even though the brothers had heard this counsel before, and knew how important it was, Oliver reminded them frequently. "People can start to forget," he told me, because these incidents didn't happen often on the State U campus; or if they did, they weren't well known.

The problem wasn't the guys themselves, in Oliver's opinion. His chapter didn't recruit assholes. "People know what is right and what is wrong," he insisted. The problem was the alcohol, he said. Alcohol changed people, and alcohol was inescapable in the Greek community. That was one reason that PhiEp designated five sober brothers per party. Whether they were stationed or floating, they knew it was their responsibility to keep the guests safe. "If they see someone hitting on a girl who's way too drunk, they tell him to back off. And they know if one of our guys is super trashed and talking to a girl, there's a chance he could say something he wouldn't normally; he could be rude or disrespectful, so they watch for that and step in if they have to," Oliver said. "At parties at other fraternity houses, we can't force them to run things the same way, but we also stress to our guys that even if we're not at our house, we should be on the lookout. There are creepy dudes out there, and you want to watch out for them."

CHAPTER 7

The Brotherhood:
Relying on a Second Family

JAKE WAS CONFLICTED. A few nights prior, Andy had held a Blackbeard family meeting. Andy, Victor, and Ty's Big had given Jake and Ty three pieces of advice for Hell Week: "Do not laugh at anything the brothers do," "Don't do anything that will get you singled out," and "Know your fucking pledge book."

Now, with two days to go before Hell Week, Jake still hadn't memorized all the fraternity minutiae: the fraternity's early history, details about the coat of arms, the BNs of every member . . . But on the second day of Hell Week, Jake would have two midterms for which he hadn't yet had time to study, on top of a 1,000-word English essay due. Ultimately, he decided to prioritize his pledge book. "I know grades are important, but I don't get threatened in my classes. I do get threatened to know my fraternity stuff," he told me.

At precisely midnight on the first day of Hell Week, the backyard double doors opened for the pledges, and a black-robed figure crooked a finger. "Enter in order," he intoned. "Pledges, you will fail." In alphabetical order, the pledges silently filed into the house. Instantly, brothers lining the hallway shouted at the pledges, "RUN!" The pledges sprinted to the end of the hall, where Z stood, his arms crossed. Preston, the chapter treasurer, collected their phones, keys, and wallets.

For the next week, the pledges, who could leave the house only for classes, were hazed in a variety of ways. They were kept up late, awakened early, and sometimes led through rituals in the middle of the night. They were allowed to eat only what the brothers gave them—usually half-meal portions and, once, a buffet of disgusting concoctions (oatmeal chili, hot-pepper Jell-O, vinegar Coke). Their "pledge tasks" included forced drinking, calisthenics, cleaning the house (which the brothers repeatedly trashed), dunking body parts in ice water, wrestling, and drunk relay racing. They had to create a skit about a gay student, "making fun about how he likes to take it in the ass," perform a stereotypical impression of a Jewish brother, and pretend to be sex-crazed personal trainers (which apparently meant they were supposed to hump an exercise ball). When they weren't involved in a pledge task, they had to stand in the Great Room and stare silently at the letters on the wall. And they had to keep a candle lamp, which represented their fervor for the brotherhood, lit and protected around the clock. Jake arrived drunk to some classes and fell asleep in others.

On Thursday night, Greg hosted the final EP session, at which the pledges were surprised to see almost every brother in attendance. Greg announced that a few select freshmen would take turns reading their porn essays. He told Logan to go first—and ordered JB (the largest pledge) to act the part of the petite white girl and Matthew (the smallest and youngest pledge) to play the guy. As Logan read the cheesy dialogue and described various positions in graphic detail, Matthew pretended to have sex with JB, bending him over a table and contorting him into various other positions. It was difficult to hear Logan because the brothers and pledges were laughing so hard. At the story's climax, a senior gave Matthew a can of shaving cream to squirt on JB as he finished. The pledges got a standing ovation.

The next day, Jake slogged to class, where Beth handed him coffee. A few minutes into the lecture, she gave him a three-page document. It looked like a play, titled "The Secret Code." A small Post-it note stuck to the front read, "Sebald Code."* Within minutes, he had deciphered her message: "Jake, I hope this note finds you well. I cannot begin to fathom the terror you must be facing, my friend. You will get more coffee in class tomorrow. Hang in there."

Jake looked up at her, overcome that someone had taken the time to do this for him. She smiled back.

That night, the officers relentlessly assigned the pledges chore after chore. Victor pulled Jake aside to ask how he was doing. He gave counsel that, to Jake, sounded ominous. "Huhhuh, listen, the week's almost over, but don't be afraid if you fuck up because there's always a purpose behind everything." *Oh no,* Jake thought, *the worst part hasn't happened yet.*

At about 9:00 P.M., Daniel came into the kitchen, irate for unknown reasons. "GO TO THE GAME ROOM NOW AND CHANGE TO YOUR SLEEP CLOTHES! GO, GO, GO!" he screamed. The pledges ran to the Game Room, changed clothes, and waited. As soon as they were barefoot, Daniel screamed, "GET INTO YOUR WORK CLOTHES AND STARE AT THE LETTERS!" The pledges changed again and raced to the Great Room. "NO! IT'S BEDTIME! GO TO THE GAME ROOM!" Daniel yelled. He ran the pledges back and forth about a dozen times.

Z strode into the Great Room, holding the candle lamp. The pledges' heads dropped. He paused for a few moments before speaking. "This candle's supposed to be the fucking passion you're supposed to show if you so desperately want to be part of our brotherhood. So why the fuck did you leave it unattended? You know what you guys did to that passion? You did this to us!" Z hurled the lamp at the wall. It shattered. The pledges shifted their bare feet.

"I need pledges to clean that," Z said. Two pledges raised their

---

* After a ringing is mentioned (a bell, a doorbell, etc.), the first word and every 11th word thereafter until the next ringing comprises the coded message.

hands. "Get a broom and dustpan and clean this shit up," Z said, and stalked out of the room.

The pledges gazed at the letters as they were supposed to, sneaking occasional awkward glances at the two guys painstakingly collecting every shard of glass off the floor. They continued to stare at the letters for nearly an hour. Staring at the single point was so mentally draining that Jake thought he might pass out.

A senior walked into the room with a chair. He sat in front of the pledges, giving them a break from the letters, and delivered a lecture on trust. At the end of his talk, he said, "It's been such an experience these last four years. I feel so welcomed and dedicated to this fraternity that I would honestly die for some of the brothers here." When he left the room, the pledges resumed staring at the letters.

After more time had passed, Daniel came in. He sat behind the pledges, forcing them to continue looking at the letters, and gave a talk about honor. Once he left, the pledges waited silently for another half hour, focused on the letters. Jake felt like he was going crazy. Three more brothers gave speeches as the pledges stood, staring at the letters both during the talks and in the long intervals between them.

As soon as the last speaker closed the door behind him, Jake sank to the floor and cried. He didn't know why, exactly, he sobbed; the lectures hadn't been nearly as intense as other activities. He told himself he wasn't in his right mind because for days he had been malnourished, sleep-deprived, overworked, and stressed. Staring at the letters for four hours without moving had pushed him past his breaking point.

Ty put a hand on Jake's shoulder. "Are you okay?"

"Oh, it's nothing," Jake said through his tears as other pledges came over to check on him. "Please just let me cry this out. Don't worry about me. I'm fine, I'm fine."

Chase came into the room and saw Jake on the floor. "Jake, you'll be first for the next activity," he said.

Jake rose slowly, wondering what he was in for now. As Chase led him to the informal chapter room, he asked, "You okay, man? You feeling all right?" When Jake nodded, Chase patted him on the shoulder. "Don't worry, it'll be all right. This is a good activity for you. And you should know that when I was a pledge, I broke down, too."

Chase showed Jake the fraternity's secret knock, and the door opened. The room was pitch black. "This is called Personal Reflection. The brothers are listening," Chase said. Jake could hear the guys rustling in their seats. "This is your time to talk about your feelings or anything you want to get off your chest."

Oh, I can do this, Jake thought. He took a shuddering breath. "I'm a very organized person. I like to have everything planned out and know everything that's going on beforehand," he said. "So as you can understand, this entire week has been a major changeup in what I'm comfortable doing." He sniffled. "But I understand why we go through this. It's a healthy experience for me to be in this situation, to not know what I'm doing, and to trust what the brothers are doing for me. I'll be all right. I know I can make it through the rest of the week if I just trust in whatever activity happens." At this, he choked up and couldn't speak again. The brothers were silent. Chase led him back to the pledges.

In the Great Room, Sebastian asked Chase if he was allowed to bring Jake to the bathroom. Sebastian sat silently with Jake, his arm around his shoulders. Within moments, two older brothers, Steven and Henry, came into the room and put their arms around Jake, too.

"Are you all right?" Steven asked.

"Yeah. I just have to get it out of my system," Jake said. The brothers patted him and went back downstairs.

"I have to tell you, Jake, I know where you're coming from,"

Sebastian said. "I haven't told anyone this, but I broke down the first night of Hell Week." Jake looked at him in surprise. Sebastian always seemed like he had it together. "After being forced to eat that food and then do all the chores at top speed, I actually decided I was going to drop." Sebastian had found Greg, who was talking with Z, and asked, "Can I drop?"

"Don't drop," Greg said.

Z even addressed Sebastian directly. "Seriously, don't drop," Z said quietly. "We want you here."

It was comforting for Jake to know he wasn't the only guy who had suffered what he decided was an anxiety attack because of Hell Week. And, he told me later, "It was nice to know I had people who really cared."

Ω Ω Ω

Oliver felt that he was possibly beginning to find his groove as a leader. His designated advocate strategy was working to help motivate not only the brothers who were neither horse nor cart, but also some of the carts. Oliver had been able to schedule an extra drug-and-alcohol-awareness presentation, and he had even used the advocates to persuade brothers to slightly scale back their partying.

When the brothers' priorities shifted, the chapter's GPA rose. As PhiEps devoted more time to the house, they spent more time studying together and pushing their brothers to do better. This sense of collaboration and competition had helped Oliver immensely when he was a freshman. "We study together as a group, making sure everyone's on task the entire time instead of dicking around on Facebook or YouTube," Oliver told me. Older brothers took turns taking all the freshmen to a reserved room in the library and staying with them for three hours, three or four nights a week, to make sure they learned college-style study habits.

Unfortunately, Oliver's presidential duties afforded him less time to study, and his GPA had dropped from a 3.6 to a 3.0. He was disappointed, but he understood that there was only so much he could take on at a time. He rationalized that it was more important for him to lead a full college life—keeping up with his presidential responsibilities, hanging out with friends, staying active on campus, watching movies—than to spend all his time studying. "I know college is a harder game. I'm not going to 4.0 college," he told me. "I could probably do better, but I'm okay giving up a little GPA for peace of mind and happiness in the long run. It's more important to focus on being a true, whole person than to be a GPA."

One night, Oliver brought a former fraternity brother to his parents' house, which was half an hour away. A member of Oliver's pledge class, Mark had been deactivated after freshman year when he didn't make PhiEp's minimum GPA. Oliver still hung out with him whenever he could.

Because his parents were on vacation, Oliver was looking forward to kicking back with his friend after a long, stressful week. He showed Mark how to climb out his bedroom window and onto the lower roof, something he had done many times over the summer when he wanted a tranquil place to relax.

He let go of the upper roof and was stepping out of the way to make room for Mark when he slipped on a wet spot. He scrabbled to maintain his footing, then reached desperately to grab the edge of the roof. He missed. As Oliver slid down the sharp incline, he realized he was falling headfirst toward a small square of cement 20 feet below.

This was not the first time in college that Oliver was forced to consider the mortality of a teenager. Several months before, a high school acquaintance texted him out of the blue: **You heard about what**

happened with Christopher? Christopher, one of Oliver's best friends from home, had transferred colleges because of his anxiety issues. Oliver had talked to him a few days prior, when they planned Oliver's visit to Christopher's new school. The texter told Oliver that Christopher had died at 19 of an overdose.

Reeling, Oliver had gone to his room. As he stared at his wall, he cycled through shock, sadness, anger, and confusion. He couldn't believe his good friend was simply not there anymore. He already felt a hole where Christopher should have been.

The next day, when Oliver was hanging out in front of the PhiEp house with Patrick, his curly-haired accountability buddy, and another close pledge brother, he started to tell them what had happened. "Yo, this just kind of went on," he began. "My friend just died." Before he could elaborate, a bunch of sorority sisters came over to flirt. Oliver excused himself and went inside to his bedroom.

Within moments, there was a knock at the door. Patrick came in and sat down on Oliver's couch. "What's going to happen now is we're going to talk about this," he announced. "I know you don't want to, and it sucks right now, but we need to talk about it. Tell me about him."

While it was difficult to start talking about Christopher, Oliver felt a little better once he did. Patrick kept the conversation going. "What memories do you have of him?" It meant a lot to Oliver that "despite the fact I didn't think I wanted to talk about it, he showed care and thoughtfulness and he knew me well enough to come in," Oliver told me. Once Oliver was ready to tell other pledge brothers about Christopher, they took over his house chores, without asking, so that he could work through his grief. They had his back, no questions, no conditions. If that wasn't brotherhood, then what was?

Oliver believed the brotherhood encouraged every aspect of the ideal man that Nationals espoused. Most of all, Oliver valued the way dedicated brothers tried to hold one another to standards intended to develop them into good people. That was what Patrick had asked Oliver to do for him as his accountability buddy. And it was working. Although Patrick didn't cut back on partying as much as Oliver had hoped, he was following a routine Oliver had helped him create that slotted times for working out and studying. Patrick was getting healthier and his grades had improved.

Brotherhood was, for Oliver, "synonymous with loyalty. Every-one's willing to do whatever it takes for each other. Sure, there's al-ways guys horsing around, but at the end of the day, I know I could count on any one of them for anything I need." Brotherhood also signified a network. Already, he had seen brothers benefit from alumni connections: One guy scored an internship with a profes-sional sports team directly from an alum, and another got a job at one of the most sought-after companies in the world because an Alumni Board member wrote him a sterling letter of recommenda-tion. Oliver, too, had an internship interview set up by an alum. "Going into the real world postcollege, and even summer intern-ships, it's helpful to have seniors or recent alumni who can recom-mend you for a job based on who you are as a person because they lived with you for years. They have connections all over the place," he said.

Even more, brotherhood symbolized for him a commitment to looking out for your brothers, the way he, Beau, and the J-Board had looked out for Javier. Javier had stopped drinking, as promised, and was less stressed out. He had even thanked Oliver for his role in as-signing the probation. "It's good to take a step back from booze when you're in that scenario. It's good to get some space from that stuff," he told Oliver.

The brotherhood *meant* something. Oliver could see that in the nostalgically misty eyes of the generations of alumni who visited the house. He already could tell that when he reached their age, he would feel the same. He knew he would look back fondly not only on the fun times but also on "my personal journey from being the shy kid to someone who led a house at 19 years old," he told me. "This place has been the biggest source of growth and development I've ever had and led to the best relationships I'll ever have. Understanding that all of those things happened here at this house is pretty cool."

At his parents' house, knowing with certainty that he was going to hit the ground, Oliver pushed off the roof to fling his body toward any direction but the cement patch below him. When he hit open air, the only thing that went through his head was: *ROLL.*

As he neared the ground, he tried to barrel-roll to disperse the impact of the fall, but he miscalculated the distance and landed on his left side on the lawn. The pain in his left foot and elbow was excruciating. Even in the dark, he could see that his elbow was awkwardly out of place.

"Oliver! Are you okay?" his friend shouted.

"No."

"I'll be right down!"

With his right hand, Oliver reached into his pocket, but his phone had fallen out. He patted the grass around him until he managed to palm the phone. *Batman would do it,* he told himself. *It's fucking time. Let's go.* He slowly typed one-handed, "How do you put back in a dislocated elbow?"

Mark burst out the front door. Calmly, Oliver finished reading and told him he was going to pop his elbow back into place.

"What?! You're going to do *what?*" Grossed out, Mark followed Oliver's instructions. He took off Oliver's sweatshirt and placed the sleeve in Oliver's mouth to bite down on. He helped Oliver move his arm in a circular motion as Oliver prepared to punch the elbow back in with his right hand.

Perhaps Oliver's years of martial arts had steeled him for moments like these. *I've been through worse than this,* he lied to himself. *I can get through it.* In much the same way he was able to stay composed while plummeting from the roof, he now adopted what he later called a "gritty mentality to do what had to be done"—and he popped his elbow back into place.

High on adrenaline and assuming his ankle was sprained, he tried to get up, but couldn't put weight on his left foot. Mark helped him inside to a couch. "It's okay, I'm good," Oliver reassured his friend. "I'll sleep it off and go to the hospital in the morning."

"Well, okay," Mark said, reluctant. "I'll be in the other room. Holler if you need something."

For two hours, Oliver tried to sleep, but he was in too much pain. At midnight, he woke up Mark, called an aunt who lived nearby, and promptly went into shock.

At the hospital, the ER doctor informed Oliver that he had indeed dislocated his elbow and, to her surprise, he had put it back in properly. "You are the toughest and dumbest person I've seen in here in a while," she said. "You could have died." Oliver had a shattered heel, a fractured ankle, and cracked ribs. He would be on bed rest at his parents' house for a week and use a knee scooter and crutches when he returned to school.

One of the first things Oliver did was delegate to Geoff and the other execs a list of tasks to take care of at the house. Then he wrote to the Alumni Board and lied. Oliver did not tell them he had been with a former fraternity brother. He knew they would ask the same question that everyone else, including his parents, had asked him: "Were you drinking?" He worried that the Alumni Board would assume he and his friend were doing stereotypical drunken fraternity antics, which wasn't the case. If they didn't believe him, the alumni's relationship with both him and the chapter would erode.

He told them he had been alone, putting up holiday decorations on his parents' roof, when he fell.

"The thing most people immediately go to is 'Must have been stupid fraternity stuff,'" Oliver told me later. "I was fine, so it didn't matter. I didn't want anyone to worry, and I didn't want to talk about it much. If I said I was putting up holiday decorations, there wouldn't be a bunch of questions."

As word of his injury spread, Oliver mass-emailed the brothers, asking them to show Geoff and the other execs the same respect they had shown him. It was a relief for him to know that he could depend on the execs to handle his responsibilities. Sometimes, when he was away from the PhiEp house, he "felt like a parent, wondering if, while I'm gone, the kids are going to be throwing a fricking house party." But each time he called Geoff to check in, the VP reported that the chapter was sound. And Chef, who regularly texted Oliver, had no complaints about the boys.

Oliver was surprised that several brothers separately came to visit him—most students didn't have cars, and it was a busy week at school. He was not surprised by the funny giant get-well card that every brother had signed, because someone had posted on their group text, **Come sign Oliver's get well card** (to which another brother had replied, **Way to ruin the surprise, you idiot**).

When Oliver's father helped move him back into the PhiEp house a week after the accident, Oliver was struck by something that he felt distinguished his chapter from others. His buddies all knew his dad already and greeted him warmly. Oliver couldn't imagine belonging to a chapter where the brothers didn't know one another's parents. Phi Epsilon welcomed parent visits at any time, beginning with the PhiEp official parent orientation each fall. During the orientation, which was geared toward parents of pledges, parents could tour the house and ask the brothers questions. "We give a spiel about safety, say it's a really good place for their sons to be, given our academic history and the types of guys we tend to turn out," Oliver told me. "We reassure them their sons aren't going to be forced to drink until they die or until a huge accident happens, that this is not a stereotypical fraternity."

Back at State U, Oliver thought he should address the freshmen. Originally, he'd planned to tell them the holiday decorations story; after all, they needed to take their chapter president seriously. But during the week at home in bed, he had spent a great deal of time considering this strategy. If he wanted his brothers to trust him, he had to be transparent. And when he noticed that the freshmen were still stressed about managing fraternity responsibilities on top of college life, he thought he could improve their morale by telling them a story about their president being a dumbass.

He called the freshmen to a meeting. He began with a motivational talk about how they needed to keep their chins up. He ended by making fun of how he had actually fallen off the roof. "They all appreciated it, and their spirits were a little lifted after that. I think it was a time for myself and them to get a little closer and for them to see me as myself rather than the president," Oliver explained later.

Actually, his accident seemed to further bond the brotherhood. No one complained about meetings or petty politics now. The brothers had all cheerfully pitched in to manage the house smoothly in Oliver's absence, and now they mobilized to take care of their president. To minimize his journeys down the stairs from his third-floor room, brothers constantly stopped by to ask if he needed anything or refilled his water bottle without his asking. Over the next several weeks, they helped him on stairways, drove him to class, ran his errands, brought him food, and filled in for him at meetings across campus. Before chapter meetings, the other execs corralled the members to their seats as Oliver made his slow, 15-minute slog down the stairs. (One brother repeatedly volunteered to carry him, but Oliver politely declined.) When, at the bottom of the stairs, he realized he had forgotten something—his laptop, his phone—brothers sprinted upstairs to retrieve them.

Oliver was deeply grateful for his brothers. They were generous with their time and compassionate with their assistance. Like family, they took care of him. They also gave him a ton of shit for being on the roof in the first place. When Oliver was sitting down, brothers often snatched his knee scooter to joyride around the house. He treasured the humor. "It's nice to laugh at that stuff. Bad shit happens every day. I fell off a roof. If I'm in a shitty situation, I'm glad people can make jokes about it, because what else can you really do at that point?" he told me.

They might have slipped up now and then, but Oliver recognized that the guys in his chapter had bonded enough so that, when it counted, their brotherhood was undeniably strong.

Ω Ω Ω

Zeta Kappa Hell Week continued with more of the same. The pledges endured additional rituals, ceremonies, and hazing. On the second-to-last night of Hell Week, all brothers and pledges were summoned to the informal chapter room. Z sounded different, unintimidating, as if he were any other brother. "Okay, so this next activity is called Compass Confessions," he said. "For the rest of the night you can look at me and call me Hunter—or Doyle, because apparently everyone calls me Doyle for some reason."

The brothers chanted, "Doy-ul, Doy-ul, Doy-ul!"

Z rolled his pale blue eyes. "That's not even part of my name. I don't know why that's a thing. Anyway, I have here a compass. We're going to pass it around from person to person, starting with the pledges, and you can talk about whatever you want."

The pledges gave bland mini-speeches about how they were happy to be part of the fraternity. When Jake got the compass, he told the group that he was close with his parents and sisters, and he missed them. "I'm grateful that everyone in my family is currently in good health, but then, I haven't been able to talk to them since last Saturday, so who knows what's happened since then." The guys laughed. "I also feel that over the almost 12 weeks of this pledge process, I've really changed as a person just because of all these new activities and people I've been exposed to."

A few turns later, the compass reached a pledge whom Jake didn't know well. "The last time my girlfriend and I had sex, I wasn't wearing anything and she forgot her pill for a few days," he said softly. He explained that she had to wait until a specific day to take a pregnancy test. She had tested two days ago, but because he wasn't allowed to talk to her, and the brothers had his phone, he wouldn't know until after Hell Week whether she was pregnant. He said it was hard not to be there for her, and stressful to think of what might happen.

His talk changed the tenor of the conversation. Sam said he was mourning the death of a cousin. Logan asked to go again. "You know, when I went, I don't believe I got personal enough with you guys." He told the group about his mother's diabetes. When he wept, the pledges nearby wrapped their arms around him comfortingly. Several other pledges asked for the compass back so they could "get more personal," too, sharing the negatives in their lives. Eric said he had lost all his good high school friends because they didn't talk to one another anymore—and one former best friend, who had joined a top-tier fraternity, had become "a fucking frat bro and really changed as a person. I really didn't have anyone I could call a friend before going into this pledge process with you guys."

Quinn told the group that he was bullied in high school, where students had constantly made fun of him. "I never really felt like

I belonged with anyone until I got into Zeta Kappa," he said through tears.

Every time a pledge teared up, his pledge brothers embraced him. And when many of the brothers spent their turns reminiscing about a brother who had recently died of cancer, the brothers hugged it out, too.

"We were really close," Jake told me later. "I never thought during Hell Week we'd do such a riveting, emotional activity. That was just the best thing we could have done. This was the final thing that really brought us together as a class, the real turning point. When everyone revealed what was going wrong in our lives and that we needed each other, it was really touching."

For an hour after Compass Confessions, the pledges were allowed to chat freely with the brothers. Now that Z had offically introduced himself, the brothers seemed ready to open up about him. "Hunter is the epitome of Zeta Kappa," Daniel explained to the pledges. "He represents our values." Other brothers described Hunter as one of the most intelligent people they'd ever met.

On the final night of Hell Week, Daniel told the pledges to change into their tighty whiteys, get their coloring books, and meet in the Game Room. Someone had jacked up the heat, causing the pledges to sweat even though they wore nothing but briefs. Wes was missing, and none of the pledges knew why. Daniel told the pledges to work on their coloring books until he came back. The pledges passed the time mostly by drawing penises.

The officers returned with blindfolds and told the pledges to hold them, line up in alphabetical order, and wait. Several minutes later, Wes, panting, ran into the room in his briefs. He found his place in line in front of Jake. "Dude, I really think I fucked up," he whispered.

"Where have you been?" Jake asked.

Wes explained that instead of coming straight back to the house after class, he took a detour to his girlfriend's dorm. She met him outside with a kiss and three bags of beef jerky—and that was when two brothers caught him. "They grabbed me, took the jerky away—I was going to bring it back for all the pledges, I swear—and told me to sprint the fuck back to the house and put on my tighty whiteys. And now I'm here."

Jake prayed the brothers didn't know about his arrangement with Beth.

Moments later, Daniel and Greg burst through the door. Daniel looked as if he were on the verge of tears. "I CAN'T FUCKING BELIEVE YOU! I CAN'T FUCKING BELIEVE YOU HAD THE GALL TO FUCKING DO THAT!" he yelled at Wes. "Do you even want to become initiated? Do you even want to fucking become a brother? I don't even think we should initiate you anymore, because you sure as hell don't fucking deserve it right now." Wes buried his head in his hands, devastated.

"You're a fucking piece of shit," Greg said quietly. "I hope you realize that. I hope your whole class realizes that." He slammed the door.

Wes looked broken. None of the pledges told him off; they understood the need to see a loved one, and—for Pete's sake—to eat. "Don't worry, you're going to get shit for it, but we still want you in our class. We're not going to ostracize you or anything," Jake reassured him.

Upon Greg's return, he instructed the pledges to don their blindfolds, put their right hand on the shoulder of the pledge in front of them, and march. When the line stopped, several brothers individually led the blindfolded pledges upstairs to various bedrooms. Jake was placed in a chair. Someone turned on loud horror movie music, the kind of eerie, skin-prickling piece that crept up on a listener, faded away, then suddenly screeched. Jake tried to sleep, or at least to get comfortable, but about every 10 minutes, a brother came in, forced him to sit up straight in the chair, and shone a flashlight close enough to pierce the blindfold. Jake felt as if he were going insane.

Several hours in, he began to hallucinate. He thought he remembered horrible conversations with the brothers, he thought he saw pledge brothers through his blindfold in the dark. He was forced to sit up straight in the chair, alone, for the entire night. After seven hours, as he later learned, he felt brothers lift him from the chair. Wobbly and disoriented, he let them guide him downstairs. There was no music there, to Jake's relief. He inhaled the silence, trying to will himself back to clearheadedness.

The blindfold was removed. Jake was in front of an altar in what he assumed was the formal chapter room. Several brothers in robes stood watching him solemnly. Z spoke: "Candidate, on this altar lies quill and parchment. For the records of this fraternity, write your name." Jake wrote carefully and neatly. The robed brothers suddenly spun him around the room while performing a call-and-response that was too quick for him to follow in his exhaustion.

Z continued: "Next, you shall prove your worthiness by writing the answers to the following." He asked a series of questions about information in the pledge book. Jake grew more confident with each question. He had studied for this. He knew the date of the chapter founding, every word of the creed, the BN of every chapter officer, and he remembered the secret knock Chase had shown him. He finished diagramming the knock and waited for the next question, careful not to look at Z.

"What the fuck was that?" Z shouted. "What the FUCK was that! Turn on the lights!"

Jake looked around, panicked. *Oh no, I messed up. I got something wrong!*

"Who is this man's brother?" Z bellowed.

Victor dashed over and grabbed Jake, claiming him.

"Get him the fuck out of here. Go! GO!" Z yelled.

Victor rushed Jake out of the room and pulled him into the bathroom.

Jake was mortified to see the older members of his family there: Andy, Ty's Big, and even the family patriarch, glaring at him. "Jake, do you realize what you've just done?" Andy asked. "You wrote a fraternity secret on paper! 'Ever conceal and never reveal, by verbal means or written word.'"

Jake was near tears. "I didn't mean to! Oh my God!"

Ty's Big gripped Jake's shoulders. "You've ruined our family name! This hasn't happened before."

Jake was shaking now. "Oh, God, please, I didn't mean for any of this to happen! I'm so tired!"

Victor covered his mouth, looking incredulous.

"Why did you write down the secret knock?" the patriarch asked.

"I thought I was supposed to give the answer! I'm really tired. I've just been up for so long," Jake said.

"Do you not realize that you've just given up everything you've stood for? Something you've been tested on your entire semester? You've failed."

Jake wiped his eyes. "What do you think we should do now?" the patriarch asked.

"I really don't know," Jake said, his voice quivering.

"Okay, listen. I'm going to talk to Z and see what he can do about this, but this hasn't happened before," the patriarch said.

"Oh, God, I'm so sorry," Jake moaned.

The brothers left the room. Alone again, Jake sobbed. After the roller coaster of rush, 11 weeks of pledging, forced drinking, hazing, sleep deprivation, and poor-for-him academic performance, plus this week of malnourishment, zero contact with his family, more forced drinking, and hours of exhausting hazing, he had jeopardized his membership at the last minute. *Have I done all this for nothing?* he agonized.

Ω Ω Ω

Oliver, now on the mend, was house-sitting for his parents when he got a panicked call from Geoff, the chapter VP. Tonight, the PhiEps were throwing one of their two biggest parties of the year, cohosted with four other fraternities. The chapter had worked hard to plan a party that met the highest risk-management standards. They had hired nine security guards and planned to keep the party contained in the front parking lot, to prevent guests from entering the house. Oliver wouldn't have missed the party, but his parents needed the help, and he would not let them down.

Three hours into the party, two city policemen had surprised Geoff at the table where he was stationed in front of the lot. He had never seen these officers before.

"How's the party looking? Would you like to do a walk-through?" he asked them, knowing that the party, which had been registered well in advance, was in solid shape.

"The party's fine," one of the officers said. "But as we were walking over, some guy peed off the deck, and we almost got pissed on."

Geoff had apologized profusely, trying to placate the officers. He shut down the party immediately, and the crowd dispersed.

Oliver told Geoff he would deal with the problem when he returned to school the next day. Two hours later, another brother called him. The police were back at the house, demanding to speak with the chapter president. "Go to Geoff's room and see if he's there," Oliver told the brother.

Geoff wasn't there; he was at one of the satellite houses. "Okay, while you go find someone they can talk to, I'll talk to them," Oliver said. "Tell them I'm happy to cooperate any way I can, and I can talk to them on the phone right now."

He could hear the brother repeat Oliver's offer. But the cops grew only more frustrated. "We need to talk to someone here *now*," Oliver heard one of them say.

"Go find Reed," Oliver told the brother. As chapter secretary, Reed was currently the highest-ranking officer physically in the house.

A few minutes later, Oliver heard Reed say courteously to the officers, "What's going on here? How can I help?"

"Are you the VP?" an officer asked.

"No, I'm the secretary."

"No," the officer said, gruff. "We're only going to talk to the president or vice president. Your lack of cooperation will be reflected in our report." The officers left.

Oliver hung up the phone and furiously flipped over a small backyard table. This was a big deal that could have serious repercussions, even though the party itself had been safe and secure. "This was a major party," he told me. "A lot of things could have gone wrong with risk management, but we went so far out of our way to make sure that didn't happen. Despite all our efforts, someone still did something they know they're not supposed to do. It's such a dumb thing. There's literally rooms in houses for you to take a piss in. Why would you do it on a police officer?"

When Oliver returned to the house the next day, Peter, an older Alumni Board member, angrily pulled him aside. He showed Oliver the police report. The officers' write-up made it appear that PhiEp had perpetrated a purposeful act against the police force, first urinating on them and then refusing to allow them to speak with the chapter president or vice president on the premises.

By then, Oliver had done enough detective work to piece together what had happened. Upon arrival, police officers were supposed to check in with the exec manning the entrance and walk through the party with that chapter officer. These officers had come through a dark, rarely used back alley next to the PhiEp house. Keegan, a sophomore who was drunk at the time, didn't see the people below the deck when he peed off it. The police shone a flashlight on his face but said nothing. Assuming friends were messing with him, Keegan flipped them off.

"The police didn't follow proper protocol," Oliver explained.

"That's not entirely your fault," Peter agreed. "That's not you guys being jerks. It's just a series of really unfortunate events."

Nevertheless, the seriousness of the police report meant that PhiEp now had to manage a hearing with the IFC. Hearings were waived for most Greek violations. But for a case like this, Oliver would have to represent his chapter in formal proceedings. He had to prepare arguments, collect evidence, and defend his chapter in front of the IFC Judicial Board. PhiEp had not had a hearing in years.

Oliver called the alum who had been chapter president the last time PhiEp had been called to a hearing. The alum explained how the trial worked. "But your situation is way different and more challenging than mine," he told Oliver. "Mine was black and white: Either we did it or we didn't. Yours is in the gray area. A cop almost got peed on, but that happened because the cops were in a place where they shouldn't be. What Keegan did was disgusting, but it wasn't illegal. But it still happened. You're stuck in a shitty position."

Oliver could either plead that his chapter was responsible for actions that were being characterized as anti-police, or he could plead that the chapter was not responsible and then fight the charges. The potential consequences were enormous. At a hearing, the IFC could put a chapter on social probation (no social events). It could force the house to go dry. Or—and this was what scared Oliver the most—they could shut the chapter down.

"The Fraternity Saved My Life": What Does Brotherhood Mean?

When Travis, a recent Virginia grad, was in college, he was initially hesitant to tell people he fell into the "queer" category of LGBTQ. It wasn't easy to explain his asexuality; with no interest in sex, he viewed relationships only as emotional connections. As a fraternity member, he said, "It was kind of weird not dating, especially at mixers, where people are forcing you to interact with girls. I didn't feel uncomfortable, but when you mix with sororities, the girls are sometimes the ones who want to hook up. Or after, you play awkward drinking games like 'Never have I ever,' or people ask, 'What was your most embarrassing hookup?' and I stayed in the background not saying anything."

After a year of brothers asking whether he was interested in someone, Travis came out. He felt comfortable enough with the membership, which was 12 percent gay, to assume they wouldn't judge him. He expected them to have respectful questions, and they did. He didn't expect them to praise him. "Wow, that's actually really cool," one brother said. "That's, like, pure," said another. "I know so many people who objectify people. They just want sex. And here you just want someone to connect to. That's emotional and not superficial." Their reactions marked the first time Travis "felt a little relief," he told me, "because it was the first time I told anyone at all. I could just keep being me."

In direct contrast to the images portrayed in the media, for many college guys, fraternities are the safe spaces on campus. In his chapter, "no one will judge you for having a 'nerdy' hobby or being part of a niche community," said Travis, whose pastimes include gaming and anime. "Many of these things I wouldn't mention to some of my high school friends, because they would think they're dumb. But in my chapter, people don't shun me for my hobbies. They ask me questions about why I'm so interested in them. For instance, I got a few of the brothers to start watching some anime. Many other people have similar experiences with their own interests, and we all feel at home."

Because his brothers so readily accepted him, Travis was able to accept himself, a sentiment that many fraternity members conveyed to me. "I've learned a lot about myself and the people I consider to be true friends," Travis said. "My fraternity has made me comfortable with all my random quirks and has allowed me to fully embrace my personality. I no longer feel the need to act differently around certain people or try to hide facets of my personality, because my fraternity has been so accepting."

For Travis and other brothers who joined fraternities for the people rather than the parties, what does fraternity brotherhood mean? How does it distinguish fraternities from other campus groups? And does it elevate relationships beyond typical friendships? Members told me that brotherhood involves constant communication and expectations that members will share their confidences, listen to others', and be supportive. An unusual aspect distinguishing brotherhood from other college friendships is that these conversations are often conducted collectively, with dozens of guys sitting in a circle or ongoing mass group texts among pledge classes. Also, fraternities often try to teach guys how to be better communicators, by public speaking and/or emotional sharing. Just as they are inspired to share their triumphs so that brothers may celebrate with them, they are also encouraged to admit their failings, doubts, and sorrows so that brothers may console and reassure them.

A recent Pennsylvania grad described "brotherhoods," Friday night events during which actives participated in sober team-building activities for a few hours. Afterward, the group sat in a circle in the chapter room, where they had the chance to say anything, whether to provoke deep thoughts or announce a graduate school acceptance. "One time, a brother came out as gay to all of us. He said he hadn't told his parents or siblings yet. He felt most comfortable with and trusted all of us," the grad said. "And I'll never forget: The biggest, toughest guy in our chapter stood up, walked over to him, and gave him the biggest hug. We all clapped and cheered. All of us were overwhelmed with emotion that night."

When a Georgia freshman from out of state confided in an older brother about his social awkwardness and communication difficulties, to his surprise, the brother encouraged him to become a campus tour guide, which successfully helped him work through these concerns. Since then, he said his brothers have offered him "constant support" through tough exam weeks, girl issues, and "the highs and lows of college life." They lend him their cars to get to job interviews, give him academic advice, help him formulate workout and diet plans, and "listen to my problems. It's comforting to know I have a network of brothers who support me and truly care about my well-being," he said. "What makes fraternities so unique in comparison to other organizations on campus is that we eat our meals together, live together, study together, and spend the majority of our free time hanging out with one another. Because of this near-constant contact, we develop intimate relationships that make us feel like we belong to a second family."

Now a junior, he said his memberships in all his non-Greek extracurriculars are directly attributable to brothers "encouraging me to branch out and explore different types of campus organizations. My brothers have pushed me out of my comfort zone and made me a more well-rounded man."

An Oregon chapter treasurer compared fraternity membership to "being in a boardroom meeting. Not everybody agrees with each other, and people have to learn to work with people they don't like, to get the job done. The fraternity system isn't just a place to drink beer and do stupid stuff with your brothers. It's a place to shape yourself to be a better man." He said that because his parents divorced when he was young, he was a shy child who kept to himself. "I wouldn't say much. I was too afraid to ask questions in class. I was deathly afraid to talk to a girl. The fraternity helped me come out of my comfort zone. It helped me grow as a person. Before, I had a hard time asking things, or talking to my parents. Now I don't have that problem. I sometimes talk too much. That pretty girl across the room? I have no hesitations about whether I'm confident enough to go talk to her. The answer is always 'no' unless you go talk to her."

The relationships in fraternity brotherhoods typically aren't fickle. They aren't allowed to be. The bonds are ritualized. Loyalty is sworn. Many of the rituals and traditions also create opportunities for brothers to ask for or provide support. Multiple fraternities regularly hold a ritual during which each member has the opportunity to speak his mind "for the good of the fraternity." In Teddy's Oregon chapter, this occurs at the end of every chapter meeting, when each brother passes around a gavel and shares something personal, asks for help, recognizes a brother who has aided them, or suggests a call to action. "If someone helped me study for a test, I can stand up and recognize him. Or I can say, 'For the good of the fraternity, I'm really struggling with this and that, if somebody could help me out,'" Teddy said. Recently, a brother used his turn with the gavel to tell the chapter that his father had just died. "He was choking up, and you could tell he was struggling. We all had a moment of silence and then gave him a hug."

An upstate New York chapter holds similar "gavel sessions" for pledges and their Bigs. "For a bunch of 19- to 20-year-olds, things got very deep. My father had entered the ICU after a heart attack, and things weren't looking good. As someone who didn't share my feelings often, especially at 19 and especially around a group of guys, I was very hesitant to share what was going on. But eventually, I broke down in tears. In one of the biggest surprises of my life, everyone, I mean *everyone*, was incredibly supportive. One brother came to me and shared his own experience with his father dying. I was even contacted by local alumni who took me to dinner, seemed honestly interested in how I was feeling, and shared their own experiences and advice," said a recent graduate of this chapter. "Because I went to college 3,000 miles away from my family, these brothers became my support. In three to four years, it's almost guaranteed someone is going to have a tough time in their life. For family issues, deaths, financial crises, and mental health issues, brothers have always flocked to help. This goes above and beyond what you expect from ordinary friends."

During brotherhood-only events at least once a month, such as a movie or an outdoor activity, this chapter created extra opportunities for members to get to know one another. "This made us hang out with each other in an environment without women, often without booze, and without other distractions. As much fun as parties could be, these members-only events are the ones I look back on most fondly." Brothers of other fraternities described similar guys-only activities: wings and water pong tournaments (which substitute water for beer), paintball, trampoline parks, casinos, sports at an ice rink.

Teddy's chapter, which is responsible for cleaning the house, rotates every resident through mandatory daily chores. On Sunday mornings, the entire chapter, including live-outs, works together to clean or fix an area of the house. When Teddy is doing his cleaning duties, various brothers (who have their own cleaning assignments) often offer to assist him, even if only to help carry toilet paper rolls for restocking. "The greatest acts of brotherhood are the small things we do for each other each day," he said. "I might be scrubbing the bathroom floor, and a brother walking in will stop and help me, or I might be struggling in a class where my brothers can help me understand the difficult concepts. Just waking up each day to the men I live with smiling and greeting me with "Sup, man' or 'Kill that midterm today, bro' can make my day. These men are my friends, and they have proven time and again to be there for me when I need them the most."

Brothers also commonly bond through philanthropy and, in some chapters, community service. While at certain houses, brothers suspect that their chapter's lip service to a required philanthropy event exists primarily to offset their less noble endeavors, other chapters genuinely believe that performing community service together can strengthen their ties and enhance their character. At Seton Hall University, the Alpha Sigma Phis rake leaves and shovel snow for any local residents who need help. Several brothers volunteer with the local emergency rescue squad, and half the chapter helps freshmen unload their cars and move into their dorm rooms at the beginning of the school year. On weekends, they volunteer at parks, food banks, churches, and other locations. "Our words are 'To Better the Man' and our brotherhood attempts to embody this through having each other's backs no matter what. But few people realize we're also the 'keepers' of the community around us, which is represented through our second value of charity," a chapter officer said. "As positive members of society, leaders, and gentlemen, we believe in setting the tone for people in the community around us. Yes, we track each individual's time spent volunteering, and we recognize these brothers through a point system that tracks these hours. But we strive not to perform charitable acts and community service because we have to but, rather, because it's the right thing to do."

At Georgia Southern University, the Omega Psi Phis, a BGLO, participate in weekly Service Saturdays, during which they volunteer for various organizations. In addition, they have raised money to pay for underprivileged children's optometrist appointments and glasses, prepared meals at a food bank and served them to impoverished residents of a local apartment complex, run back-to-school supply drives to fill backpacks that they distributed to local elementary schools, and hosted a free cookout in a poverty-stricken neighborhood, complete with games for children and a face-painting booth staffed by the brothers.

"Service bonds fraternity brothers because it brings a good feeling you just can't resist, putting yourself aside and thinking about others. It makes us a whole lot closer," said a member of that chapter. The brother, who also was close with his college football teammates, said his fraternity bonds are stronger. "Football was just an on-the-field thing. We hung tight, but my fraternity always keeps contact with each other. It's a never-ending relationship. It's an actual brotherhood. It goes beyond ourselves. We reach out to each other's families to see how they're doing. We didn't do that in football."

While some fraternity traditions should have faded with the times, one of the best carryovers from these group's historical origins is the idea that the brotherhood is an on-campus family. A difference between friends and family is that family bonds are presumed to be lifelong, which is how fraternities frame their relationships. The lingering terminology reassuringly bolsters this idea: *Big Brother, Grand-Big, founding fathers, house moms.* The ninth value listed in one fraternity's code of conduct is "I am my brother's keeper." Some chapters call back to that mission statement in their daily lives. "When someone helps a brother out, we say, 'That was a really number-nine move.' Or when we need help, we say, 'I need a number-nine favor,'" a Delaware brother said. "That's a sacred thing to us, so people take it seriously when you say something like that. The sense of brotherhood goes past petty differences. There's no way you can be best friends with all 50 guys, but I'd do as much as I can for any one of them."

The brotherhood can be an important source of solidarity, information, and guidance for culturally based chapters. Many members of LGLOs, for example, are first-generation college students, for whom peer support is crucial. On an Idaho campus that is 95 percent white, all but one brother of a Latino chapter are first-generation students, and many members are first-generation US citizens whose families work in the fields. "No one in my family ever went to college. I didn't know what the first step was or what to do. I was thrown out there, and it was like, 'Good luck!'" the chapter president told me. "It feels weird when you're the only nonwhite person in the classroom. You feel like you don't belong here, like you were not meant to be in that classroom studying that subject. It helped just knowing people who went through the same experiences I did. We go through these struggles together, and we can conquer them together."

The chapter helped a student who is part of the DACA program (Deferred Action for Childhood Arrivals) figure out how to pay in-state tuition, saving him about fifteen thousand dollars a year. When members can't afford textbooks, the chapter provides them. And the brothers welcomed a prospective member with poor grades who wanted to drop out of college by bringing him to "study table" with them and giving him resources. "He did a one-eighty and now excels as a leader on campus, which he says is because we held him to a higher standard," the president said. "We're always going to find ways to help out a brother or someone who's interested in us. And we all want to give back to our own community." The brothers also often visit their high schools to inspire other Latino students.

Many BGLOs and LGLOs also participate in "strolling," or "stepping," in which they display their fraternity's trade steps, calls, and hand signals as a show of group identity. Stepping, a combination of dance, sport, stomp, and verbal play, originated in the mid-1900s among black fraternities and sororities to express Greek loyalty. It is a phenomenal display of synchronicity and coordination based on stylistic elements derived primarily from African-based performance tradition.

Studies show that LGLO membership helps students adjust to college, stay in school, develop leadership skills, and "provide a sense of belonging on campus." In one study, LGLO members said that *el hermandad* (the brotherhood) provided their strongest support in college. Fraternity membership introduced them to fellow Latinos, connected them to internships and other opportunities, and provided friends who motivated them academically, held them accountable, and with whom they had meaningful discussions.

Likewise, gay/bi/trans/progressive fraternities improve bonds among brothers with education, resources, and guidance about their sexual identity. "It gives me a space to be myself in the context of more than just myself. I can identify and present how I want, and my brothers will still be there to stand up for me no matter what," a sophomore told me. "It can be really hard, especially here in the South, to find people who understand the experiences you've had. Delta Lambda Phi is a really good space to talk to anyone about anything. We're always going to be there to pick each other up when we fall down and build each other up even if we're at the top. And our current trustee said he wants to be the last white cis male trustee of Delta Lambda Phi. It meant the world to me as a Hispanic trans man that he's willing to give minorities a space to speak."

Regardless of the composition of the group, fraternity brotherhood is intended to encompass "love and respect, reliance and dependability, trust and growth. It provides a conceptual foundation for the relationships that are developed within the fraternity. A stranger is *expected* to become your best friend," said an Indiana student. "There's a sense of intimacy attached to brotherhood. Friendship in the digital age is much different than brotherhood. Friendships can become nothing. A lot of friendships are selfish:

'What are you giving me?' In the brotherhood, it's 'What can we give each other?'"

After a rocky freshman year during which he tried to commit suicide, a Michigan student joined an NIC fraternity as a sophomore. "I remember praying constantly for anything to get me out of the hole I was in. I rushed because I thought maybe surrounding myself in a more positive community would be better than the potheads and the druggies I hung out with because I thought I had no one else." Chapter officers of the fraternity he approached told him they would give him a chance, "but if you make us look bad, we're going to kick you out."

The process of learning the chapter's values and bonding with guys through mandatory study hours, community service, and rituals gave him a "sense of stability in a time in my life when I needed it most. After my flop of a freshman year, having a group of men who accepted me with my faults was the show of brotherhood and companionship that I so desperately needed. Brotherhood was vital to my rehabilitation process," he said. "They could see me trying to reconcile with myself. I started feeling more comfortable with myself, feeling at home knowing I had somewhere to go, not sitting alone in my room in this pit of focused dread and anxiety. It was as little as just having someone to sit with, which I didn't have freshman year."

He cherished rituals such as "Views," a more intimate form of interviews in which one or two pledge brothers were locked in a room with a brother to ask him questions about himself. The brother was not allowed to open the door until he felt the pledges had thoroughly gotten to know him, and vice versa, at which point the guys hugged. Views could last one to six hours. "Our chapter took Views very seriously. If you have time to go to a bar for four hours but not for an hour to talk with a brother, the group doesn't want you. This developed in my mind over time a sense of my commitment to the group, teaching me to choose what's worthwhile. What's real gratification, sticking my dick in someone, rolling a molly, or developing an emotional bond? I was developing an emotional bond with myself through talking to these guys."

Now in an honors undergrad program, an achievement he attributes to his fraternity experience, he said, "I learned the process of establishing a greater sense of self, a sense of character, an understanding of the weight of my words, the gravity of my actions, the expectations that coincide with 'contribution,' and how to accept my shortcomings. The fraternity gave me a space to learn about myself after a tumultuous time where I was so unhappy with the person in the mirror that I would rather [have] kill[ed] myself than be that person. I'm forever in debt and grateful to those people. The fraternity saved my life."

Ω Ω Ω

Jake desperately tried to stop crying and to compose himself. He so badly wanted to be a part of this brotherhood. Chase came into the bathroom, blindfolded him, and returned him upstairs to his chair. The horrendous music flipped on again.

This time, though, after only a few minutes, somebody lifted Jake from the chair and guided him out of the room. When his blindfold was removed, he was back at the altar in the darkened chapter room.

Z spoke quietly. "If you truly believe you wish to learn more, repeat this oath after me," he said. "I have erred, but I seek absolution."

Shaking, Jake began to repeat the words—and then heard a chorus of voices behind him say the same. He glanced over his shoulder to see all his pledge brothers standing in solidarity.

"First Rite is about mercy," Z said. "It is about how to let go of your past and continue on with your life despite the mistakes you've made."

Z gestured for Jake to join the other pledges. The lights went on. "If you believe you made a mistake during First Rite, please step forward," Z said. Jake stepped forward. The other pledges stepped forward, too. Z stared at the group for a few seconds, then stepped forward as well. The brothers lined up along the walls also took a step forward. The freshmen looked at one another, processing what this meant: It was part of the ritual to make a mistake so that every member learned he could ask his brothers for mercy. Every guy in the room had failed First Rite—this must have been the failure that Victor had cryptically warned Jake about. Jake was moved to his core.

The pledges were led out of the room, blindfolded again, and lined up in the hallway outside the basement. One by one, pledges entered the room and did not come out. As he waited his turn, Jake leaned on the wall, half-asleep. Finally, his blindfold was removed and he was in front of the door. Greg, robed, gestured to Jake, who did the secret knock. "Who waits at the door of this lodge?" asked a brother from within the room.

"A candidate for initiation into the Holy Order of Zeta Kappa," Greg said. After an additional exchange in English and Greek, the door opened. There stood Preston, also robed. "The gates of secrecy and honor have been opened to you. Through this door you must pass alone," Preston said. He gave Jake a candle. The room was draped in black. Robed brothers holding candles formed two lines from the doorway to a closed coffin, on top of which rested what looked like a human skull. Preston nudged Jake forward. He walked slowly between the lines toward the coffin.

"All that is born must die; such is the law," said Z, who stood next to the coffin. Two by two, the brothers extinguished their candles as Jake passed them. "The flickering taper, failing in the dark"—

Z reached over and snuffed out Jake's candle—"is emblematic of the life of him who shuns the kindly light of friendship's torch and treads in gloom his solitary way. But he who, choosing wisely, enters here shall pass with fleet step through the shadowy vale to find beyond the figured gates of death the light he seeks within our brotherhood."

Two brothers came up behind Jake, startling him, and tied his wrists together with twine. Z removed the skull from the coffin and, with the help of another brother, opened the lid. Jake was pulled backward into the arms of multiple brothers, who picked him up and placed him into the coffin. The lid closed on top of him. Jake tried not to hyperventilate.

Brothers picked up the coffin and carried it around the room. Jake could faintly hear them chanting something about "the resurrection of the dead." The coffin was lowered to the floor. Jake began to sweat. He heard the brothers singing but could barely make out the words beyond "brother, among brothers rise." The coffin was hoisted once more. Finally, the lid was raised and two brothers lifted Jake out, draped a white robe over him, and led him to the altar in the corner of the room. They told him to kneel on one knee and place his bound hands on the altar.

The brothers encircled him and Andy. Andy told Jake to repeat after him an oath in Greek and English. When Jake's hands were unbound, Andy pinned a Zeta Kappa pin on Jake's robe and showed him the fraternity's secret handshake.

Six brothers came forward, each of whom gave Jake the secret grip. The last brother, Victor, led him to the hallway, where he saw most of the pledges sitting silently. "Congratulations," Victor whispered.

After the rest of the pledges went through the ritual, the freshmen were led back into the basement room. The lights of the room blinked on, and the brothers removed their hoods. They said in unison to the pledges, "Hail, brothers! Hail, our Zeta Kappa brothers!"

Then, cheering, they whipped out their penises and helicopter-dicked for several seconds. The pledges cheered, too. The penises were resheathed, and the entire group gathered in a circle, cheering and shouting. *We made it!* Jake thought. It felt like "an enormous load had been lifted from our shoulders," he told me later. "It was such a great feeling." He had finally become a brother.

The brothers hugged the freshmen, made sure they were okay, and laughed off the events of the night. Jake learned that in First Rite, every pledge was set up to fail. The significant difference was the order in which the pledges experienced the ritual. As punishment for breaking Hell Week rules, Wes had gone first, and had to spend the next seven hours in his chair listening to horror music and believing he had made another irreparable mistake. (While he sat in the chair, brothers also repeatedly slapped him.) After Jake's Personal Reflection confession that uncertainty made him uneasy, the brothers had decided he would be the last pledge to undergo First Rite. Otherwise, they thought he would be too hard on himself when he returned to the chair. "We all knew how valuable the ritual would be to you, and that you'd be devastated if you thought you messed it up," Kevin, the academics chair, said. "But, man, we got you good! You were shaking and everything!"

Jake also learned that the loud music was intended to drown out the sounds of the brothers screaming at the pledges, and that until recently, the pledges were nude for the ritual. The chapter had modified the tradition to tighty whiteys because, they reasoned, "Who really needs to see that much dick?"

The brothers produced a bong and the bottles of alcohol the pledges had been instructed to bring; families met to carry out their own traditions. Jake's family downed countless shots of Southern Comfort. "You'd better fucking do it right this time," Ty's Big warned. Jake did, filling the shot glass to the rim, then tossing the drink down his throat.

The brothers told the initiates to put on their polos and khakis for a group photo outside. The new class of brothers proudly gathered on the lawn, grinning from ear to ear, equals at last. And then the brothers doused them in warm beer, sprayed them with cold water, and dumped bags of sugar on them. The message, to Jake, was "We may be brothers now, but we're still too far down the totem pole to get the same respect as the older guys." He didn't mind, though. He was surrounded by best friends like Ty, Sebastian, and Logan. Also, he was too drunk to care.

The following week, Jake received his exam grades. On his physics test, he got the worst grade he'd ever earned in his life. He got an F.

CHAPTER 8

What Makes a (College) Man: How Students View Masculinity

THE NIGHT AFTER INITIATION, Beth asked Jake to help her practice lines for her drama class. She led him to "a secret place" she had found in a nearby classroom building. Jake followed her up a spiral staircase and through an unlocked door that led to a flat roof. Beth sat down and patted the space next to her. "This is my place of meditation. I love to just sit up here and read or look at the view," she said. She pointed at the sky. "See? The stars look really nice tonight."

Jake (in his words) nerded out. "Oh, yeah! That one's Orion; you can see his belt. And I'm not a hundred percent sure, but I think that one's Betelgeuse," he said.

"It's amazing to think that none of what we do even matters in the long run of the universe," Beth said.

"Yeah, all these feelings we have toward each other right now will probably have no effect whatsoever on how the course of time plays out," Jake said, then kicked himself for being depressing. "But, you know, once we decompose, our energy is brought back to the universe in lower life-forms. The circle of life and all that."

"Aw yeah, talk about circles; they turn me on," she said.

"Please, you think that's sexy? I'm a personal fan of dodecahedrons myself," Jake flirted. He cringed when he said it, but somehow it did the trick. Beth leaned in, and they kissed, slowly, gently, their lips barely touching. She wrapped her arms around Jake's neck and passionately pulled him closer. He felt transported.

When they broke apart, Beth looked into his eyes. "Jake, I have really strong feelings for you," she said.

Jake couldn't believe it. No other girl had ever outright told him that she liked him. "I have really strong feelings for you, too," he said. They never did get to practicing Beth's lines.

By semester's end, Jake and Beth had gone out several times. Other than Ty, Jake didn't tell his brothers about her. He thought they would bug him about how he'd lose valuable opportunities for sorority hookups at parties if he was committed to a girlfriend. He didn't think that, as a GDI, Beth would be comfortable if he brought her to the house. And their relationship felt like an escape from the responsibilities of life in a fraternity house.

As the class with the least seniority, the Fall 2017 Class was now known as jibs, for "junior initiated brothers." They still were occasionally hazed, usually by guys like Tanner, who ordered them to take long pulls of liquor at various fraternity functions. But as brothers, they finally could attend chapter meetings, where they observed the politicking to try to secure sorority matches. The officers stressed that moving up the middle tier was the chapter's "most important mission."

For Greek Week in the spring, the Zeta Kappas were pleased they'd be matched with a sorority at the top of the bottom tier. They were angling for a solid middle-tier sorority match for Homecoming next fall. The officers believed their plan was realistic because of what they called their chapter's "momentum." Whereas in the fall they had been able to score mixers only with Beta Sig, Alpha Rho, and one other sorority, their reputation had slowly improved as brothers and pledges began dating or hooking up with girls in other chapters. "We've propelled up the rankings," Jake explained to me, "and we need to continue to make good use of that through our philanthropy, our mixers, and as a brotherhood. I definitely believe the officers when they say we're on the rise, especially now that we've almost secured Theta Ep for Homecoming."

The jibs learned the meanings behind the rituals, traditions, and some of the hazing activities. "It's a bullshit response that 'there's a reason behind everything.' But now that I'm done with it, I can see it isn't *all* bullshit. There were reasons behind things, especially the rituals," Jake said. "So I've definitely been enlightened. But I haven't learned some sort of super secret that could change my life."

Jake was most interested in hearing about Z. The brothers told the jibs that their Z had been one of the tamer Zs in recent memory. Previous Zs, they said, had hazed the pledges more harshly, embarrassed them in front of sorority sisters at mixers, screamed at them often, and even regulated their time in the bathroom. Z, the brothers said, represented the value of joining the fraternity. "He's the one man in charge of deciding whether you're in as a brother," a Z-Kap said. "There would be no value in becoming a brother, no purpose, no reason people would be so desperately seeking to stay if there weren't a Z to make it such an exclusive and difficult thing to get into."

Hunter told the jibs, "As Z, I make sure the opportunity to join the brotherhood is placed at the highest possible value. I set up a remarkable challenge for the pledges to undergo throughout the semester. I want them to feel the excitement, the rush of continuously being unworthy and working up to that point of being initiated. And if the pledges mess up, it's my job to set up an experience that would make the class seem unworthy to join and also remorseful for their actions."

Jake bought into it. "That explains why he's there and why we can't look at him," Jake told me. "If he wasn't there and there was no challenge to become initiated, the importance of being a brother wouldn't be set into your mind beforehand. You wouldn't have a sense of responsibility and duty once you were a brother if you didn't feel like you had to earn it."

"Do you value your brotherhood because you had to work for it?" I asked him.

"Because we had someone constantly telling us we're unworthy and forcing us to do stuff, it's made being initiated so much more rewarding in the end. It did add value to becoming a brother. It wasn't just some other club; it was an experience in itself to get to this point," Jake answered. "Which is symbolic for why you can't look at Z. He's the manifestation of the brotherhood you aren't worthy enough to be a part of yet. If the pledge master's goal is to make sure the pledges are close, then Z is the carrot on a stick. He's the person who makes us want to become a brother, makes us see the importance of it through the hazing. And the purpose of the hazing is to make sure not only that we bond, but also that we feel joining and becoming a brother is an honor."

"And do you believe that?" I asked.

Jake paused to consider the question. "Several weeks ago—even two weeks ago—I'd be like, 'That's a load of bullshit.' But now, when I'm on the opposite side, I kind of do believe there really is a good purpose behind Z. We weren't worthy yet for the fraternity," he repeated.

"How do you feel about the hazing now?"

"There needs to be a big disclaimer about the hazing we experienced. There's a purpose behind each hazing. There's no beating or something that could really injure us. My pledging process seems relatively tame compared to what more intense, higher-tiered fraternities do, which involves physical shit," he said. "I'm going to do as little as I can as an older brother to haze the new class. That's just not me. I'm still against it. I still believe we can progress and make the experience valuable with less hazing. But I will say that, yes, it was effective at making joining a much more valuable experience, and it made me so much closer—inseparable—with my pledge class.

It introduced me to the traditions of the brotherhood, and at some points it was fun. But I could see how it could be morally or ethically wrong."

"What about the forced drinking? Over the summer, you were terrified of that," I pointed out.

"I can't believe my biggest concern was that I'd be forced to drink," Jake said. "I wish I could talk to Summer Me and say you're going to go through worse stuff than drinking. Drinking now is a lot easier. I've built up a lot more tolerance. I'm definitely not as lightweight as I was the night I accepted the bid. Back then, I was still uncomfortable with drinking. I've definitely changed in that respect."

"Have you changed in any other respects?" I asked, then went for the deep dive. "Fraternities say they help boys become men. Has that journey begun for you?"

"That's a bullshit thing to go for, for manhood. Ooh, I'm so masculine!" he joked. "I think college would have done that to me anyway. It's not about becoming a man. My balls didn't dramatically grow in size this semester. It's about brotherhood. I never had a brother. I never had a connection with a group of guys before, a solid connection with a group of people I could trust. Now I've found that. I'm more well connected and I have people to depend on. It's not who you are but who you know."

Ω Ω Ω

Oliver was working on his IFC trial strategy when Wyatt, a freshman, texted him to ask if he had a few minutes to chat. Yeah, come to my room and we can talk about whatever's on your mind, Oliver replied. Although he was stressed about the upcoming trial, he would always make time for a brother. Meanwhile, he had put his chapter on temporary social probation, backing out of every scheduled party.

When Wyatt came in, smiling bravely as if he was trying to mask his nerves, Oliver gestured for him to sit on the couch. After some casual small talk, Oliver asked, "So, man, what's going on? What did you want to talk about?"

Wyatt paused. "So, um, I just wanted to kind of talk to you about how I've been feeling lately. I've previously had some issues with depression and anxiety, and, um, they're coming back and causing some issues for me."

"Are you seeing someone for it?"

"Yeah," Wyatt said, slouching.

Oliver nodded. Peers had come to him for help before. In high school he had talked a classmate down from suicidal thoughts. In his experience, guys in these situations needed someone to talk to so they wouldn't bottle up their feelings. "First of all, I appreciate you telling me. It takes a lot of courage to talk about things like this. What do you think is causing these issues to resurface?"

Wyatt considered the question. "Um, I think it has a lot to do with all this dramatic change and new environment. I've never lived on my own and this whole experience just kind of feels like, um, being thrown in the deep end. I just don't know if going Greek was the right fit for me. I don't know if I'm the right person to do this."

"Obviously, it's your choice if you want to stay or go," Oliver said. "But stick around a little bit and get out of your comfort zone. I never thought I'd go Greek. And now here I am with this opportunity to talk to you about this stuff. I've found that if you get out of your comfort zone, it can take you in a really cool direction if you allow it to."

"Yeah, but, um, on top of that, everyone around me seems like they're just ahead of me and doing so much more. I feel like they have their life and school planned out already and I'm just sitting here far behind them."

"Well, man, I totally get why you're feeling that way. The thing is, everyone does. But every time we come across a change like this, it's important to remember a few things. The first is, things are different, but that doesn't mean you made the wrong decision to be here. Remember what brought you here and remember what your goals are. You don't have to have everything figured out right now. I certainly don't. You're surrounded by amazing people, but you're one of those amazing people yourself. Don't lose sight of that. Everyone brings something unique and special to the table."

"Thanks, man. I really do appreciate that. I'm not sure. It still makes me nervous."

"Of course. A piece of advice I got a while back, and it's one of my favorite things anyone has ever told me, is 'If it is to be, it is up to me.' You can make your own fate. I've been where you are, and I know it's scary, but I also know you can get through it. Like really any challenge that comes up in your life, you just have to calmly look that beast in the eyes and say, 'Sorry, not today. Today is my day,' and then go prove it. I challenge you to see if you can beat those inner demons. I know you can."

Wyatt sat straighter for the rest of the 20-minute conversation. As they wrapped up, he said, "Thanks a lot, man. I guess it's just nice to really feel some one-on-one guidance."

"I've got your back and will be here to support you every step of the way, along with all the other guys. That's what family does: We have each other's backs. If you're ever feeling stressed or uncomfortable, you should come let me know, and we'll work through it together."

"Thanks so much. This whole thing has made me feel a lot better. I guess it just helps to talk things out sometimes."

Oliver believed what he told the pledge. On several occasions, whether to Oliver alone or to a larger bunch of brothers, in person or over group text, other PhiEps had expressed appreciation for the chapter's support. A few had sought the brotherhood's help with handling their parents' separations. One of Oliver's friends, suffering through a breakup with a long-term girlfriend, texted the chapter his gratitude that he had "a family here" to support him. And talking to Wyatt made Oliver remember how, when he was stuck or stressed, he had almost always felt better after seeking Diego's advice. Now that Oliver was in an older brother role, he was delighted to be able to pay it forward.

In the midst of preparing for the trial, Oliver finally permitted himself to unload his own feelings. During a "Fourth Quarter," the after-after-party tradition during which the few brothers still awake shared their thoughts and feelings, a brother turned to Oliver and said, "Your turn."

Oliver tried to dodge him. "Oh, hey, I'm good. Let's talk about you guys."

"No, dude," another brother said. Oliver had always been there for the brothers. Now they wanted to be there for him. "It's time to talk."

So Oliver did. He talked about girl stuff and future goals. Mostly, he told them why he wasn't "big on the whole sharing my emotions thing." Ever since his young family friend had been beaten by his father, Oliver had wanted to be stoic. If he was a rock, he'd be tough enough to handle everyone else's pain. "I've always wanted to see how much weight can I carry on my shoulders, how much I can actually take," he said.

"You don't have to do that, man. No one can do everything alone," a brother said.

"Family's got family's back, no matter what," said another.

"Yeah, I can be stubborn about it," Oliver agreed. "Maybe if I'm clearly not opening up about something, definitely ask me."

Oliver was surprised by the relief, gratitude, and warmth he felt in confiding in this motley group of guys. He finally realized that allowing himself to lean on people—as when Patrick helped him grieve Christopher's death and when the brothers made his life easier after his injury—was not a weakness.

"It feels like lifting a fricking load off my chest," Oliver told me later. "I guess when you get so fixated on going it alone, you forget you have people who want to be there for you."

"It's Okay to Cry": The Pressures of Masculinity and How Fraternities Can Ease Them

Too often, when the public hears about boys in college, the context is negative and woman-focused: sexual assault cases, for example, or boys' dreary academic performance compared to girls'. Media coverage about college guys usually laments the problems they cause rather than exploring the challenges they face. Discussions of "toxic masculinity" can leave boys feeling even more misunderstood, because they so often leave out a key point: Those forces certainly hurt girls on campus, but they can suffocate the boys, too.

College usually marks the first time boys begin to determine their identity away from family, home, and the anchors they have known since childhood. It's a moment when they look to their peers to confirm or question preconceived notions of masculinity, to help them figure out what it means to be a man. And experts say that the college years, when these students are somehow expected to independently transition from boyhood to manhood, are also the stage at which they feel the most vulnerable. Researchers have described boys' freshman year as characterized by separation anxiety, loss, and grief. At the same time, these teens frequently feel they can't express those feelings because, as a growing body of evidence suggests, college boys are strongly pressured to be "masculine."

What does it mean to be masculine in twenty-first-century America? Masculinity is a performance, a collection of behaviors and attitudes, a balancing act between a man's values and his reaction to his interpretation of society's expectations. There can be multiple forms of masculinity, depending on a subculture's standards and a man's self-esteem. But in the United States, researchers have characterized the 11 prevailing expectations of masculinity as: having the drive to win at all costs, desiring multiple sexual partners and casual relationships, suppressing and controlling one's emotions, engaging in risky behaviors, having a tendency to engage in physical aggression, wanting to dominate situations, asserting independence, viewing work as a major life priority, having power or control over women, appearing heterosexual, and desiring status in society. "There are lots of ways of being masculine, and lots of masculinities, but I'd say the 11 in our scale reflect some parts of the dominant culture's normative ways of being masculine," said Boston College education professor Jim Mahalik. Clinicians and academics now commonly use this scale in their work with and studies about men.

But just because these are prevailing cultural norms doesn't mean all men want to act this way. They follow these expectations, and tolerate these behaviors among peers, because they want to be accepted by other men. "Most men don't want to be the kind of men they have been taught to be, but do not always know that other men share this discomfort," scholar Alan D. Berkowitz wrote in *Masculinities in Higher Education*. "For a norm to be perpetuated it is not necessary for the majority to believe it, but only for the majority to believe that the majority believes it."

The result is a cycle in which many people who think these characteristics define "real men" then adopt them to establish their own masculinity. Other men observe their behavior, assume it represents the masculine norm, and follow suit. Subcultures form in which men who align with these expectations are rewarded while those who do not—whether they express their emotions, have other priorities, or aren't heterosexual—might be alienated or ridiculed.

Most men want to "do the right thing," but they feel compelled to "fit in with what they think is true for other men," Berkowitz wrote. "Men drink more alcohol (than they would otherwise), have more sex, blame sexual assault victims, talk and act in sexist and homophobic ways, and watch with silence when men degrade women verbally and physically because they think that these other men support these behaviors more than they really do." Adolescent boys are not the only ones vulnerable to conformity: A man's perception of how much other men drink is the strongest influence on how much he will drink.

Surveys have found that most college guys don't endorse traditional masculine norms, but they believe that most other men do. More specifically, college men overestimate their peers' use of alcohol and other drugs, amount of sexual activity, desire to hook up, willingness to use force to have sex, acceptance of homophobia, and tolerance of behavior that degrades women. They don't necessarily know what their peers truly believe because they might worry that probing conversations are unmasculine.

At many schools across the country, fraternity brothers told me that, in general, the guys who are considered most masculine are the ones who hook up the most and, especially among underclassmen, the ones who party. ("If you're hooking up with girls, that's seen as more masculine than someone who drinks but doesn't hook up," a New Jersey junior said. "Both are definitely attached to being masculine, but the drinking idea fades with age.")

Being athletic or buff is another common indicator at some schools. To be masculine at a Florida college, "you gotta be very fit; that's the first thing. Either you're good at sports or go to the gym a lot," said a sophomore there. "You also got to be very outgoing and social. Good-looking. Love to party. Another part of being masculine is being able to talk to girls, play the field really well, hook up.

And especially on my campus, having high-up positions or a good job." A brother from California said that "a 'zero-cares' attitude makes you more masculine."

Many studies have found that men who endorse traditional expressions of masculinity (such as Mahalik's eleven) are more likely to engage in risky behaviors that increase their chances of illness, injury, and death. College students who follow this path are more likely to drink more, get depressed, and commit sexual assault. And it is common for men to become emotionally isolated because they worry that opening up, seeking intimate friendships, and showing affection are perceived to be feminine behaviors. NYU psychology professor Niobe Way has characterized boys' late adolescence as "a time of disconnection and loneliness." Between the ages of 16 and 19, the suicide rate for boys skyrockets to four times the rate for girls.

Now consider the predicament of a new college student, a boy who is expected to become a man, who faces these masculine "norms" discouraging him from expressing his emotions or seeking intimacy—important tools for forming meaningful connections—at precisely the time when he is most vulnerable and alone. At precisely the time when he most yearns to make friends.

Enter fraternities.

Fraternities appear to offer ready-made friendships without threatening a student's masculine status on campus. By calling members "brothers," fraternities seem to promise the kind of supportive relationships that could alleviate a freshman's separation anxiety, loss, and grief. In the introduction to this book, I wondered why, with the negative stigma and scandalous headlines, a college boy would still want to join a fraternity. When one considers that fraternities are the most visible answer to the conflict between acting masculine and finding friendships, it's easy to understand the allure.

These organizations even commonly state as a purpose that they teach members how to be a "better man": Delta Sigma Theta, Delta Sigma Phi, and Alpha Sigma Phi's mottoes are "To better the man"; Kappa Gamma promotes the "whole man," and Theta Chi the "resolute man"; and Sigma Tau Gammas aspire to reach "the highest ideals of manhood." By making these claims to students at just the life stage at which they are trying to figure out what masculinity means, fraternities appear to provide both the companions and the guidance to help a boy transition to manhood.

For many students, acceptance to a fraternity is a relief because they feel like they won't have to navigate college alone. "The initial transition is the most difficult part. There's an expectation when you first come in; all the college guys, though they may not be in reality, put on this façade of your typical college douchebag. As a freshman, if you're not like that, it's hard to find the people you fit in with who you'll be hanging out with for the next four years," Teddy said. "When I came here, I didn't know anybody. I didn't even know where the dining halls were, so I had to ask random people, 'Hey, do you know where the food is?' Once I joined this organization, it was easy to ask, 'How do I print something out at the library?' or 'What database can I use for this class?' Rather than being the scared little freshman not knowing what the hell I'm doing, it was nice to feel like 'Oh, this is my place now. This is where I fit in here.' "

Brothers told me that because the point of fraternities is to form close friendships, they bonded more quickly and with more guys than they would have if they hadn't been Greek. "Guys are more expected to hold emotions back and be a person who has everything in control on the outside. Classes and organizations only get you so far in terms of getting you out of the work mentality and having personal connections with people. So for guys, it's much more difficult to meet someone who you'd call a lifelong friend or who'd get you through college," a Florida sophomore said. "There's always the fear of not being accepted anywhere. It'd be very tough to open up to people if you didn't already have a fraternity as a catalyst for your emotions."

Fraternities ritualize intimate emotional expression with activities specifically designed to encourage brothers to confide in one another. During one fraternity's "Dragon's Breath" ritual, an officer sits at a bonfire or in a dimly lit room and reads a list of 100 statements. The members raise their hands if they agree and, at certain points, discuss their experiences. The statements begin gently: "I have been outside the country," and then plunge into deeper topics. One of the statements is "I have sexually assaulted someone." A senior told me, "People are honest. One time, someone raised their hand for that one, but it was more like, 'I was at a party, we both got very drunk, we started making out, her friend said she was too drunk, and I felt like shit.'"

An Iowa fraternity ends every chapter meeting with a ritual called "Good of the Order." As with gavel sessions, the brothers are encouraged to reveal their deepest thoughts; after each brother's turn, he says, "Love and respect." A junior told me that "the most thoughtful and insightful conversations are held during the Good of the Order." On one occasion, a brother told the group he was depressed and feeling suicidal. Brothers hugged him, a few started to cry, and many of them said they would "do anything and drop everything for him." The junior gave him resource information, which he knew about because the chapter had attended mental health presentations. "You'd never expect it from him. He was always such a happy guy," he said. "It was one of the most touching experiences I've ever witnessed. The amount of support that brother had was insane. I'm tearing up right now remembering it. He's thriving right now."

A powerful moment in the ensuing conversation occurred when an older brother told the group, "It's okay to cry. It's okay to open up. You don't have to 'be a man.' That's just a societal thing that shifts people's views and promotes harmful stress." The junior remembered, "That really hit home. Because sometimes I overlook that and I think, *I can't do this because I'll be thought of as a pussy.*" Even if boys have heard this message before, it can resonate more when it's relayed by an in-group peer who has already established masculine bona fides.

Self-disclosive friendships among boys have been significantly associated with higher self-esteem and lower levels of depression. Experts say that one way to improve boys' mental and physical health, as well as school performance, is to encourage friendships that defy masculine stereotypes by sharing thoughts and feelings. Many fraternities already do that.

This book has included several members of open-minded chapters that embrace a variety of students' philosophies and orientations. There are plenty of earnest, good-hearted fraternity brothers who accept students for who they are and who genuinely believe they can teach members to be better men. And when older brothers and alumni model healthy versions of masculinity, younger members often follow suit. A hallmark of BGLOs, for example, is their strong focus on alumni relations, which exposes members to successful and engaged black adults. Men can also join black fraternities after college, a practice that emphasizes the lifelong connections available to members. "My fraternity has given me access to a network of successful black men who I would not have known otherwise," a Tennessee BGLO senior said. "Before college, I had rigid ideas about what achievement was. To me, it was just monetary success. Now that I'm part of my fraternity, I see that success means being a good family man and good husband, identifying a faith you can take seriously, being involved in your community, and being physically and mentally healthy. Having brothers who are serious about success and achievements in all those different fields has given me a new understanding of what black masculinity is."

But here's where good intentions can go astray: Different chapters have varying beliefs about what it means to be a "better man." Studies show that white fraternities and sororities commonly cling to harsh, conservative notions of gender roles. They are more restrictive than other college groups; they often believe fraternity brothers should be "real men," as defined by traditional expectations, and sorority girls should be feminine, passive, and deferential. (Fraternities are more likely than sororities to have stereotypical attitudes about gender.) Researchers found that Greeks are more likely to offer bids to "women who appeared to be extremely feminine and men who appeared to be extremely masculine," thus perpetuating the cycle. Even when a new recruit initially doesn't hold stereotypically masculine views, like Jake, the processes of pledging, traditions, chapter and alumni interactions, and parties can encourage groupthink and eventually change his mind-set.

In all-male groups such as these, there also might be more pressure to conform to the group's standards of masculinity. Behavior that is perceived as normal can actually become the norm. That may be why research shows that, generally, fraternity brothers are more likely than other students to endorse casual sex, objectify women, accept aggression toward women, and/or pressure peers to hook up. This is not to say that all or most members espouse these views, only that many are taught that these views are normative.

Academics call exaggerated traditional male gender role behaviors "hypermasculine." Because many fraternities endorse hypermasculinity, while non-Greeks also participate in drinking, hookups, and questionable behavior, fraternity members might be more likely to take this conduct to an extreme. College men who embrace masculine standards such as sleeping around, taking risks, and being competitive are also more likely to drink to get drunk. They might assume that getting drunk is a masculine thing to do, and that drinking will make them exhibit more masculine characteristics such as aggression, bravery, and emotionlessness.

But here's a surprise: It turns out that those conventional masculine expectations don't have anything to do with being a man. Scientists have discovered that there's no biological basis for believing that boys are innately tough, independent, or stoic; actually, in infancy, boys are more emotional than girls. Yet while girls are permitted to express their feelings, boys are taught to suppress them. "But this doesn't mean men aren't experiencing the same feelings," neuroscientist Lise Eliot wrote in *Pink Brain, Blue Brain.* "In laboratory studies, men respond even *more* intensely than women to strong emotional stimuli such as a violent movie or an impending electrical shock. The catch is that their responses are mostly internal: compared to women, men undergo greater increases in heart rate, blood pressure, and sweating when confronted with highly emotional situations."

Other studies have shown that close, solid friendships might be more important for boys' psychological development than for girls'. University of Maine psychologist Cynthia Erdley found that the quality of friendships was associated with loneliness and depression only for boys. While her study focused on younger boys, she told me her findings "suggest that boys, who generally have lower quality friendships than girls, are left more vulnerable to psychological difficulties when they have less supportive, intimate friendship experiences."

When boys are taught that their desire for close male friendships is against their nature, "we gender and sexualize a socio-emotional need that's essential for our survival as a species," Niobe Way said. "We're essentially saying don't act human." This message tends to sink in during late adolescence, when cultural pressure to act "manly" intensifies, and boys disconnect from their emotions while at the same time long for their close male friendships of boyhood, she said.

The biggest danger, Erdley added, "is that boys do not get the support they need from their friends, and this leaves them vulnerable to loneliness, anxiety, and depression symptoms. And males are more likely to lash outward when they are depressed."

Notably, non-Western cultures don't have the same prejudice against male intimacy. It's acceptable in many countries for male friends to hold hands or shed tears. Only in America and American-influenced countries are boys' emotional skills and intimate same-sex friendships ignored or insulted, Way said. It's possible, then, that fraternities are such a distinctly American phenomenon because other cultures don't force guys who seek these relationships to form a separate social structure.

Why do fraternities so often express hypermasculinity in destructive ways despite the risks to themselves and others? Boys could be internalizing the clash between culture and nature. Chapter 1 mentions that in the early twentieth century, when homosexuality became a label and a recognized sexuality, fraternity activities suddenly seemed suspicious. According to Nicholas Syrett, "While they might well date women with varying degrees of seriousness, many expected a brother's chief commitment to be to his fraternity." (Recall how older Zeta Kappa brothers told Jake during rush about dumping rotten trash on guys who lavaliered their girlfriends, signifying his commitment to her.) "They attempted to maintain this commitment in the face of a society that increasingly understood intimacy between men to be sexual."

Today, many fraternities continue to struggle with reconciling a shared desire for male intimacy with a fear that expressing such a desire will be perceived as weak or effeminate. Even in chapters that are no longer homophobic, hypermasculine standards ingrained for nearly 100 years demand that brothers avoid appearing feminine or gay. But rituals, traditions, and living conditions can encourage them to bond by baring their souls and comforting one another, which allows for levels of vulnerability and male intimacy that contradict but operate within the fraternities' own hypermasculine standards.

Also, many fraternity brothers forge affectionate friendships and/or engage in recruitment discussions about the physical attractiveness of male rushees. Some brothers participate in nude or seminude all-male rituals, as in Jake's chapter (which also wielded dildos). And recruits and pledges want fraternity members to desire them as brothers. The *ASHE Higher Education Report* observed, "This is a challenging concept for men to express when most language they know at their age about desire depicts a romantic or sexual connection, rather than an emotionally vulnerable relationship." If brothers believe their activities could be considered to have gay overtones at the same time as they consciously or subconsciously are trying desperately to portray themselves as "not gay," then their hypermasculinity could be an overcompensation. To put it more bluntly, many fraternity brothers are so worried about losing their masculinity in the eyes of other students that they make up for it by doing stupid things.

This type of overcompensation is an example of what gender theorists call "precarious manhood." The term is based on the idea that a guy believes he doesn't automatically "have" masculinity; instead, he is expected continually to earn it, prove it, and hope not to lose it. The theory suggests that when guys think they are losing masculine status, they often overconform to stereotypically masculine behaviors and attitudes to try to regain it. This fear of powerlessness or loss of control, according to researchers, is why male friendships so frequently revolve around joking or sexual humor, which "allow a needed connection without being self-disclosive or emotionally intimate, that is, with little vulnerability." It's arguable, then, that problem fraternities' attitudes aren't caused only by deep-rooted homophobia. There might be other reasons that members can feel emasculated.

Consider pledging, for example. Whether or not pledges are hazed, they might feel uncertain, believing they are probationary members at the bottom of the fraternity hierarchy. "There's a lot of fear when you don't know what's going on, and you feel like a little boy being yelled at by all the big kids. You don't feel like a man," a recent Massachusetts grad said. During their pledge period, several guys in his class overcompensated by creating a challenge they called "Team Savage": They voluntarily drank a Solo cup of their own urine (talk about toxic masculinity). "It's disgusting, but it made them seem tough and strong, and they gained their status back in the house. Team Savage meant you were one of the hardest partiers. You didn't get anything for doing it; you just felt more masculine."

It's possible that even the desire to form close male friendships could make college guys feel vulnerable and therefore more likely to engage in risky or sexist behavior to counteract their self-doubt. Because they are socialized to hide their emotions, *Guyland* author Michael Kimmel observed, "boys feel effeminate not only if they express emotions, but even if they feel them." Popular culture even feminizes close male friendships with the term *bromance,* which both uses the language of desire and attempts to make the concept more palatable by joking about it.

When we think of patriarchal masculinity, typically we think of women as the victims. But boys, too, can feel stifled by these narrow gender norms. The performative aspect of masculinity can be stressful for guys who feel compelled to pretend to fit society's expectations of men; psychologist William Pollack famously referred to "the mask of masculinity." In one study of college students, the *Journal of College Student Development* reported, "This performance was like a mask that they put on in an effort to cover up the ways in which they did not meet these expectations and in order to present to others someone who would be seen as a man." Guys felt pressured to display characteristics they didn't necessarily identify with. One participant described his reaction as "putting my man face on."

The students found society's expectations of college men to be so limiting that they couldn't live up to them. They became insecure about their masculinity and reacted by overcompensating to prove their manhood. Some of their resulting behaviors included activities they later regretted, such as "making homophobic comments, objectifying or demeaning women, drinking to excess or competitive drinking, or suppressing their own emotions."

When I talked to fraternity brothers, most didn't bring up the word *masculinity* without prompting. But some of them did raise a distinction between guys who embodied hypermasculinity and those who were comfortable with more varied gender roles: *fratty* or *frat bro* versus *fraternity man*. Teddy described a "fratty" guy as "someone who's associated with wealth and a typical party douchebag." (On some campuses, students refer to this kind of brother and/or his actions as "FAF," for Frat as Fuck.) A Michigan junior said, "A frat bro is an exacerbation of fraternity culture. It's not real. It's on video. It's a six-second show of someone doing something for a camera," performing for social media, a description that sounds a lot like putting a man face on. Think Jake's fraternity versus Oliver's. Or Kirk's first chapter versus his second.

Kirk's two chapters "have completely different definitions of masculinity," he said. In his current chapter, "everyone thinks masculinity is more of a problem than a badge of honor." In his first chapter, "no one knows what *toxic masculinity* means. People would be very confused if you meant *masculinity* to mean anything but 'drinking beer, muscles, and macho man.'"

Kirk was thrilled when he met the brothers of his current chapter. "I came from a place where I joined because I liked one of the guys, but I didn't really like the whole misogyny toxic masculinity stuff. Here, I found a close brotherhood that didn't match the stereotypes of a fraternity. Where people could have their own individual identity. You're not put in a box. There weren't all these ideas about masculinity." The guys in his new chapter were so determined not to be frat bros that they banned the word *frat*. When a new member running for office—the leading contender—said in his speech, "I really want to help this frat" instead of "fraternity," the chapter voted against him.

One day when I spoke with Kirk, he had just spent a weekend visiting his first chapter. On Saturday night, they partied. On Sunday, they drank, watched football, and talked about girls at the party, girls whom brothers were dating, and sports. When Kirk returned to his current chapter, "Someone was talking to me about Tunisia and asked if I'd seen *Charlie Wilson's War*. We talked for an hour about the 1980s Afghanistan conflict. Multiple people joined in, and then a guy from Pakistan talked about the refugee crisis."

Oliver's chapter, too, was relatively healthy partly because it didn't emphasize hypermasculinity. The brothers were exposed to a variety of productive masculine expressions, such as hard work, passion for hobbies, and individualism. It was okay, in Oliver's chapter, to be offbeat, to be dorky, to be gay. It's not surprising that his chapter had fewer alcohol and sexual assault issues—and was more vigilant about preventing and addressing them—than a stereotypical fraternity. And studies show that when male teenagers prioritize work as a measure of masculinity, they are, like Oliver after freshman year, less likely to engage in heavy drinking because getting drunk could harm their work or academic performance.

Many chapters like this exist; we simply don't hear about them because they aren't embroiled in headline-making scandals and because they focus more on their members' inner qualities than their chapter's external image. A Rhode Island brother came into college with "the view I gotta go in and drink well, get a lot of girls, never show emotion, always tell everyone classes are going great, I'm not having any issues. I was trying to make it look like I knew what I was doing, that I could fit in and have a great time, even though I wasn't sure of myself. But I wasn't finding the traditional hookup scene and what I'd seen in the movies."

Second semester, he rushed a fraternity in search of that atmosphere. To his surprise, the fraternity's alternative views on masculinity made him reconsider prioritizing toughness and hookups. "When I found this community—yeah, it had partying and the social aspects, but it also had the idea that you can do all that stuff without having to put on a show. You can be yourself entirely in front of these people. I didn't think you'd find a fraternity who wanted to have a great time and also wanted to talk about toxic masculinity and sex assault on campus. That was eye-opening. It changed me."

The chapter altered his views on masculinity because of the attitudes that older brothers modeled. "These were people I respected who were incredibly intelligent and had the right worldview, so I committed to that community. When they talked about checking yourself, doing the little things like not looking at a girl too long or making anyone feel uncomfortable, it started to make sense to me," he said. "Also, the most successful people in my fraternity and on campus were genuinely being themselves. I wasn't a douchebag at heart, just thinking [acting traditionally masculine] was how you become successful in college. When I saw these leaders in my fraternity having success without being those guys, I realized, *Wow, I don't have to do that if I don't want to.*" Now he proudly calls himself a feminist.

A midwestern brother told me he was unsure how to interpret

the traditional standards of masculinity he encountered at college, where he became plagued by anxiety after two sorority women were dissatisfied with his sexual performance. "I had really bad premature ejaculation. I didn't know it was a problem until I got to college. Sorority girls talk. I don't think anybody was having good sex in high school. In college, you understand what sex really is. With pornography, there are performative expectations of what a man should be. You assume everyone's fucking well. It was a very emasculating thing to deal with," he said.

When he confided in his brothers, they told him there was more to "being a man" than how he performed. They reassured him that the problem was in his head and he could get past it. "Being able to communicate to other males about it was helpful. They wanted me to feel confident in bed; I was anxious not only talking to women, but when I got home with a girl," he said. "I had this collision of the masculinity I had grown up with and what it was to be a man in college, the sensation of a frat bro. But my chapter didn't have any frat bros. They wanted the gentleman fraternal man. They provided a good example of what it was to have this different sense of masculinity: fraternity men who could be comforting, have fun, and get work done. They had that great balance."

Experts say that because fewer than half of US states are required to teach sex education, teenagers are learning about sex from porn—and the guys I interviewed agree. Their smartphones provide easy access; a University of New Hampshire survey found that 93 percent of male college students had viewed online porn before the age of 18. But the easiest free porn available can emphasize male dominance (and worse), giving guys a skewed view of how they're expected to perform. "The over-the-top and misleading way porn portrays sex can cause a man to feel he isn't performing well enough, and even lead him to do things that look good on Pornhub but aren't effective in the real world. Performance anxiety is pretty common among men my age. Your mind begins to wander to *Am I performing as well as I should? Is this as great as it was made out to be? Why isn't she making tons of noise like they normally do?* When you think these things, it makes you perform worse," a newly graduated New England brother told me. "Women are treated terribly in most porn. They're often portrayed as a man's plaything that should do whatever the man desires. This instills a sense in guys that you're at your most masculine when a woman is submitting to you. Many men understand porn is different than real, intimate sex. On the whole, though, porn sets unrealistic and potentially dangerous standards of masculinity that too many young men feel they have to meet."

But many young men rise above dangerous standards, too. A 2014 study interviewed selected members of 44 chapters of a predominantly white NIC fraternity who "challenge[d] stereotypically masculine norms through their commitment to academic excellence, involvement in campus leadership and service, responsible alcohol consumption, engagement in respectful antisexist friendships with women, and the consistent denouncing of homophobia and racism within their male peer groups." The students exhibited behaviors, such as confronting brothers who behaved poorly, that demonstrated what education professors Frank Harris III and Shaun Harper call "productive masculinities." These nontraditional expressions of masculinity have been linked to better health, safety, and school engagement for college men.

Similarly, I spoke with brothers who interpreted the goal of making their brothers "better men" as helping them to become better *people.* They believed it was their responsibility to hold brothers to high standards of tolerance and cooperation. They were able to create a subculture in which brothers were rewarded for being good guys. In the "love and respect" Iowa chapter, for example, when a new member wrote "faggot" on a group text, several members called him out: "Dude, that's not okay," they replied. "Don't say that word." The junior told me, "No one in my fraternity likes that word, out of respect for our two gay members. We definitely have checks and balances." The new member said he wouldn't use it again.

This is not to say the job is easy, particularly in chapters that, like Jake's, are accustomed to praising stereotypically masculine behaviors such as getting drunk and having a lot of casual sex. Brothers at other schools told me their strategy for improving the chapter is to recruit new members who already genuinely believe in good values. During recruitment, "We look for leaders who will help us achieve our goals," said a New Jersey junior. "Greek life can be a little dangerous; all colleges have demographics of people engaging in risky behavior. We want people with decision-making skills and good judgment, like a responsible adult. A guy who comes in talking about parties and how he can drink is the last recruit we're looking for. That doesn't correlate to being a good brother to other people. It's about being selfless and looking out for the brother next to you."

The students in the "productive masculinities" study held brothers accountable by using formal disciplinary procedures to enact consequences, much as Oliver and his brothers handled Javier's alcoholism. They also prioritized getting good guys into leadership positions to ensure the chapter remained healthy. This may be easier to accomplish in smaller, mid- to lower-tier chapters. Top-tier fraternities and sororities commonly follow more rigid rules about masculinity and femininity. And because they are often more conformist than lower-tiered groups, their members might feel more pressure to comply with those rules. An upper-middle-tier brother told me, "There's a correlation between how high a tier a fraternity is and how masculine the guys are."

. . .

Gender theory also offers a more nuanced look at partying than the public, and perhaps fraternity brothers themselves, are aware of. First, partying could be considered a way to publicly express many traditional masculine behaviors at once: risky behavior (drinking), competition (for girls, sex, or drinking game bragging rights), suppressing emotions (drinking again), promiscuity (hookups or sex), breaking rules (drinking, yet again), and heterosexuality (dancing with or hooking up with girls). For fraternity brothers, partying can be a way to experience these hypermasculine markers together. The next morning, when they regale one another with stories about their hookups or antics, they reaffirm their masculine status.

Second, many students come to college expecting a permissive environment in which drinking and hookups are part of the college adventure, the proverbial "four years of freedom." If students view college as a break in between the restrictions of childhood and the responsibilities of adulthood, then partying is a way to take advantage of that, to indulge, explore, and let loose before being expected to fulfill adult obligations to work and family. "You want to forget for at least one night that you're ultimately trying to make a career and future for yourself," said a Mississippi brother. "There's a sense that now is the time to have as much fun as you can because it's all downhill after school. One reason people party is they don't want to think about the fact that it's going to end. These four years are probably the most fun I'll get the chance to have."

By situating partying in this way, students might consider it a normal step on their path to manhood. "These partying behaviors [are] how college men are encouraged to conform to society's expectations," college administrators Keith Edwards and Susan Jones observed. "The emerging theory helps frame college men's partying behaviors . . . not as deviant, but as conforming performances men feel they must put on to be seen as men. Rather than seeing men who party as ignoring social norms or irreverent to authority, instead student affairs educators may understand them, in part, as men who feel trapped by social norms as they understand them and confined by the authority of society's expectations."

Many college students and, notably, less privileged fraternity brothers such as members of black and Latino fraternities don't equate partying with masculinity. In one study, "Most of these men expressed strong disapproval of college students who seem more interested in partying than studying and advancement. Inverting many of the same meanings the more privileged men used to construct selves as youthful, adventurous, and masculine, these upwardly mobile men draw on ideas of maturity and social responsibility to depict college partying as foolish and self-indulgent."

Instead of viewing college as a time of freedom from responsibilities, many of these fraternity brothers see it as a time to buckle down, begin to take on adult responsibilities, and improve their job qualifications. For them, not partying and not drinking heavily illustrate a masculinity characterized by responsibility, control, and commitment to hard work. "We're college students. We still go out. But we believe that blacking out and hard-core crazy drinking games sound ridiculous. We're trying to get away from the machismo attitude of masculinity," said an Idaho Latino fraternity brother. "We have jobs and are part of organizations where we want to get as much experience as we can because these four years go by in a blink of an eye. And we know our skills have to be just as honed as everyone else's when we enter the job market, because we never know what kind of biases there might be."

Several versions of masculinity lie somewhere in the middle. For Teddy's Oregon fraternity, masculinity is about balance. "If someone is completely opposed to partying with us at all, and the excuse is 'I have all these responsibilities,' that's a turnoff. Yes, we respect that you work so hard, but if you can't ever relax and hang out with your friends, then what's the point of working so hard?" he said. "The guys in the house who get the most respect are the ones who don't party a lot, but when they do, they have a lot of fun with us, and the rest of the time, they're working really hard, and we understand why they're not always with us."

What Could Help

While white fraternities have a reputation as being macho womanizers, they weren't always that way, and they don't have to remain so. It is possible for college guys to have intimate male friendships without feeling the need to overcompensate with a show of hypermasculinity. And students are healthier for it.

Fraternities' interpretations of masculinity can affect the larger student body. Even if they constitute a minority of men on campus, fraternities, like athletes, are visible, and they are perceived to be popular and influential. (Some brothers told me they believe fraternities are more influential because there are more fraternity members than athletes on campus, and fraternity brothers have more time to party.) Studies show that many college men view fraternity brothers and male athletes as "the embodiment of ideal masculinity on campus"; that's one reason students frequently regard the masculine characteristics associated with them, such as being fit, competitive, and promiscuous, to be ideal masculine qualities.

Fraternities aren't solely to blame for this hierarchy. Think of the attention that colleges pay to their football and basketball teams. Schools often glorify (mostly men's) athletics rather than promote friendship and emotional intelligence. Many fraternities follow that example, prioritizing athleticism and the expressions of masculinity promoted by the athletes themselves. Some scholars say that because there is a "hierarchy of masculinities in which some will have more privilege than others," school administrators should better recognize college men who excel outside of Greek life and sports.

Another way universities could help college guys would be to increase their consistent exposure to less stereotypical interpretations of masculinity. A handful of once- or twice-yearly presentations about alcohol abuse, sexual assault, and hazing is a Band-Aid reaction that condemns what brothers might do without addressing why they might be compelled to do it in the first place. To get to the root of fraternity issues, universities and national offices would be better served by concurrently trying to reframe how students perceive gender roles. Programs, presentations, and courses about masculinities, and better male-specific resources, could help fraternity brothers understand why they feel pressured and present more varied representations of gender roles. A university's investment in this type of programming would benefit the entire campus. Students won't become aware of "productive masculinities" unless people teach them what those are.

In the study in which participants spoke about wearing a mask, the students eventually came to terms with the parts of their identity that didn't fit the stereotypical gender role. "In these specific ways, such as being more sensitive, choosing not to drink or have sex, or being involved, they had accepted that, as individuals, they were just different kinds of men," researchers concluded. "In doing so, they were able to take off the mask by being more emotionally available, avoiding meaningless sexual relationships with women, speaking up against sexism and homophobia, or avoiding partying aspects of the college experience altogether." The students could overcome the pressure to demonstrate traditional masculinity because of their exposure to other expressions of masculinity, whether in courses, literature, or interactions with others.

It is both sad and illuminating that the greatest treasure for many fraternity members is an activity that should be commonplace but can seem unique and once-in-a-lifetime to them *only because they are men*: opening up to other guys. Chapter expectations that they will share confidences and support one another create a cozy space in which they can, simply, talk. For a college guy, "it's really liberating. You're free to talk about your ideas without the fear of somebody chastising you or being like, 'You're a dumbass,'" Teddy said. As colleges weigh whether to eliminate single-sex groups, they might consider whether their schools provide other safe spaces on campus in which guys can comfortably confide in other guys. Multicultural, LGBTQ, and women's centers might facilitate these valuable opportunities for many students. But straight white males need supportive communities, too.

A New Jersey brother told me there are many topics he wouldn't have been able to discuss with anyone if he weren't in a fraternity. "The day-to-day things that get you down? Those are the things a fraternity's there for. If I went to a friend in my pledge class and told him about a problem I was having, he'd talk to me for four hours," he said. "When you're entering college, it's tough to make friends. It's not like men are social butterflies coming right out of high school. Before I found my chapter, I didn't have that many friends, only a couple guys I had a good understanding of. In the fraternity, it was natural and easier."

One day when the brother was "really down" about his relationship with his parents, he confided in his pledge class. "I had eight other guys listening to me, talking to me about my issues: parental stressors, pressures I felt moving off to college, how relieved I felt to be out of high school but still sort of hurting when I went home."

The conversation both made the brother feel better and drastically improved his relationship with his parents. "It's not even that
they proposed a solution. One thing someone said that I'll never
forget was 'You never told this to anyone?' I said, 'No, I had no one
to talk about this with.' This could have eaten away at me. For a lot
of guys, just sharing stuff with someone helped so much. I wouldn't
have had the chance to talk about things as minuscule as I try to
make them seem because I'm a guy, so I'm not going to talk about it.
We diminish the importance of something that's important to us so
we don't have to bring it out into the world. But saying it to these
people in a safe space is very helpful. And probably saves a lot of
lives. The mental health resource is huge. When people try to tell
you you don't need anyone, that's BS. You need other people to talk
to and listen to you. Fraternities give that sort of outlet."

Ω Ω Ω

When school resumed after Winter Break, Jake moved into
the sleeping porch with the rest of his pledge class. He was glad
for the company because it distracted him from his heartbreak.
Near the end of vacation, Beth had called to tell him she had met
someone else.

Jake threw himself into the weekly mixers, where he hooked up
with several girls, even though he considered all the interactions to
be "unsuccessful dates." He made good on his promise to Ty; at a
party where both of them were attracted to the same girl, Jake
backed off so Ty could dance with her alone. And he looked forward
to the Alpha Rho mixer scheduled for after the spring pledge period,
where he hoped he might run into Laura. (He didn't think he could
contact her before then without seeming awkward.) Because of his
public string of mixer hookups and the brothers' assumption that
he'd gotten together with Laura last semester, Jake garnered such a
reputation in the chapter that the brothers, impressed and proud of

how far he had come, nicknamed him "Frat Daddy." This time, he didn't ask them to call him Jake.

The day before Spring Rush, all active Zeta Kappas attended a rush meeting at the house. Shawn, the rush chair, delivered a Power Point presentation explaining the chapter's recruitment rules and traditions. Jake was surprised at how methodically the week was choreographed. Some of the brothers were assigned to teams. If you liked a recruit, you were supposed to hand him off to the second-level brothers, some of the chapter's most sociable guys. Second-level brothers brought the recruits they liked to a member of the Rush Committee, the group of experienced brothers who ultimately decided whether a recruit deserved a bid.

"When you think a kid's a real goob or a scrub, like kids who are very awkward," Shawn explained to Jake's pledge class, "you give them to a walkout brother and tell someone on the Rush Committee why you want to walk them out." The Rush Committee member would meet the recruit and, if he agreed, pass him to another walk-out brother, who would escort him to the door with a send-off much like the one Jake heard from Kappa Tau.

"Whatever you do," Shawn continued, "don't get a rush boner. I'm looking at you, Sanders."

Chase nodded. "So true. I get my largest boners during rush."

"Don't get so excited when a new kid walks in that you want to give him a bid. We're going for quality over quantity. They need us more than we need them," Shawn said. "If they're a scrub, they're a scrub. They're unredeemable, and you've got to walk them out."

As rush began, Jake quickly learned what the brothers looked for: confident guys with good personalities. Because Zeta Kappa was moving up the ranks, the brothers wanted to recruit more people who were involved on campus. And, to Jake's disappointment, looks were also a priority.

On the first night of Spring Rush, Jake met Josh, an articulate freshman who had already attended both Zeta Kappa open houses that day. A smart overachiever like Jake, Josh kept up his end of a good conversation. When Jake asked what he wanted to get out of a fraternity, Josh gave the right answer: "Those kinds of tight-knit relationships you can have in a brotherhood." Jake thought Josh was great. He introduced him to a second-level brother.

That night, after the recruits left the rush party, the brothers gathered in the Great Room. Shawn plugged his laptop into the TV and scrolled through a list of every recruit who had come to the party, showing their profile pictures one by one and asking what brothers thought of their conversations. The chapter discussed whether to give each boy a bid the next night, introduce him to more brothers, or walk him out.

Shawn pulled up Josh's profile picture. Josh happened to be overweight. "This kid is absolutely fucking ugly. Let's get him out of here," a brother said.

At once, several members of Jake's pledge class disagreed. "Yeah, he's not the best-looking person, but I had a decent conversation with him," Jake offered. "He said all the right things." The chapter decided to give Josh another chance to talk to more brothers.

On the second day of rush, Josh again came to both open houses and the rush party, signaling that Zeta Kappa was his first choice. After the party, when Shawn scrolled to Josh's picture, a junior declared, "Look, I know some of you had really good conversations with this kid. But the fact is, we're always going to bid kids who can hold a good conversation and give the right answers. At this point, it boils down to his overall looks. There are other kids who are much nicer-looking and able to show themselves off more than this kid."

"I can't believe you're judging him by his looks! We should be judging them by their character," Steven said. "I loved the conversation I had with Josh. He seems like a really nice person who'd be dedicated to pledging and becoming a brother."

The argument grew heated. "Get the scrub outta here!" a brother shouted.

"What the fuck is wrong with all of you?" JB said, visibly upset. "This kid has come to every single one of our open houses and every single rush party and you decide that alone doesn't prove he's worthy of a bid? You just have to look good to get one?"

"We aren't going to be able to move up our tier if we're giving bids to below-average-looking kids," an officer argued.

"Does anyone really believe this one kid would jeopardize our chapter's image?" JB retorted. "I mean, come on, are you all so full of yourselves that you believe Josh will be the only ugly guy here?"

As brothers yelled at one another, a guy in Jake's class muttered, "Shit, I wonder what happened when they were reviewing me." Jake was thinking the same thing. Had there been a debate over whether to walk him out?

By the end of Spring Rush, after a draining week of talking to, and about, as many recruits as possible, Zeta Kappa had given bids to 16 freshmen. Josh was not one of them. A brother walked him, weeping, out the door.

Jake assigned himself the job of trying to convince the recruits on the fence to accept their bids. One freshman was a good student who worried about the time commitment of pledging. "Oh, you'll be able to manage all your classes alongside it," Jake told him. "Don't worry. At Zeta Kappa, we value our classes above everything else. If you have any scheduling concerns, we will definitely allow for absences." Once Jake was through with him, the freshman agreed to accept the bid.

When Jake told me this, knowing that his own first-semester GPA was the worst of his life, I asked him, "Did you really believe that or were you just sweet-talking him?"

"You know, that's the thing, isn't it? When you sweet-talk these kids—I don't even know anymore. Am I just trying to get him to join or am I really meaning what I'm saying? I was able to pass all my courses, but pledging damaged my grades. If I was in high school, I would be utterly destroyed by my GPA, really upset. But now I'm satisfied I got that, considering most of my time was spent pledging. But you can't tell these kids that. And you know what's worse? When a kid comes up and asks how was pledging for you."

During Shawn's initial rush presentation, Jake had asked him, "What is the best course of action if they ask about hazing?"

"Whoa, whoa, whoa!" several brothers interjected. "Don't talk about that." "Zeta Kappa is a nonhazing fraternity."

"Tell them your pledge semester was a lot of fun and allowed you to bond with your class very well," Shawn answered.

So when one of the new pledges asked Jake about hazing, Jake followed orders. "Personally, my pledge semester was a lot of fun," Jake told him. "There'll be lots of events, and you'll have lots of activities to do with the rest of your class, and from that you're going to really bond with them and you're going to become best friends for life! Isn't that right, Ty?"

Ty nodded. "Yeah, we're really good friends now, thanks to the pledge semester. I didn't know Jake before, but now I know him really well."

When I asked Jake what went through his head when he answered the pledge's question, he said that besides the bit about his friendship with Ty, "I straight-up lied to this kid! I want kids to get from this book that they should still join Greek life as long as hazing is done in moderation and without the intent of hurting anyone. But even so, I'm just straight-up lying to every pledge I talk to about how everything's going to go! It's such a strange conversation because you're never telling them the truth. You're telling them what they want to hear."

"Why do you do that?" I asked.

"Because, in the end, once you get through all the challenges and strife and pledge book learning and Hell Week and suffering, then you get a solid group of guys you know you can trust for the rest of your life. And I guess people use that to justify all the hazing, because they believe the ends justify the means. That speaks a lot about how the process works. As long as it makes you into a better person, does it really matter what you go through?"

Ω Ω Ω

Oliver devoted most of his nonclass waking hours to preparing for the hearing. He grilled brothers to make sure he had the facts straight. He studied the scripted format for the hearing and prepped every word he wanted to say in each section. He played devil's advocate, coming up with possible arguments the IFC could hit him with and developing his counterarguments. He put his schoolwork aside and scanned the IFC Constitution to find the precise wording for any rules that applied to his case.

He met with Peter and another alumnus to discuss their options. Still unclear about the hearing's specific format, Oliver consulted two of his friends on the IFC Judicial Board that would oversee the hearing. One of them was the president of the neighboring house.

Two days before the hearing, when Oliver revised his notes, he realized there was something missing from his arguments. If he used the three-step process that he had developed for his own chapter meetings, his presentation adequately described what happened and why it happened, but it was missing the integral third step: the specific measures the chapter would take to address the problem and prevent it from happening again. He barely left his room until he figured out a plan.

Finally, it was time for the trial. Oliver met Geoff and Peter at the student union. All three were in suits, as per IFC hearing regulations. Oliver had brought Peter because he was on the committee that had hired State U's director of fraternity and sorority life. Before the trial began, Oliver had Peter introduce him to the director, hoping to show him that "we're not bad guys, so his impression of me was not only 'the president of the house whose guy peed on the cops.'"

Sitting at the conference table with the director were the 11 members of the IFC Judicial Board and the IFC's presiding officer. The presiding officer, a senior, pointed Oliver to the seat at the head of the table and then read the list of charges. "Do you plead responsible or not responsible?" he asked.

"We plead responsible," Oliver said.

"Now you have the opportunity to talk about what happened and give us any information that might affect the sanction we give you," said a board member.

For the next 40 minutes, Oliver talked the Judicial Board through the sequence of events, displaying photos on his iPad of the locations he mentioned. He showed them where the officers should have checked in for the walk-through, and the alley where they had surprised Keegan. He illustrated how it would have been impossible for Keegan to see the officers, or anyone, enter the alley.

Then he explained why the police report was inaccurate. Coincidentally, one of Oliver's brothers had a friend whose father was a city police officer. The father talked to the officers, who, in describing the story, had used the phrase "almost peed on." The father texted his son, who captured a screenshot of the conversation for PhiEp. "The cops said they got peed on, but that was not true," Oliver told the board. "Here's a screenshot of a conversation with another city PD member." They looked at his screen. "The police don't traditionally do this. They broke the protocol we've always had." Oliver referred to the IFC Constitution, which detailed this protocol in depth. "This is something no one would ever be prepared for. I'm not telling you this to justify what my member did, but to emphasize that this was not a malicious act toward the police department. It was just a stupid mistake."

He fielded a few minor questions from the board and moved on. "We shut the party down at nine. They came back at eleven. Even if the party went the full duration that we registered it for, it would have been over at ten. The police had no reason to come back. It was unexpected, and I don't blame Geoff for not being around; there was no reason to think he should be. I offered to talk to them on the phone, but they declined. Our secretary was present to talk to them. We answered the door, and they refused to talk with anyone but Geoff or me in person. That's not necessarily inappropriate, but we set our own chain of command. If I'm not around, it goes to Geoff; if he's not around, it goes to Reed. We have that chain because Geoff and I can't be around all the time. We are people, and we have things to do, too. It was unfair of them to put that in the report."

Oliver paused again for questions, none of which was tough. Then he continued: "There are two parties who could be held responsible for what happened, Phi Epsilon and the individual, so we need to address each one. The party went really well, and we had no trouble. While responsibility does lie on us as a fraternity, the police report was about the act of one person. So I want to provide tangible solutions, goals, and ideas about what our punishments should be. We've done this so far: We found out who is responsible, and here are the steps we want to take to move forward."

Oliver told the board that his first reaction was that maybe the chapter should deactivate Keegan, "chopping off the hand to save the body." But he recognized that "when Keegan isn't drunk, he's a phenomenal PhiEp. He's everything a PhiEp should be." After the party, Geoff had screamed furiously at Keegan. Keegan's roommate told Oliver that Keegan had cried himself to sleep.

Keegan had done some dumb shit before, Oliver told the council, but only when he was drinking. "So clearly the problem has to be addressed through alcohol." Oliver had already put Keegan on indefinite social probation and barred him from drinking on campus. Oliver had also scheduled counseling appointments for Keegan with a PhiEp alum who was a psychologist. An alum who knew some city police officers set up a few ride-alongs to give Keegan a better sense of the officers' perspective. And Oliver booked a meeting with the police department for Keegan and the chapter to apologize to the officers face-to-face.

"Keegan is at peace with the consequences. It's better than being removed," Oliver said.

As for the house, Oliver explained that he had put his chapter on temporary social probation and set up additional risk-management meetings. "We are already taking responsibility, and I am punishing us for you. In addition, we'll hopefully get in some community service requirements for a percentage of our members that you feel is a comfortable number. It's what I think you should be telling us to do. And here's another idea for what you can enforce on us," Oliver said, setting up his slam dunk.

He had thought this one through carefully. He had to satisfy the IFC, but he also had to come up with a solution that pleased the alumni and his brothers. The alumni were angry about the multiple violations. They wanted to see something done to prevent future incidents, but they didn't want to see the house put on long-term social probation, which would make it harder to recruit new members. The brothers needed a consequence that wouldn't undo all Oliver's hard work to motivate them and that would keep them devoted to the chapter.

"I'm fully aware that the actions of a member of my fraternity jeopardized the relationship between State U, the police, and the Greek community; made my house look terrible; and did not represent State U well. I'd like to respectfully ask that you look through our case history. Most of the things on here are not serious. On some occasions, the head of the IFC forgot to turn in our party permit." Oliver asked the director of fraternity and sorority life to confirm this for the board, which he did.

"We have had more serious incidents, including the one I'm now here for," Oliver said. "I've looked at the incidents, and there's clearly a trend. The serious problems happen when we party at our house with another fraternity. So I propose we should not be allowed to host other fraternities at our house, because our party room is small, so the parties get incredibly hectic or are held outside. Look at my track record. Risk management is something I pride myself on, and I feel I've had a lot of improvements in that area. But it's hard to control when other fraternities come over. They think they can do whatever they want, and it becomes a nightmare. I have no issues with my guys on our own—just when other houses come over. So until we prove we can handle it, we shouldn't be allowed to do those types of parties. We've already done more than what the IFC would have asked us to do to address this situation."

Oliver mentally crossed his fingers. He thought the IFC would appreciate the proposal because it showed that he was serious, he recognized the problem, and he had good solutions. If it worked, his proposal would appease the alumni, who had told him the brothers were "throwing parties you can't handle." And while he didn't admit this to the IFC, the brothers didn't want other fraternities at their house anyway.

The presiding officer spoke. "These all sound like great ideas, but how will you follow through with this? What are some consequences if you don't follow through?"

"I haven't thought about it, because we're going to follow through," Oliver said. Most of the brothers on the Judicial Board laughed.

"Okay, well, if there's nothing else, give us 15 minutes," the presiding officer said. "We're going to talk about what we think your sanctions will be. Can you wait outside, please?"

Outside, Peter told Oliver, "You did a really good job," and left for work.

Five minutes later, the director of fraternity and sorority life came outside. "If you guys want to come back in, we've made a decision."

At the table, the presiding officer smiled at Oliver. "We're going to go with your plan. That sounds good to us. Update us in four weeks, and keep us in the loop."

"That's great. Thank you," Oliver said.

Later, when he and Geoff got back to the house, the brothers would swarm them to ask about the verdict. Oliver would explain the ban on cohosting parties at the PhiEp house and announce, "This is our punishment." The brothers would cheer: "That's not a punishment!" "We just got a gift!" "You got us out of hosting parties we'd get in trouble for." When Oliver would call Peter, the alumnus would say, jubilantly, that Oliver was following in Trey's illustrious footsteps, even though he was a year younger.

But for now, once Oliver and Geoff were outside, past the windows of the student union, they slapped a sweet, crisp high five. Then, because they were in suits, they immediately started quoting *Step Brothers*.

"Prestige Worldwide!" Oliver said. "We're here to fuck shit up."

"I feel like a lightning bolt hit the tip of my penis!" Geoff answered.

As they strutted down the sidewalk, Oliver felt like a leader at last.

CHAPTER 9

Good Fraternities vs. Bad Frats: How to Tell the Difference

THE HAZING BEGAN with the spring class's Bid Dinner, the pledges' first official activity. From the hall where Jake hung out with his date, he watched brothers force the pledges to play games and to chug for 10 seconds when they lost. One freshman staggered past Jake, shouting, "Holy shit, I've had a lot to drink!" Ty uploaded to the Fall 2017 private Facebook page a video of a pledge barfing all over an upstairs bathroom.

As various guys stumbled out of the bedrooms, Jake's date—a random setup—laughed. "There's so much going on! Everyone's acting so goofy. It's like watching a fraternity sitcom," she said.

Wes gleefully barreled into the hallway. "Dude, I'm hazing these kids so bad, shouting at them to drink and shit," he said. *He's going to channel all the anger taken out on him on the new kids,* Jake thought. *It's a chain of abuse.*

Jake vowed again to be "the nice brother," he told me. "I'm going to make an effort to really talk to them. I have no intention to make them drink. I'll participate in the other hazing activities, but I'm not going to be an individual dick to these guys."

His resolve lasted two days.

During the pledges' first weekend, the brothers' group chat exploded with conversations about hazing the new guys. They decided to target a couple of pledges who had awkward Facebook pictures. One of them dropped the fraternity within the week.

Several brothers were eating lunch at the house when a brother made a joke about Jake. Everyone laughed—that was fine with

Jake—but Austin, a pledge, laughed the hardest. "That made me want to haze him, to haze all these kids. Now I want these kids to go through the same shit we did. I'm actually having those thoughts now. They're trying to be overly chummy, patting me on the back when I talk to them, but they only just joined! They're trying to become a brother without going through all the shit yet. They gotta know there's a hierarchy in place and they've got to overcome these challenges before they get to be on my level. Before they get my friendship," Jake told me.

"That's a new perspective for you," I said.

"All of our attitudes have changed over time. We were just getting hazed, and now that we're able to laugh off everything, we lose the feelings it caused us and we're desensitized enough to want to haze the next class. And that's how the cycle goes." The brothers told Jake it happened every semester: The pledges assumed that after Bid Dinner hazing, they were on par with the brothers. That's why the chapter gave them pledge pins so quickly after that night. Jake explained, "The pins are to put them in their place, to remind them they're still different from the rest of us. They're still inferior."

Jake joined the other brothers in yelling at the pledges, threatening consequences if they didn't memorize their pledge books. He gave Austin impossible questions for the practice interview. He had little sympathy when one of the pledges threw up after the 5:45 A.M. jog. And when Austin told him, "You brothers should give pledges more credit and respect just for *trying* to follow all your orders," Jake didn't let it go. He posted Austin's quote on the secret Z-Kap Facebook page to which the pledges didn't have access, and let the comments fly. Brothers called Austin a pussy and resolved to haze him more. At the next EP, Daniel, the new Z, roared at the pledges, screaming about their unworthiness until Austin, in particular, cowered before him.

As the pledge period progressed, four more pledges dropped

out, three of them because they couldn't afford the initiation fee, dues, and house fees.

Jake enjoyed his status as a brother because "the weight, stress, and anxiety that was brought upon me as a pledge has been lifted and transferred to the new pledges." But Jake's class still had to follow "BN" commands from older brothers. At mixers, brothers would command, "BN: Drink this!" or "BN: Set up the beer pong table!" Jake was unfazed because he was so pleased that the brothers were including his class in committees and training them for future leadership roles.

These opportunities included participating in hazing the new class. Inspired, Jake volunteered to play a part: "conductor," one of the guys at EP who awakened the sleeping pledges by flashlight, hooded them, and dragged them upstairs. He learned that just before the ritual began, the brothers planned which pledges would get "extra hazed," which Jake hadn't experienced as a pledge because the brothers didn't think he could handle it. For certain pledges' rituals, brothers were naked, wagging their penises at the pledge when the pillowcase was raised. Sometimes they even smacked the pledge on the crotch.

During Jake's first overnight ritual as a brother, he and the other conductors were instructed to mess with a few of the pledges, shoving them around while they were blind beneath the pillowcase. They were lenient with Will, an obedient pledge who reminded Jake of his former self; Will had diligently copied every word of the pledge book by hand in a composition notebook, to better memorize the information. When Will's conductors forgot to put the pillowcase on him before they ran him down the hall, Will put it on himself.

For Austin, Jake's team took a different approach: After they hooded him, they stuck him alone in a dark closet for two minutes. When they ran him down the hallway, they spun him around eight times instead of the recommended three, until he was falling-down dizzy. When they dragged him up and down the stairs, Jake purposely didn't tell him when to step, so that he tripped several times along the way.

"I feel like a really fucked-up version of Santa. I decide who's naughty and nice and then deliver swift justice through these hazings. I feel really bad saying this," Jake told me. "I have my limits as to what I'm comfortable making other people do. I'll participate in some of these hazings mainly because I know the outcome and that they won't get hurt, but I'm not going to force them to drink. I don't think I've got it in me to do that. I try to draw a line somewhere."

"Do you feel you've changed?" I asked Jake.

"Yeah, I'd say so. The whole pledge process really scared me shitless at points. So this semester, at first I didn't want to see anyone go through the stuff I had to. But then I heard about what the older brothers went through, which was a lot worse, and with even more forced drinking. I figured the pledges are going to recover from this," Jake said. "What's changed my view is I've learned to trust that the brothers don't go too far with anything they do to these pledges. Like at Bid Dinner, a brother announced beforehand, 'Let's make sure we don't send any of these guys to the hospital. Really control what you make them do.'"

I asked Jake what he now thought about the EP overnight ritual that he'd so despised as a pledge.

"Looking back, it was a real pain to lie on the floor for that long. However, when I'm doing this with my class and helping Z out, it's just something we all laugh off. We think they can take it because we took it in the past. That goes along with a lot of things that've happened this semester. We don't consider this something bad, because we all had to deal with it, too. Every single class before them had to do the same thing. It's tried and true. Also, Z makes sure there's no risk for anyone getting hurt. All that happens is they get scared. He's a mature guy who just wants them to get that excitement from the pledging process, not anything that could damage them forever. It's funny thinking how much I've changed since the summer, when I was basically deathly afraid of even the word *hazing*."

While Jake didn't force the pledges to drink, other brothers did, at tailgates, mixers, Spring Stripper Night, and throughout Hell Week. Several pledges drank until they vomited. During Hell Week, the brothers hazed the spring class worse than they had hazed Jake's class. Jake was part of the team that woke up the pledges before six one morning for an extra hazing activity.

Near the end of pledge period, Jake broke his vow of being "the nice brother"—and felt guilty about it afterward. At a mixer at another fraternity house, he ordered a pledge to pile two plates high with chicken wings and bring them back to the Zeta Kappa house. As the pledge carefully attempted to balance the plates on the long walk without spilling them in the snow, Jake taunted him— "Hurry up, you're too slow!"—forced him to take a long, unnecessary detour around the back of the house, teasingly swung the door closed a few times before letting him inside, and heckled him as he attempted to maneuver upstairs, carrying the heavy load to the Great Room.

After Jake dismissed the pledge, Greg, who was hanging out with a few brothers in the Great Room, told Jake, "You know, you could have used my car."

"Yeah! I completely knew that!" Jake said.

"Hey, man, I'm proud of you," Greg told him.

"Why'd you do it?" I asked Jake when he recounted this.

"I just thought it was funny and would be something funny for the brothers to see. I took advantage of the rules."

"What'd you think about it later?" I asked.

"Later that night in bed—that's when I think about everything that went on during the day—I felt like, *Aw, man, I've really changed.* I thought, *Oh wow, maybe I* am *turning into a dick.*"

Ω Ω Ω

PhiEp annually held a ceremony in the Formal Room, where the seniors gave speeches about their fraternity experiences and handed down fraternity relics to their Littles. Each senior talked about the significance of the object or about the person to whom he was passing it down. Some of the speeches were serious, others funny. At the end of the ceremony, Diego stood up on a storage table, and the room hushed. Perhaps more than any other senior, Diego had the brothers' unwavering respect and admiration. He no longer had a Little; his Littles had been ROTC like him and had ended up leaving the house. Diego talked about his hope that the chapter would keep "moving forward in a positive direction" and how happy he was to have been a part of it. "We can't be complacent. We can't just sit here and be neutral, because being neutral is the same as going backward," he said. "We need to be constantly working to better ourselves in every aspect of life."

The room snapped in agreement, but Diego wasn't finished. "I have one more thing. Oliver, can you come up here for a minute?" Oliver joined him on the table. Diego slung an arm around his shoulder. "At a time when not a lot of people wanted to lead, Oliver stepped up, and without any leadership experience, he had the balls to take it on anyways," Diego said. "I just wanted to point out how great a job he's doing and how people should strive to follow his example. He's going after it, he's dedicated, and he's hardworking. Oliver's ability not only to take on the presidency at such a young age and with no experience but to do it successfully is very impressive." Diego hugged him and presented Oliver with a book about leadership skills from the military perspective. Hearing such kind words from a role model inspired Oliver beyond measure.

Oliver's first national fraternity conference, the annual spring meeting of PhiEp national and chapter officers and alumni, was an epiphany. At school, Oliver constantly berated himself because he believed his chapter wasn't meeting his standards: the Carnival debacle, the apathy, the party violations. But the longer he sat through conference meetings and breakout sessions and talked to fraternity officers, the more he realized that his chapter was relatively progressive.

The lecturers spent a surprising amount of time explaining what was to Oliver basic information about how to have a successful fraternity, how to motivate people, and what sexual assault was and how to reduce risks. Many of the students in attendance seemed never to have seen (or paid attention to) a presentation about sexual assault, which in Oliver's chapter was mandatory. The risk-management ideas that seemed so cutting-edge to the audience, most of whom were asking questions that Oliver thought chapter presidents should already know the answers to, were protocols that Oliver's chapter had instituted years ago.

Even when the conference presenters lectured about leadership skills (what makes a good leader, "how to get people behind you"), information that seemed revelatory to other audience members was business as usual to Oliver. The presenters explained, for example, the idea of "motivating the middle."

"There are going to be workhorses, that small margin of people who are always ready to work, and then there will be the lazy guys who won't do anything," they told the audience. "Find the guys who are teetering on the edge, motivate them to do better, and bring them over to the workhorse side of things." Oliver had done all that and more, using his designated advocate strategy.

Oliver told me, "It was eye-opening because everything at the conference was new information to these guys. That's all basic stuff we cover in a week. A lot of issues in fraternities happen because people aren't prepared. It's very easy to be prepared."

In one session, a fraternity officer asked what to do if a party got out of hand. Oliver shared his chapter's "sober brothers" protocol. Other students were astonished that the State U chapter required certain brothers to be sober for the night. "Whoa, it's crazy that you guys do that!" one guy said.

As Oliver socialized with the attendees, he gleaned that the trouble his chapter had gotten into this year was nothing compared to what some other PhiEps had experienced. "The other presidents are all great guys, but they have a different culture than we do," he told me.

Oliver was taken aback to learn that even the concept of a mandatory annual philanthropy event was apparently new to most of the chapters. "Some of the other chapters had their own events, but our Carnival was still more successful than most if not all the other chapters'. So when I thought it had failed this year, I was harder on myself than Nationals would have been on me," he told me.

After a cocktail hour on the final night of the conference, Oliver sat at a ballroom table with Geoff and a few members of the State U Alumni Board at the black-tie dinner and awards ceremony. As the national president announced the smaller awards (Best Philanthropy, Most Improved Chapter), Oliver reflected on his tenure. He believed he had prodded his chapter further in the right direction. Their average GPA was above 3.5, first place among all State U fraternities. They had had no problems since the "pee" incident. Javier was sober and stable. Wyatt, the pledge plagued by anxiety, was now a happy, more confident PhiEp. And even Oliver had become better at asking his brothers for help and opening up to them about his uncertainties.

Although Oliver had set it as his reach goal, he didn't expect to win the award for Most Outstanding Chapter. There were other competitive PhiEp chapters, and some that had restarted successfully. Oliver was, in his opinion, too young and inexperienced a leader to bring home the award, but he was proud of the work he had done. His chapter continued to buck trends because, he said later, "We want to pave our own path and do the right thing and not just be another fraternity, but a strong, beneficial part of the Greek community."

Oliver recalled a recent conversation with an alum in which he brought up the period when the chapter was shut down. The alum had told him their chapter would "either be thriving and not like a stereotypical fraternity, or you will be shut down." Oliver had half joked, "Or we could just foster a group of very average guys." He was surprised at the intensity of the alum's response: "No way. That's not what we do here. Average is not something we find acceptable." The Alumni Board's outlook, Oliver told me, "circles back to: If we're not embodying the values we hold so dear, then the board does not feel comfortable having us running a fraternity. And that makes sense to me. It keeps everyone on their best behavior, developing as people. And it works."

The announcer paused. "The award for Most Outstanding Chapter . . . State University chapter."

As the alumni at the table clapped him on the back, Oliver, stunned, grabbed Geoff to walk together to the podium to receive the plaque. *Holy shit,* Oliver thought among the cheers, *this was my first real leadership experience, and I just achieved my biggest goal.* He sent a photo of the plaque to the chapter's group text. Word spread quickly; within a minute, Trey called to congratulate him.

At the first opportunity, Oliver and Geoff went to the bathroom.

As soon as they were sure they were alone, they whooped. "Nice!" Oliver yelled. "We fucking did it!" Geoff shouted. They high-fived and hollered for a while before emerging from the bathroom once again cool and collected.

The national officers did not give any speeches about the award winners. There were no press releases or explanations in the fraternity magazine. Did the State U chapter win because its members had overcome challenges? Because the protocols they considered standard were advanced compared to chapters in other parts of the country? Oliver didn't know. The officers never told him. But there was one particular moment, which happened shortly after he returned to State U, that made him think his chapter deserved the award without question.

One night, in the middle of a house party where Oliver was the sober exec, two freshmen came to him to report an issue: One of their pledge brothers and a freshman girl, both wasted, had just gone upstairs to the sleeping porch. "This guy was just trying to hook up with a girl in the porch, and they were both way too drunk. And he was generally being a douche," one freshman explained. The freshmen had rounded up every pledge brother at the party to intervene as a unit. While one boy told the girl he was going to walk her home, another, with a backup, said to the drunk guy, "Hey, dude? You can't do this."

Oliver listened to the freshmen carefully. Because the girl was a non-Greek from the dorms and had come to the party alone, she didn't have anyone looking out for her. (He explained to me, "When people from the dorms come over, they think it's going to be exactly like the stereotypes and then end up being the ones binge-drinking.") He told the freshmen they had taken care of everything that needed to be done that night and that he would talk to the guy in the morning. The freshman would not remain in the fraternity.

It was in this moment, not at the awards ceremony, when Oliver realized the value of the leadership experience he had gained in PhiEp. He had learned the power of communication, the effectiveness of humor, and the importance of compassion. And his charges had listened. The freshmen had averted a potential crisis safely and discreetly. To Oliver, this meant that Phi Epsilon had successfully trained the new pledge class about the dangers of sexual assault, risks that could lead to it, and how to prevent it from happening. Under Oliver's reign, there had been zero sexual assaults by members of their chapter and, as far as Oliver knew, not even a hint of disrespect toward women. The newest class of Apple Pie Boys had stayed true to their gentlemanly fraternity values. The future was bright. Oliver couldn't have been prouder.

Ω Ω Ω

The night of the Alpha Rho mixer, one night after Zeta Kappa's spring initiation, Jake started drinking early to boost his confidence in case he ran into Laura. He planned to apologize for not hooking up with her the night he didn't want to jeopardize his chances with Beth. *That was a mistake,* he thought now. He wanted to ask Laura for a second chance. In the Zeta Kappa house, he searched for her in room after room.

He had been on plenty of dates this semester, nearly all of them set up by his brothers, but not with anyone he wanted to pursue. At one mixer, a brother set him up with a hot sorority sister whom brothers told him he had hooked up with on the bus. Jake didn't remember, because he had blacked out from the SoCo with which he had overfilled his thermos. (Although he threw up several times while blacked out, he told me later that he would continue to drink Southern Comfort because "It's the family drink, so I have to be able to drink that.")

He liked the sister and might have seen her again, except for what Andy told him the next day: "Hey, if you'd had sex with her, we could have been Eskimo bros!" Jake had to ask him what that meant. Because the sister had been Andy's "slam"—they had slept together many times—if Jake had sex with her, then he and Andy would bond by having shared "the same igloo." It turned out the girl supposedly had also had sex with at least 10 other Zeta Kappas, including one of Jake's pledge brothers, who had taken her home and slept with her the night Jake blacked out.

This turned Jake off. "I don't want to take anyone on a date anymore who has gotten with so many guys from my own fraternity!" he told me later. "It's been weird enough to be with girls who have done it with our guys right on that very bus sometimes. The whole concept of an Eskimo bro is very weird for me. I haven't even had sex with anyone!"

Yet when Jake hooked up with girls he chose on his own, the brothers disapproved. One girl was sweet, friendly, attractive—and not a stick figure like many of her sorority sisters. (She was perhaps a size eight or ten.) But the brothers told Jake she was a whale. On another night, Jake drunkenly hooked up with a nice sorority sister. The next day, Andy posted on the chapter Facebook page, tagging both Jake and Jake's Big, as if Jake were casting shame on the family, **Heard you got with a fatty last night. Tell me that's not true, Jake.** Caught in front of an online audience and trying to spin the narrative into "something funny," Jake replied in the affirmative with a fat joke.

Jake, Andy wrote back. **Come on, man. You deserve better.**

"That's how you justify it. You think whales are below the standard of the brotherhood. It's very objectifying," Jake told me. "The way our chapter ranks girls and sororities is purely based on looks, which sucks. A lot of the guys can be very picky."

"Picky or mean?" I asked.

"Yes," he said. "It comes up a lot. It's terrible. In our own Fall '17 group chat, guys post profile pics of girls who aren't good-looking, and the guys make the rudest comments, calling them whales, saying a guy is 'out harpooning.' Sometimes they're potential dates for sorority mixers. Even if a girl is mildly round and it's not even that noticeable, they'll still be chalked up as a whale. The brothers will say they don't want 'fat bitches' in our house. That's how they make sure we all think we're better than getting whales."

"Does the brothers' judgment matter to you?"

"It's had some effect on me, but I still consider myself to be very lenient."

I read Jake something he told me after his first Bid Dinner back in the fall: "Hopefully through this I don't turn out to be some guy who judges girls on their looks. That's just not me."

For a moment, Jake was quiet. This was the first time I had called him out on one of his direct quotes. "So back then, yeah, I think I definitely went too far vowing never to judge a girl by their looks. The sad truth is you judge everyone by their looks," he said. "I still believe character counts, especially if they have a great sense of humor and are really chill. But it isn't true to say I don't judge girls by their looks. Maybe I was trying to be a white knight back then."

"Okay, what if you meet a chill girl with a great character and a similar sense of humor whom you know your brothers would call a whale? Would you be less likely to ask her out?"

He said yes. "If I bring someone like that, I'll get looks from other guys as soon as I get in the house. I will get made fun of. They'll classify her as a whale based solely on her looks. They'll talk to me about it the next day. It's sad, but it's just the atmosphere of the fraternity to judge first on looks."

I switched gears. "Do you think you're in a better place having gone through the fraternity?"

"Yeah, I'd say so, after the process of becoming a brother. When

I started off at TC, I was a 'geed,' a 'goddamn independent.' I was skeptical about the Greek system, and thought it was filled with bros and jocks who just want to roofie girls' drinks all the time."

"Are you a better person?"

"Yes. The fraternity has given me a lot to be involved with around campus. On a more personal level, it's made me into a more confident person. Greek life has introduced me to some brothers who are genuinely some of the most motivated, involved, and sometimes the most intelligent guys I've come to know. That's an experience, getting to know every single one of them and what I can take from them," Jake said. "But that does come with a change from what I considered myself to be before I joined."

"A positive or negative change?"

"Back then, I was considered very polite and quiet, a guy who wouldn't want to offend anyone. You become a better speaker and someone who's a lot more extroverted. But now I'm not like the completely polite guy anymore. It's like you become very outgoing, and that in itself has its pros and cons in any situation."

Jake was in the Great Room when he saw Laura walk in the front door with three sisters. After all the thought and preparation that had gone into this moment with a sorority sister he had genuinely liked for months, Jake did what came to him naturally: He panicked. *Oh shit, oh shit,* he thought, running away. Upstairs, a sophomore brother caught him in the hall. "Yo, dude. What's going on?"

Jake filled him in. "And now, oh my God, Laura's here. I don't know what to do, I don't know what to do!" Jake said. "I'm only one drink in, and I'm not ready enough."

The sophomore grabbed Jake by the shoulders and looked him squarely in the eyes. "Look, man. You're a fucking stallion. You did this before, you can do this again. Just go up and talk to her. You can do this."

"Okay. You're right," Jake said. Pumped from the pep talk, he returned downstairs, but Laura was gone. Dismayed, he squeezed through crowds of people packed in the narrow halls and common areas, drinking as he hunted for her. *I need to consume as much alcohol as possible so I can at least bear my own conversation skills,* he told himself. He couldn't find her anywhere.

He navigated the stairways for half an hour until he decided to go to the sleeping porch to catch his breath. That's where he found her, chatting with some of her sisters. *I don't know if I can do this,* he thought, and then: *Why the hell not? I'm just going to go start a conversation.* He walked up to her circle. "You guys got the right idea being up here where it's a lot cooler than when you're downstairs with 50 people crammed in a hallway," he said. The girls engaged. They talked as a group until a brother came upstairs and redirected Laura's friends toward a separate conversation, leaving Laura and Jake alone.

When Laura's friends went downstairs, Laura didn't join them. Jake and Laura spent the rest of the mixer walking around together, drinking and talking. At one point, a senior made eye contact with Jake, gave him a large bottle of beer, and said, "Hey, man, keep it." ("I think he knew I was trying to score with her, so he probably wanted to help me with that," Jake told me later.) Jake and Laura shared swigs from the bottle. When Jake saw Matthew, his youngest pledge brother, making out with a girl—Matthew's first kiss, Jake knew—Jake took a picture of the couple kissing and posted it on the fraternity Facebook page with a thumbs-up.

Back in the Great Room, a brother played "Piano Man" on the guitar while onlookers sang along. "We gotta sway with each other!" Laura said. At the end of the song, Jake and Laura looked at each other, laughing. Their eyes locked. *I have that feeling that I want to kiss you, but I don't know if you want to kiss me, but I can kind of sense it,* Jake thought. They leaned in at the same time. They made out for the rest of the night.

When the house started to empty out, Jake said to her, "Hey, listen, I really enjoyed tonight with you. It's been really fun. I wanted to ask . . . Did you want to do anything else with me tonight?"

"Well, my roommate is in her boyfriend's room tonight," she said.

"Well, is she now? How convenient," Jake said, thinking, *This is a sign from above.*

In Laura's room, they got naked quickly, even as they began to sober up. After a while, Jake asked, "Do you want to have sex?"

"No, I'm really sorry, but I'm saving that for someone who I really love," Laura said.

"Okay, I respect that. I do have a condom, though," Jake said.

"No, I'm really sorry. But I can do other things," she said, and gave him his first blow job.

When she finished, he returned the favor (his first time, too), until she whispered, "You said you had a condom, right?"

"I'm a virgin," Jake admitted.

"Me, too," she said. And then they both were not.

The next morning, after he left her room, Jake wrote in the Fall '17 group chat, I like sex.

Immediately, the "Likes" multiplied. The comment thread snaked. **FRAT DADDY**, his pledge brothers wrote. Word spread from there. As soon as he got to the house, brothers congratulated him and patted him on the back. He was watching a beer pong game when Eric loudly proclaimed in front of a coed group of onlookers, "I would just like to mention how proud I am of my man Jake here for finally doing it."

Jake sheepishly ducked his head. Another brother said, "Yo, as soon as you're done with that beer, I'm getting you another one to congratulate you."

When Victor and Andy heard the news, they took Jake aside and pulled up Laura's Facebook profile to see what she looked like. Andy appraised the photo and gave Jake a thumbs-up. "Proud of you, man," Andy said.

Jake basked in his Grand-Big's validation. "Getting that recognition from him was such an amazing feeling. It made me feel very important, like I've finally achieved his approval. He was hard on me before [about hooking up with a non-skinny girl] because he knew I could be better," Jake told me. "Now it feels like I finally joined the club. Now I've had that experience of having sex for the first time, its own rite of passage. So socially, I feel more on equal footing with the rest of the fraternity."

Jake reflected on how drastically his attitude toward hookups, relationships, and girls had changed since the fall. "Remember how I used to be like, 'I don't want a relationship with someone in a sorority'? I thought I'd get a relationship with someone in my class instead," he told me. "But you know what, it turns out the opposite has happened. I've had more luck with frat parties than I have in class. My opinion changed completely about girls in sororities and forming relationships. A lot of people in Greek life do that, just hook up at a mixer without going on a date first. It's not a big deal anymore. I used to be against a lot of that—meeting girls at mixers and hooking up, thinking there's no possible way you can consider there to be any consent if they're drunk. But I'm finally used to that life. As long as there's consent, I think it's fine."

Jake sounded lighter, giddy, relieved. He sighed happily. "It felt really good to get that all out of the way before the year ended. It finally felt like it's paid off, being in a fraternity."

"Why?" I asked.

"Because I lost my virginity."

Much of that conversation would have stunned anyone who had known Jake before college. After spring finals, though, Jake delivered even more surprising news. He had not heard from Laura again, though he'd tried to ask her out. When they'd attended the same party, she avoided him. So he went out with the girl who'd supposedly slept with at least 10 Z-Kaps. "Now I'm an Eskimo bro!" he told me, laughing. "And she used to be Andy's slam! I couldn't stop thinking about him as I was fucking her, which was annoying. I'm Eskimo bros with like 10 guys in the fraternity. It's still weird, it's a big deal. But I try to play it off as if it isn't."

How to Find a Healthy Chapter That's the Right Fit

Was it fair to end Jake's story with the last lines of our final interview of the academic year? I asked myself this question many times. Jake was conflicted about becoming an Eskimo bro, but he was so worried about how his brothers perceived him that he pretended that he wasn't. And he was happy with his fraternity experience for reasons other than sex. He found the friends, confidence, and sense of belonging he had craved during his first days of college. Months later, after the hard-core seniors had graduated, Jake would initiate discussions with his pledge class about how to make the chapter's culture less "frat bro." When we chatted, on the phone or over meals, I could still hear the sweet, earnest boy he was before he arrived at Town College.

But fraternity life had changed him, and he was self-aware enough to know it. Because his attitude toward several issues had shifted, when he was in the fraternity bubble he didn't always seem like that sweet, earnest boy: He hazed pledges, felt superior to freshmen his age in the newer pledge class, drank "one sip short of alcohol poisoning" (his words), and made a fat joke about a girl he'd hooked up with. His story sometimes felt like a mild early-season *Breaking Bad* arc, fraternity style. He did and said things that would have horrified him before he joined Zeta Kappa. Did it matter that he displayed these behaviors less often than some of his brothers and that he felt conflicted about what he did? Did it redeem him if he acted like a different person outside the fraternity than when he was in it?

When I read Jake his quote from the fall about not judging girls by their looks, he said, "I like these conversations because this is what I use to reflect on how things are going in my life. When you're in a fraternity, it's like an echo chamber. You kind of get lost in the opinions that encompass the entire house. But these questions you ask make me think about what I said a year ago and if it's still true." He thought to himself for a moment and then admitted, "But I've changed as a person."

That's one of the dangers of fraternities, the echo chamber that can cause a good guy to do, say, or condone things he normally wouldn't. It underscores the difference between Oliver's Phi-Eps, who valued individuality and urged gentlemanly behavior, and Jake's Zeta Kappas, whose primary mission was to improve their tier.

Fortunately, many of the brothers I interviewed belonged to chapters that seemed more like Oliver's than Jake's, healthy communities that emphasized friendship and acceptance. Oliver became more responsible, more confident, and more of a leader because of his fraternity experience. Kirk became more open-minded. Teddy found a supportive second family. Ben created one. In truth, fraternity culture is more nuanced than "good versus bad." Jake's fraternity gave members some positive opportunities (e.g., Compass

Confessions) to confide in one another, receive comfort, and form solid friendships. And even "good" fraternities such as Oliver's can make mistakes that could lead to negative outcomes.

Also, chapters can change. A former national leadership consultant told me that his fraternity's former CEO liked to compare fraternities to chain restaurants. "If fraternities were a franchise, they'd be the worst franchise in the world. You're dealing exclusively with 18- to 22-year-old men, and as soon as they're educated and know the rules, they graduate, and then you've got a new crop of young men who know nothing and make the same mistakes," he said.

At a Massachusetts school, a brother made it his mission to improve his chapter's culture. A gay student in a house that hosted an annual kinky stripper event, he wanted the fraternity to be a welcoming space in which "my queer and female friends are treated with respect and dignity." He had daily conversations with brothers about his vision, insisted that forced drinking and strippers were damaging to the brothers and the chapter, found allies in the house, and took on leadership roles. The chapter's hazing activities, which were mostly of the answer-questions-wrong-chug-this variety, "weren't safe and created larger issues, drinking issues that made people quit their sports teams and think partying and drinking was everything," he said. "I stood in front of a room of 60 guys bigger and stronger than me and said, 'This is wrong. It's going to get us in trouble. It clearly messes with kids, and we shouldn't force people to do it.'"

Eventually, he and his friends successfully eliminated the entire pledge process and replaced the stripper event with a casino field trip. "I pushed harder and harder, and opinions changed. Parties became less about binge-drinking and getting the hottest girls and more about having a cooler event. I was so proud I was able to do that. I had to be confident in myself and tell them this is what's going to happen and why it should happen."

Vastly different chapter cultures can exist on the same campus. A midwestern university hosts a welcoming NIC chapter that's 25 percent nonwhite on a campus that's 88 percent white. The percentage of gay, bi, and transgender members ranges from 10 to 30 percent depending on the semester; the chapter makes accommodations to make sure these brothers are comfortable. This brotherhood also has the highest fraternity GPA on campus, wins school social events, and facilitates in-house trainings on gender identity and transgender vocabulary. But another chapter just across the street screams racial and homophobic slurs at its members.

We have to assume that, given their powerful presence and popularity among students, fraternities aren't going anywhere anytime soon. The variables are what parents can do to guide their children through the experience and what educators and fraternities will do to make the environment safer. The most important measures that parents and students can take are to communicate and gather information. I hope this book will make it easier for families to have these discussions.

But how do you distinguish one chapter from another if you're not already part of the system? Some schools are better than others at honestly supplying easily accessible, thorough information. Rider University's website, for example, offers details about each chapter's policies and violations, successes, risk-reduction measures, and relevant statistics.

To get a sense of overall campus culture, families can read through a school's annual security report. Updated every October and available on university websites, the report lists campus crime statistics, efforts taken to improve campus safety, and policy statements about issues, including alcohol/drug incidents and the prevention of/response to sexual assault. As part of the report, each school's required biennial review, which covers alcohol and drug use, "gives a sense of the party culture," said Alison Kiss, executive director of the Clery Center, which helps schools improve campus safety. "It should also list a number of resources for students who aren't partiers. Do they keep their gym lit later? Do they list alternatives to drinking to let you know there's a social life outside of the party culture?"

Kiss cautioned parents and students that schools reporting zero sexual assaults or alcohol violations might not necessarily be safer than other campuses. "I would look deeper into the schools reporting violations to see if they have policies and services for their students, because they're actually talking about it. There's not a culture of silence. At the colleges that aren't reporting, we most often see they're not talking about it, so students don't know where to get help and report."

Colleges and universities must do a better job of providing this information to parents, students, and prospective students. As my researcher and I found, this data gathering is tedious, but it is worthwhile. We found helpful information when we compiled every publicly available online report of historically white national fraternity hazing, racism, sexual assault and harassment, violence, alcohol or drug abuse, deaths, and other red flags that we could find between the 2010/11 and 2017/18 academic years.* For example, Alpha Delta Gamma, Phi Lambda Chi, Phi Mu Delta, and Tau Delta Phi—small national fraternities—have had very few incidents in the 2010s. Some larger fraternities, such as Pi Lambda Phi (which does not have a history of excluding minorities) and Sigma Tau Gamma, have had relatively few incidents for their size.

The biggest surprise in our research was that although the seemingly relentless barrage of media headlines suggests that fraternities are spiraling out of control, the number of incidents has actually

---

* Not all incidents are publicly reported, of course, and some schools and fraternities might have more incidents than others due to higher membership numbers or more thorough campus reporting protocols.

been declining since 2016. It is hard to say whether the decrease is attributable to greater university or national officers' vigilance, an upsurge in social media evidence (and the accompanying public outcry) that pressures schools or Nationals to shut down offending chapters, or, one would hope, a general improvement in the behavior of many fraternity brothers and the sense of accountability they convey to new members. In any case, it is an encouraging development.

This direction could continue if schools step up their authority over Greek organizations; many chapters don't have consistent oversight by fraternity adults. Universities typically have trained on-site personnel who are qualified to manage college students. Fraternities do not. National officers aren't necessarily educators, and advisors I spoke with couldn't recall required training sessions or prerequisites for the role.

Good boys shouldn't feel they have to fight against a system to stay good. And as an Ohio chapter advisor told me, "As college students evolve, and we see more international, first-generation, and 'nontraditional-age' students coming to our campuses, the very notion of tradition, a hallmark of fraternities and sororities, is up for debate." If fraternities wish to thrive, and to provide the kind of safer, healthier spaces that would make them a more positive contributor to campus culture rather than a potential danger, then they must evolve as well.

Advice for Parents and Students

Here are some more ideas to increase the likelihood that students will have a healthy Greek experience. (For additional tips, as well as advice for educators and fraternity adults, please visit www.Alexan draRobbins.com.)

For Parents and College Applicants/Students Considering Greek Life

Visit Campus on a Party Night

Faculty advisor Nathan Holic suggested that prospective students and their parents assess campus safety in person on a party night. "What is the alcohol culture like? If the campus community feels safe, I'd feel comfortable about my sons joining any student organizations they found worthwhile. If there are real issues with alcohol at that campus, it's a good bet that fraternities will share that issue."

Ask Culturally Based or Gay/Bi/Trans/Progressive Chapters Their Opinion

If you plan to rush NIC chapters, you might get a sense of their character by talking to a member of a multicultural or gay/bi/trans/ progressive chapter. A southern Delta Lambda Phi brother mentioned that on his campus, "ATO was super sweet about accepting our pronouns and making sure others use them." That acceptance could be a clue that a chapter doesn't promote dangerous hypermasculine standards.

Look for Signs of Healthy or Unhealthy Chapters

First, check the college website to make sure the fraternities a student is considering are actually recognized by the school; if they haven't agreed to campus rules, they might no longer be recognized, a potential red flag. Brothers I interviewed also suggest that recruits look for these signs:

- "Do they make an effort for the university they are representing? Do they attend the football games or just leave after getting plastered at tailgates?"—a Texas brother
- "If chapters have parents or family days, that's a good sign."—a Pennsylvania alum
- "Look at the physical house's condition. There are some things fraternities can't change financially, but if the house isn't clean and if you can tell that no one cares, that could indicate that people aren't responsible."—Oregon recruitment chair
- "At schools where rush is shorter, cues about whether the chapter hazes could include the language that brothers use to talk about women, and how 'cool' the fraternity is."—an Illinois brother
- "Talk to service, philanthropy, and scholarship chairs to see whether they're passionate about those areas to determine if a fraternity is more than a drinking club."—a Maryland alum
- "Do they accomplish the little things: Do they hold the door for women? Do they ensure that everyone is safe at a party? I believe being a gentleman is something every fraternity man should strive for. I wouldn't want to be a part of a chapter where that culture isn't present."—the Texas brother

Ask the School What Kinds of Rules and Oversight It Has for Its Greek System

Parents might feel better sending their kids into systems that are heavily regulated by the school rather than left to the supervision of off-site national officers. In 2015, for example, Dartmouth banned hard alcohol on campus, eliminated the pledge period for all Greeks, postponed recruitment, required a male and a female active faculty advisor, and mandated that chapters use at least 15 percent of their social/programming budget for financial aid. Since Dartmouth enacted these reforms, only one national fraternity chapter there has committed a publicly reported infraction at the time of this writing.

Inquire About a Fraternity's Record

Many schools aren't as forthcoming about Greek infractions as they should be. Parents can call the office of Greek life or student life, the dean, or the IFC advisor for information about a fraternity's record. But even if a fraternity has a good record, it doesn't necessarily promote a healthy culture; this step is just a starting point.

The culture of a chapter can change by semester, but schools with several different fraternities committing gross violations year after year might indicate a broader campus cultural issue. And it's possible for a fraternity to continue operating even if it has had several recent infractions.

Ask Substantive Questions at Recruitment

Brothers offered these suggestions:

- "If there's one intrinsic quality this group places above all others, what would it be? You'd hope for similar answers from the lot. And I'd like to know what brothers are doing outside of fraternity activities. You'd want to make sure that brothers have lives outside of the group, that their identities aren't completely predicated on their fraternity life."—a Michigan brother
- "'What are your favorite school events?' There's no point in joining a fraternity with members that aren't involved with the school. If they say, 'The party we throw in the spring is pretty sick,' then you'll know that chapter isn't involved with the university and the university probably doesn't like them."—a Texas brother

- "Did you always want to go Greek? Why did you rush?"—a Washington State brother
- "What does brotherhood mean to you?" "What opportunities are there for new members?"—a recent Pennsylvania alum
- " 'What's your favorite sorority and why?' Sororities have reputations just as fraternities do, and knowing their favorite one will give you an idea of who they are as a chapter and what their values are."—the Texas brother

Consider Rushing Later

"If parents are really concerned about hazing, they should encourage their sons to rush as sophomores. Sophomores are more likely to know what to expect from pledging, because they're better friends with the kids, and often aren't hazed as much as freshmen."—an Illinois brother said. Also, because sophomores are more likely to know members, they might have a better sense of a chapter's priorities.

Ask Brothers the Difference Between Service and Philanthropy

"Every chapter is going to make a great sales pitch about philanthropy during Rush Week, but the fraternity whose members can actually tell you the difference between service and philanthropy is probably the one you want your son to join. Not every group will get their hands dirty with real service or mentoring projects. Service and dedication to one's community is the only real way for fraternities to survive this century; a bunch of young men working together to make their communities a better place," said Nathan Holic, author of *American Fraternity Man,* a fictionalized take on the role of a leadership consultant.

For Fraternity Actives

Take Easy Steps to Make Parties Safer

Here are some small changes fraternities can make that can have a big impact: Provide water, nonalcoholic beverages, and food alongside the usual drinks; students who want to limit their alcohol consumption can hold a Solo cup of ginger ale without people knowing the difference. Get a coatrack and keep it by the front door so women don't have to drunkenly search for their jackets in bedrooms. Offer a quieter common area near the main party space for people to have conversations away from the music without having to go to a bedroom. And take sober monitors/brother roles seriously.

Ignore the Tier System

Your tier shouldn't affect the quality of your brotherhood. Many Greeks told me they hate the system but feel they have no choice but to cater to the rankings. But you do have a choice. You have the choice to prioritize the quality of your brotherhood over superficial labels—and you'll be happier for it.

Partner with Non-NIC Fraternities and Other Organizations

Inviting culturally based, LGBTQ, academically focused, and other groups to partner in an activity both exposes members to different views and increases the fraternity's visibility on campus. Participating in LGBTQ ally programs can also help men broaden their ideas of gender identity and feel less pressure about their own masculinity.

Adjust the Living Space

A recent study found that simply moving furniture around helped fraternity brothers think differently about their living space. When certain rooms were designated as study spaces and outfitted with large tables that brothers could easily reconfigure to work individually or collaboratively, students were happier and more focused on their academics.

Stop Following Tradition for Tradition's Sake

Let's be blunt: It's the twenty-first century. One of the worst rationales for doing something is "This is the way we've always done it." Greeks can do better than that.

Involve Parents

Welcome parents of recruits, pledges, and brothers. At least one fraternity has even invited fathers to join as "alumni initiates," with an initiation ritual and annual banquet. By getting parents as involved as possible, fraternities can increase both transparency and member engagement.

An Iowa fraternity hosts several "Moms'/Dads' Weekends," when parents tour the house with members and meet brothers. "We usually have meetings with our house director and staff where our parents can ask questions or bring up any concerns. It's really a great way to get them involved and make sure we're level-headed. Staying open and honest with parents about the chapter can go a long way," a brother said. "This weekend is our 'Moms' Day.' Our schedule includes a mother/son dance, optional wine-tasting event, tour through the campus garden, and a gift basket auction. The proceeds from that auction go to our philanthropic organization."

He suggests that parents ask questions such as "What can we do to stay up to date with the chapter?" "Can we create an email string for the parents that provides updates?" and "Are there more events we can create to visit and learn more about the chapter?"

Replace the Pledge Period with Community Service

The activities could still be challenging and bond new members, but without the danger. Actual community service, rather than fundraisers, requires more mental and/or physical strength than memorizing alumni bond numbers or doing forced shots—and is ultimately much more rewarding.

Increase the Role of Big Brothers

The *ASHE Higher Education Report* pointed out that the role of Bigs isn't formally structured. "Rarely, if at all, are these relationships used to introduce new members to academic resources, to engage new members in the values and purpose of the organization, to educate new members on ethical decision making, or to cultivate leadership skills. The existing composition of these types of relationships among collegiate members seems to be a missed opportunity for learning and personal development."

Exempt Members' Parents from Secrecy Rules

No fraternity oaths should prohibit members from being open with their parents about any aspect of their college lives.

Merge the Interfraternity Council (IFC) and Panhellenic Council (PHC)

Just as the BGLOs have a multigendered council, so, too, could the historically white Greek groups. If fraternities and sororities were governed together, the women would be more likely to have equal voices and the men would be more accountable for their behavior.

Be a Force for Good

Fraternities can reach boys in a way that other organizations and authority figures cannot, because they've established their bona fides as masculine peer authorities. Be real campus leaders: Use your fraternity's money and resources to support the groups and messaging that boys—in your chapter and outside it—so desperately need.

NOTES

Chapter 1: Joining: Why Go Greek?

12 *"a collapse in the American construction of masculinity"*: Leonard Sax, "Many Boys Today Define Masculinity Negatively," *New York Times,* December 21, 2015.

12 *the majority of high school dropouts are male:* See, for example, www .childtrends.org.

12 *American College Health Association survey:* American College Health Association National College Health Assessment, Spring 2017.

12 *It's not always easy for boys to make friends:* See, for example, Rhaina Cohen et al., "Guys, We Have a Problem: How American Masculinity Creates Lonely Men," *NPR: Hidden Brain,* March 19, 2018.

12 *Boys comprise 75 percent of 15- to 19-year olds who commit suicide:* At the time of this writing, the most recent US suicide statistics report 1,537 male suicides and 524 females. "QuickStats: Suicide Rates for Teens Aged 15–19 Years, by Sex—United States, 1975–2015," *Morbidity and Mortality Weekly Report,* 2017.

12 *a 50 percent increase in the number of new pledges:* Correspondence with NIC spokesperson Heather Matthews Kirk. Thank you to Ms. Kirk for responding to my many questions.

12 *about one million current undergraduate members:* Ibid.

12 *one out of every eight American students:* Caitlin Flanagan, "The Dark Power of Fraternities," *The Atlantic,* March 2014.

12 *more than nine million strong:* "Greek Life Statistics," The Fraternity Advisor, http://thefraternityadvisor.com/greek-life-statistics.

13 *Between 2005 and 2017, at least 72 boys died in fraternity-related incidents:* "Sigma Alpha Epsilon Deaths Most Among Frats," Bloomberg.com, December 30, 2013; Hank Nuwer, "Hazing Clearinghouse."

13 *it is specifically the fraternity experience that causes students to be more likely to rape:* See, for example, John Foubert, "'Rapebait' E-Mail Reveals Dark Side of Frat Culture," CNN.com, October 9, 2013.

13 *Even colleges that have had fraternity scandals don't necessarily see enrollment numbers dip:* For example, at the University of Pennsylvania in the fall of

2016, an unrecognized fraternity mass-mailed a sexually suggestive email to freshman girls. Outraged students plastered the campus with printouts of the email, captioned, "This is what rape culture looks like." At rush a few months later, recruitment numbers for IFC fraternities doubled. (Esha Indiani, "Fraternity Recruitment Reportedly Doubles," *Daily Pennsylvanian,* January 11, 2017.) Two years after reports surfaced that Dartmouth Sigma Alpha Epsilons allegedly forced pledges to "swim in a kiddie pool of vomit, urine, fecal matter, semen, and rotten food products; eat omelets made of vomit," and "chug cups of vinegar," the chapter reported that it "had attracted more new members in each of the past two years than in any of the previous five." (Tyler Kingkade, "SAE Dartmouth Chapter Looks More Popular Than Ever 2 Years After Hazing Allegations," *Huffington Post,* March 21, 2014.)

13 *According to the most recent American Freshman Survey:* Kevin Eagan et al., "The American Freshman: National Norms, Fall 2016," Cooperative Institutional Research Program at the Higher Education Research Institute at UCLA; J. Patrick Biddix et al., "The Influence of Fraternity and Sorority Involvement: A Critical Analysis of Research (1996–2013)," *ASHE Higher Education Report* (Jossey-Bass, 2014), hereafter *ASHE Higher Education Reports,* 2014.

13 *At DePauw University:* "Most Students in Fraternities," *U.S. News & World Report,* https://www.usnews.com/best-colleges/rankings/most-frats.

13 *at MIT:* MIT Office of the Provost, Institutional Research, Common Data Set, 2015–2016.

14 *Fraternities raised $20.3 million . . . male college population:* This is the NIC's most recent GPA statistic. NIC Fraternity Statistics, http://nicindy.org/press/fraternity-statistics/.

14 *Some black Greek-letter organizations (BGLOs) offer merit-based scholarships to members:* Correspondence with Kenneth R. Barnes, international executive director, Omega Psi Phi fraternity.

14 *36 Greek senators and 122 Greek representatives:* Correspondence with NIC spokesperson.

14 *Forty percent . . . since 1910:* Maria Konnikova, "18 U.S. Presidents Were in College Fraternities," *The Atlantic,* February 21, 2014.

14 *are members of black sororities or fraternities:* Alexandra Robbins, *Pledged: The Secret Lives of Sororities* (New York: Hachette, 2015).

14 *Martin Luther King Jr. and W. E. B. Du Bois:* See, for example, Rashawn Ray, "Fraternity Life at Predominantly White Universities in the United States: The Saliency of Race," *Ethnic and Racial Studies* 36, no. 2 (2013).

35 *Ben:* Interviews with the author.

36 *College in the 1700s . . . would not follow that path:* Bobby Lawrence McMinn, "A Content Analysis of the Esoteric Ritual Manuals of National College Social Fraternities for Men," Dissertation Abstracts International: Section A, Humanities and Social Sciences, 1979; Nicholas Syrett, *The Company He Keeps: A History of White College Fraternities* (Chapel Hill: University of North Carolina Press, 2009).

36 *At the turn of the eighteenth century . . . strict regimen:* Lisa Wade, "How American Colleges Became Bastions of Sex, Booze, and Entitlement," Time.com, January 6, 2017.

36 *The resulting uprisings . . . high expulsion rates:* Syrett.

36 *in 1806:* Alain Touraine, *The Academic System in American Society* (Abingdon, UK: Routledge, 2017).

36 *To deter . . . who accepted the protesters:* Syrett; Wade.

36 *seniors at Union College:* Syrett; https://www.ka.org. Phi Beta Kappa was technically the first Greek-letter college organization, but it was not a social fraternity. It began as a secret society in 1776 and, unlike the burgeoning literary societies, limited its membership and shrouded its activities in secrecy. The Yale PBK chapter, which allegedly conducted meetings in a building owned by Freemasons, was so mysterious to outsiders that, on four separate occasions, nonmembers broke into the office of the PBK secretary to steal documents. During the anti-Masonic fervor of the 1830s, PBK was stripped of its secrecy, and soon reemerged as the country's preeminent honor society. It is possible that the Union College students who formed Kappa Alpha were inspired by the school's PBK chapter; two of them were members. See, for example, http://www.sjsu.edu/getinvolved/frso/history/usfslhistory; and McMinn.

37 *Originally, students formed . . . speaking competitions:* Syrett.

37 *believed the names made them seem more elite:* Ibid.

37 *Their secret passwords, handshakes . . . Members were white and Protestant:* Syrett; McMinn.

37 *Fraternities' priorities . . . a disregard for college rules:* Syrett.

38 *unsuccessfully tried to shut them down:* Wade.

38 *By joining an organization . . . smoking, and profanity:* Syrett.

38 *After the Civil War . . . rank the fraternities by their wealth:* Ibid.

39 *In the early 1900s . . . Big Men on Campus:* Ibid.

39 *fraternities flourished even in Canada:* W. Stewart Wallace, ed., *The Encyclopedia of Canada*, vol. 2: *Toronto* (University Associates of Canada, 1948).

39 *11.74 percent:* Syrett.

39 *As networking . . . Catholics, and Jews:* Ibid.

39 *fraternity for women in 1870:* KappaAlphaTheta.org.

39 *The first Catholic fraternity:* See, for example, Jeff Yang, "Have Frat Boys Finally Jumped the Pop Culture Shark?", WSJ.com, March 8, 2013.

39 *first fraternity founded by Jewish students:* Marianna R. Sanua, "Jewish College Fraternities in the United States, 1895–1968: An Overview," *Journal of American Ethnic History* 19, no. 2 (Winter 2000).

39 *first Chinese fraternity:* Yang.

39 *first Latino fraternity:* https://www.phiota.org.

39 *Phi Mu Alpha Sinfonia:* https://www.sinfonia.org.

39 *Alpha Kappa Psi (1904) and Delta Sigma Pi (1907):* https://akpsi.org; https://www.deltasigmapi.org.

39 *Alpha Phi Alpha:* http://www.apa1906.net/history.

40 *didn't focus on women at all . . ."cloud of disgrace":* Syrett.

41 *"While their numbers . . . with fascination":* Beth Bailey, *From Front Porch to Back Seat: Courtship in Twentieth-Century America* (Baltimore, MD: Johns Hopkins University Press, 1989).

41 *The public considered fraternity:* Wade.

41 *"Rating and Dating Complex" . . . "black list of the fraternities":* Willard Waller, "The Rating and Dating Complex," *American Sociological Review* 2, no. 5 (October 1937).

41 *Brothers in the top-ranked . . . "a non-fraternity person":* J. K. Folsom, *The Family: Its Sociology and Social Psychiatry* (Oxford: Wiley, 1934).

42 *by what they were not (boys, feminine, gay), resisted:* Konnikova.

42 *continued their discriminatory policies . . . admit whites only:* Syrett.

42 *4.8 percent of male students:* Beth McMurtrie, "The Fraternity Problem," *Chronicle of Higher Education,* August 7, 2015.

42 *his Dartmouth fraternity days:* See, for example, Review of Chris Miller, *The Real Animal House: The Awesomely Depraved Saga of the Fraternity That Inspired the Movie—A Wildly Exaggerated Memoir, Kirkus Reviews,* November 1, 2006.

42 *expecting to party hard:* George Dowdall, *College Drinking: Reframing a Social Problem* (Westport, CT: Praeger Publishers, 2009).

42 *The alcohol industry . . . "part of college life to drink":* Wade.

42 *In 1984, when the legal drinking age:* McMurtrie.

43 *By the early 1990s:* Ibid.

43 *Delta Lambda Phi:* dlp.org; also see, for example, Patrick Saunders, "Georgia State's Gay Fraternity Fostering Brotherhood on Campus," *Georgia Voice,* November 10, 2016.

43 *Latino Greek-letter organizations:* Diana Moreno and Sheila Sanchez Banuelos, "The Influence of Latina/o Greek Sorority and Fraternity Involvement on Latina/o College Student Transition and Success," *Journal of Latin/Latin American Studies* 5, no. 2 (July 2013).

43 *The widening gap in graduation . . . inadequate university guidance and support:* See, for example, "Closing the Latino-White Completion Gap," *The Education Trust,* December 14, 2017; Meredith Kolodner, "College Degree Gap Grows Wider Between Whites, Blacks and Latinos," *The Hechinger Report,* January 7, 2016.

43 *Most ethnic and culturally based fraternities . . . :* See, for example, Ray, "Fraternity Life at Predominantly White Universities"; Walter M. Kimbrough, "The Hazing Problem at Black Fraternities," TheAtlantic.com, March 17, 2014.

43 *Today, approximately 13 percent:* This is how I arrived at this statistic: According to the most recent National Center for Education Statistics data (2016), there are 3,667,428 males enrolled full time in four-year degree-granting postsecondary institutions. Subtract the males enrolled full time in four-year for-profit institutions (162,153), and the figure is 3,505,275. This number is supported by a search in the NCES Integrated Postsecondary Education Data System. The total number of undergraduate members of the fraternities and umbrella organizations that have this information and responded to my inquiries is 444,235. This number is a conserative rough estimate because some groups either don't know or perhaps don't care to report their undergraduate membership numbers (many non-historically white groups have graduate school and/or older members).

43 *Greeks tend to have a higher social status:* Kristen Jozkowski and Jacquelyn Wiersma-Mosley, "The Greek System: How Gender Inequality and Class Privilege Perpetuate Rape Culture," *Family Relations* 66 (February 2017).

43 *"socialization sites," where new freshmen: ASHE Higher Education Report,* 2014.

43 *Members are still . . . business arenas:* Ibid.

43 *at least three billion dollars:* McMurtrie.

44 *"There's pressure":* Interview with the author.

44 *"The idea of tiers":* Ibid.

45 *Sororities' tiers . . . :* Interviews with the author.

45 *"looks, partying hard":* Interview with the author.

45 *"This money can . . . doesn't need it":* Ibid.

46 *"Everything in Greek life . . .":* Ibid.

46 *when his brothers . . . "that's an issue":* Ibid.

46 *When Ben founded . . . "The petty politics!":* Ibid.

47 *stories circulate . . ."the top-tier fraternity":* Ibid.

48 *Teddy works . . . "for a reason":* Ibid.

48 *visibility rather than likeability:* See, for example, Kathryn M. LaFontana and Antonius H. N. Cillessen, "Children's Perceptions of Popular and Unpopular Peers: A Multimethod Assessment," *Developmental Psychology* 38, no. 5 (2002); Hongling Xie, Yan Li, Signe Boucher, Bryan C. Hutchins, and Bev-

erley D. Cairns, "What Makes a Girl (or a Boy) Popular (or Unpopular)? African American Children's Perceptions and Developmental Differences," *Developmental Psychology* 42, no. 4 (2006). See also Kenneth H. Rubin, William M. Bukowski, and Jeffrey G. Parker, "Peer Interactions, Relationships, and Groups," in *Handbook of Child Psychology* (Hoboken, NJ: John Wiley and Sons, 2006).

49 *"I wish people would understand"*: Interview with the author.

49 *Fraternities exist . . . "feeds on itself"*: Interview with the author.

Chapter 2: House and Hierarchy: What Happens Behind Closed Doors

73 *Kirk*: Interviews with the author.

74 *"At regional conferences"*: Interview with the author.

75 *"Obey the law and live the Ritual": Phi Kappa Psi Risk Management & Insurance Guide,* updated August 2013. "These policies have been adopted by more than 40 fraternities and sororities."

75 *One fraternity's ritual book . . . "cynicism and selfishness"*: Various fraternity ritual books.

75 *Various secrets have overlapped:* See, for example, McMinn.

75 *"Firing Squad" . . . "respect your differences"*: Interviews with the author.

76 *Another major fraternity . . . "closest we'd ever been"*: Interviews with the author.

76 *a ritual helped members . . . :* Interview with the author.

77 *"Something many young student . . . best for the friendship"*: Ibid.

77 *Ben's South Carolina . . . "this organization forward"*: Ibid.

78 *If a Google employee . . . "members' agency"*: Interviews with the author.

79 *misdemeanor sex offense:* Nicholas Bogel-Burroughs, "Sex Offense in Cornell Fraternity Leads to Probation for Chapter's Ex-President," *Cornell Daily Sun,* April 11, 2017.

79 *"Everyone hated" . . . "a clear divide"*: Interview with the author.

79 *interesting study from 1996 . . . places to sit down:* A. Ayres Boswell and Joan Z. Spade, "Fraternities and Collegiate Rape Culture: Why Are Some Fraternities More Dangerous Places for Women?" *Gender and Society* 10, no. 2 (April 1996).

80 *distinctions made in that study:* Interviews with the author.

80 *At a southern school . . . "more of a process"*: Interview with the author.

80 *A Virginia brother . . . higher-tiered houses:* Ibid.

81 *"You only hear . . . loyalty and pride"*: Ibid.

81 *Many brothers struggle . . ."promoted nonetheless"*: Interviews with the author.

81 *A New York chapter president:* Interview with the author.

82 *their behavior shifted with the setting:* Boswell and Spade.

Chapter 3: Pledging: "Earning" the Letters

116 *it is a crime in 44 states and Washington, DC:* http://hazingprevention.org /home/hazing/statelaws.

116 *Yet 73 percent of Greeks:* ASHE Higher Education Report, 2014.

116 *Binghamton University . . . "was going to die":* Peter Applebome, "At a Campus Scarred by Hazing, Cries for Help," *New York Times,* September 18, 2012.

116 *Conor Donnelly:* Anthony Borrelli, "Student Death: Why Did BU Freshman Climb Balcony?" PressConnects, April 4, 2017.

116 *at least 17 pledges:* http://www.hanknuwer.com/hazing-deaths.

116 *The most frequently reported hazing:* ASHE Higher Education Report, 2014.

116 *College hazing began . . . :* Syrett.

117 *Twenty-first-century . . . sensational incidents:* Lipkins, interview with the author.

117 *Wilmington College:* Valerie Strauss, "Fraternity Pledge Loses Testicle in Hazing Stunt," *Washington Post,* November 12, 2013.

117 *Hofstra University:* Nicole Hensley, "Hofstra University Fraternity Accused of Hazing Pledges with Swastikas, Vomit and Hot Sauce During 'Hell Night,'" New York *Daily News,* December 7, 2016.

117 *University of Tennessee:* Strauss.

117 *Washington and Lee:* "Washington and Lee University Suspends Phi Kappa Psi over Taser Hazing, NBC News, March 11, 2015.

117 *In 2018 . . . 10 years:* Dakin Andone and Evan Simko-Bednarski, "Fraternity Banned from Pennsylvania for Pledge's Hazing Death," CNN, January 10, 2018.

117 *During a retreat . . . brain injury:* See, for example, "Ex-Frat Officer Testifies Against Brothers in Pledge's Death," Associated Press State and Local, December 1, 2015; "Frat Member Charged with Murder in Pledge's 2013 Death Breaks Down in Tears at Arraignment," New York *Daily News,* October 23, 2015; Jay Caspian Kang, "What a Fraternity Hazing Death Revealed About the Painful Search for an Asian-American Identity," *New York Times Magazine,* August 9, 2017.

118 *The national office . . . "no-hazing policy":* Jamie Altman, "5 Pi Delta Psi Fraternity Members Could Face Third-Degree Murder Charges," *USA Today College,* September 15, 2015.

118 *it turned out that . . . not the concept:* Interviews with the author; see also David DeKok, "Hazing Was Condoned, Former Frat President Testifies in Pledge Death Case," Reuters, November 30, 2015; Michael Rubinkam, "4 Ex-Fraternity Members Get Jail in Pledge's Hazing Death," Associated Press, January 9, 2018; Kang.

118 *All chapters of Pi Delta Psi . . . pledge books:* Sam, interview with the author.

118 *to give pledges . . . "obtaining them":* Ibid.

120 *(FSPAC) . . . federal anti-hazing bill.:* See, for example, Tyler Kingkade, "Frat-PAC Lobbies Congress for Tax Breaks, to Stop Anti-Hazing Law," *Huffington Post,* July 25, 2013; John Hechinger, *True Gentlemen* (New York: Public Affairs, 2017).

120 *95 percent of hazed students . . . hazing incidents:* Novak Institute on Hazing, cited in Karl Etters, "Convicted FAMU Hazer Crusades Against Culture of Abuse," *Tallahassee Democrat,* September 18, 2015.

120 *"on paper" . . . "drive away":* Interview with the author.

121 *nine out of ten college students:* ASHE Higher Education Report, 2014.

121 *his chapter didn't haze:* Interview with the author.

121 *belief that it is their responsibility:* Interviews with the author.

121 *"pro-hazing, pro-drinking . . . bitch for years":* Interview with the author.

122 *Pat:* Interview with the author.

123 *"hazing is a necessary evil":* Interviews with the author.

123 *means of group survival:* Robert B. Cialdini, *Influence: The Psychology of Persuasion,* rev. ed. (New York: Collins, 2007).

123 *"cognitive dissonance":* Leon Festinger and James M. Carlsmith, "Cognitive Consequences of Forced Compliance," *Journal of Abnormal and Social Psychology* 58 (1959).

123 *In 1959, researchers . . . group was valuable:* Elliot Aronson and Judson Mills, "The Effect of Severity of Initiation on Liking for a Group," *Journal of Abnormal and Social Psychology* 59, no. 2 (1959).

124 *In the 1960s . . . worthless group:* Cialdini.

124 *"future society members . . . survival":* Ibid.

124 *"Hazing has become . . . handed to us":* Interview with the author.

125 *For 2017 Penn State pledge . . . kinds of alcohol:* Sara Ganim, Emanuella Grinberg, and Chris Welch, "In Video of Penn State Hazing Death, Victim Looked 'Like a Corpse,'" CNN.com, June 13, 2017; Gio Benitez and Emily Shapiro, "Ex-Penn State Frat Member's Text: 'I Don't Want to Go to Jail for This,'" ABC News, July 10, 2017.

125 *Towson University Tau Kappa Epsilons:* Petula Dvorak, "Time to Dismantle Fraternities and the Sexism, Rape Culture and Binge Drinking They Encourage," *Washington Post,* September 15, 2016; "Towson University Suspends Fraternity Amid Hazing Allegations," WBAL-TV, April 7, 2016.

125 *"life-threatening" amount of alcohol:* Sarah Maslin, "19 and Coming into His Own, Until a Fatal Night of Hazing," *New York Times,* May 21, 2017.

125 *18 drinks in 82 minutes:* Colin Dwyer, "Penn State Student Given 18 Drinks in 82 Minutes Before Hazing Death, Prosecutors Say," NPR.org, November 13, 2017.

125 *His subsequent drunken . . . 12 hours:* Maslin.

126 *"make sure the pledges":* Sam Ruland, "Messages from the Night of Bid Acceptance to the Days Following Piazza's Death," *Daily Collegian,* May 9, 2017.

126 *waited two hours to take him to the hospital:* See, for example, Andone and Simko-Bednarski.

126 *national president reportedly instructed:* See, for example, Kang.

126 *One of the defendants testified . . . an excuse:* See, for example, DeKok; and Chris Pleasance, "President of New York Fraternity Where Pledge Died During Hazing Reveals the Rituals Were Encouraged and Members Would Cook Up Excuses If Someone Got Hurt," *Daily Mail,* December 1, 2015.

126 *"did not have the authority":* Ibid.

126 *"pledge educator":* See, for example, Tracy Connor, "Student Tried to Cover Up Frat Link in Fatal Hazing: Cops," NBC News, November 2, 2015.

126 *Piazza's mother told the* Today *show":* "Hazing in America," *Today,* NBC, September 18, 2017.

126 *major hazing incidents . . . caught hazing:* Research conducted by the author.

126 *"It's very difficult . . . its own existence":* Interview with the author.

127 *"planned failure":* Aldo Cimino, "Fraternity Hazing and the Process of Planned Failure," *Journal of American Studies* 52, no. 1 (2016).

127 *chapters set up pledges to fail:* Ibid.

127 *"If hazees believe":* Ibid.

128 *"The things we did . . . it is now":* Interview with the author.

128 *Yet many fraternity chapters . . . within chapters that haze:* Ibid.

128 *taking weekly classes . . . "I'll never forget":* Ibid.

128 *A Pennsylvania chapter . . . "strengths and weaknesses":* Ibid.

129 *upstate New York . . . "mission of the chapter":* Ibid.

130 *When Ben founded . . . "and it worked":* Ibid.

Chapter 4: Why Are Students Drinking?

143 *major public health concern:* See, for example, Adam E. Barry, "Using Theory-Based Constructs to Explore the Impact of Greek Membership on Alcohol-Related Beliefs and Behaviors: A Systematic Literature Review," *Journal of American College Health* 56, no. 3 (2007).

143 *Fraternity members drink more:* ASHE *Higher Education Report,* 2014.

143 *more likely to be diagnosed:* Aesoon Park et al., "Risky Drinking in College Changes as Fraternity/Sorority Affiliation Changes: A Person-Environment Perspective," *Psychology of Addictive Behaviors* 22, no. 2 (2008); see also Barry.

143 *"are the single largest provider":* "The Role of Fraternities and Sororities To-day," *The Diane Rehm Show,* NPR.org, August 26, 2014.

144 *the more involved a student is: ASHE Higher Education Report,* 2014.

144 *Drinking is one of the oldest:* See, for example, Barrett Seaman, *Binge: Campus Life in an Age of Disconnection and Excess* (Hoboken, NJ: John Wiley and Sons, 2006).

144 *In 1639 . . . run out of beer:* Susan Cheever, *Drinking in America: Our Secret History* (New York: Twelve, 2016); Olivia Munk, "Timeline: Beer at Harvard," *The Crimson,* October 9, 2014.

144 *"a symbol of good fellowship" . . . "proper wines with food":* C. C. Fry, "A Note on Drinking in the College Community," *Quarterly Journal of Studies on Alcohol* 6 (1945).

144 *changed where they drank it:* William H. George et al., "Effects of Raising the Drinking Age to 21 Years in New York State on Self-Reported Consumption by College Students," *Journal of Applied Social Psychology* 19, no. 8 (June 1989); Wade.

144 *"collegiate life was far too drenched . . . 1980s":* Wade.

144 *drink more often . . . non-Greek parties: ASHE Higher Education Report,* 2014.

144 *77 percent of freshmen "drink to get drunk":* Bradley O. Boekeloo et al., "Drinking to Get Drunk Among Incoming Freshmen College Students," *American Journal of Health Education* 42, no. 2 (January 2011).

145 *"liquid courage":* See, for example, Derek Kenji Iwamoto et al., "College Men and Alcohol Use: Positive Alcohol Expectancies as a Mediator Between Distinct Masculine Norms and Alcohol Use," *Psychology of Men and Masculinity* 15, no. 1 (2014).

145 *drink as a social lubricant:* Ibid.

145 *"I am terrible with girls sober":* Interview with the author.

145 *"to satisfy their [emotional] dependency":* Rocco L. Capraro, "Why College Men Drink: Alcohol, Adventure, and the Paradox of Masculinity," in *College Men and Masculinities: Theory, Research, and Implications for Practice,* Shaun R. Harper and Frank Harris III, eds. (San Francisco, CA: Jossey-Bass, 2010).

145 *highest rates of alcohol-related problems:* Richard Grucza, "Binge Drinking Among Youth and Young Adults in the United States: 1979–2006," *Journal of the American Academy of Child and Adolescent Psychiatry* 48, no. 7 (July 2009). Thank you to Rick Grucza for further clarifying this information for me.

145 *looked the other way:* See, for example, Seaman.

145 *easy majors and no-Friday-class schedules:* See, for example, Elizabeth Armstrong and Laura Hamilton, *Paying for the Party* (Cambridge, MA: Harvard University Press, 2013).

145 *"It's societal in that we're told"*: Interview with the author.

146 *underage students continue*: Interviews with the author; historically, see Dowdall; Capraro.

146 *college students misperceive*: Derek Kenji Iwamoto and Alice Cheng, "'Maning' Up and Getting Drunk: The Role of Masculine Norms, Alcohol Intoxication and Alcohol-Related Problems Among College Men," *Addictive Behaviors* 36, no. 9 (September 2011). See also Derek K. Iwamoto and Andrew P. Smiler, "Alcohol Makes You Macho and Helps You Make Friends: The Role of Masculine Norms and Peer Pressure in Adolescent Boys' and Girls' Alcohol Use," *Substance Use and Misuse* 48, no. 5 (April 2013).

146 *they increase their own*: Alan D. Berkowitz, "How College Men Feel About Being Men and 'Doing the Right Thing,'" in Tracy Davis and Jason Laker, *Masculinities in Higher Education: Theoretical and Practical Implications* (New York: Routledge, 2011); Capraro; Lori A. J. Scott-Sheldon et al., "Alcohol Interventions for Greek Letter Organizations: A Systematic Review and Meta-Analysis, 1987 to 2014," *Health Psychology* 35, no. 7 (2016).

146 *"Students sometimes aspire"*: Interview with the author.

146 *Black students drink less*: See, for example, Kimbrough; Caitlin Flanagan, "How Helicopter Parenting Can Cause Binge Drinking," *The Atlantic*, September 2016.

146 *"the most privileged subset"*: Flanagan, "How Helicopter Parenting."

146 *twice as likely . . . where they were*: Kathleen Brown-Rice and Susan Furr, "Differences in College Greek Members' Binge Drinking Behaviors: A Dry/Wet House Comparison," *The Professional Counselor* 5, no. 3 (2015).

147 *intervention programs that work . . . such a program*: Scott-Sheldon et al.

147 *even when a fraternity*: Brown-Rice and Furr.

147 *chapters with a house binge-drink*: See, for example, *ASHE Higher Education Report*, 2014.

147 *to own fake IDs*: See, for example, William R. Molasso, "Fake ID Use Among Fraternity/Sorority Members," *Oracle: The Research Journal of the Association of Fraternity/Sorority Advisors* 2, no. 1 (2006).

147 *"I'll go to happy hour" . . . steep*: Interviews with the author.

147 *Louisiana State University: Greek Tiger: A Guide to LSU Fraternities & Sororities*, 2017, https://www.lsu.edu/students/greeks/files/2017_FinalGreekTiger_Web.pdf.

147 *At other schools*: Interviews with the author.

147 *more likely than other students . . . "the thing to do"*: Various sources cited in Barry.

148 *"At the end of the week"*: Interview with the author.

148 *"a quintessential fraternity activity"*: Ibid.

148 *pledges are socialized*: See, for example, Scott-Sheldon et al.

148 *"as a kind of education"*: R. L. Leavy, "An Alternative Source of Information on a Popular Topic: A Course on Drinking," *Teaching of Psychology* 6 (1979). Cited in Barry.

148 *full membership in the group*: G. D. Kuh and J. C. Arnold, "Liquid Bonding: A Cultural Analysis of the Role of Alcohol in Fraternity Pledgeship," *Journal of College Student Development* 34 (1993).

149 *pledges who believe:* Barry.

149 *David Bogenberger:* Clifford Ward, "22 Former NIU Frat Members Guilty of Misdemeanors in Death of Pledge," *Chicago Tribune,* August 5, 2015.

149 *Maxwell Gruver:* Alexandra Bacallao and Corky Siemaszko, "New Details Emerge as Ten Charged in LSU Fraternity Hazing Death," NBCNews.com, October 11, 2017; Katie Reilly, "'Those Families Are Changed Forever': A Deadly Year in Fraternity Hazing Comes to a Close," Time.com, December 21, 2017.

149 *Andrew Coffey:* Ibid.

149 *Matthew Ellis:* Tony Plohetski, "Texas State Pledge's Death: Autopsy Shows Blood Alcohol Content of 0.38," *Austin American-Statesman,* February 9, 2018.

149 *neither an unusual pattern . . .:* Nuwer, correspondence with the author.

149 *"We aren't holding back":* Interview with the author.

150 *members of fraternity and sorority chapters:* Barry.

150 *"There's a lot of peer pressure":* Interview with the author.

150 *They're bingeing on hard alcohol:* Interviews with the author; Seaman.

150 *often downing as much as they can:* Interview with the author.

150 *Pregaming . . . won't serve teenagers:* Interviews with the author; see also Jennifer P. Read, "Before the Party Starts: Risk Factors and Reasons for 'Pregaming' in College Students," *Journal of American College Health* 58, no. 5 (2010); Joseph W. LaBrie, "Identifying Factors That Increase the Likelihood for Alcohol-Induced Blackouts in the Prepartying Context," *Substance Use and Misuse* 46, no. 8 (2011).

151 *students who attended . . . campus events:* M. J. Paschall, "Relationships Between College Settings and Student Alcohol Use Before, During and After Events: A Multi-Level Study," *Drug and Alcohol Review* 26, no. 6 (November 2007). Thank you to M. J. Paschall for further clarifying information for me.

151 *This style of fast-paced . . . "and fighting":* LaBrie.

151 *"older brothers believe":* Interview with the author.

151 *linked to masculinity:* See, for example, Robert Peralta, "College Alcohol Use and the Embodiment of Hegemonic Masculinity Among European American Men," *Sex Roles* 56, no. 11 (June 2007).

151 *cultural symbol of manliness:* See, for example, Iwamoto and Cheng; Samantha Wells, "Linking Masculinity to Negative Drinking Consequences: The Mediating Roles of Heavy Episodic Drinking and Alcohol Expectancies," *Journal of Studies on Alcohol and Drugs* 75, no. 3 (May 2014).

151 *More than two-thirds:* Peralta.

151 *fraternities encouraged drinking:* Syrett.

151 *Guys who can't . . . "are deemed manly":* Iwamoto and Cheng.

152 *"maxing out . . . ":* Interview with the author.

152 *a major reason college women:* Amy M. Young et al., "Drinking Like a Guy: Frequent Binge Drinking Among Undergraduate Women," *Substance Use and Misuse* 40, no. 2 (2005).

152 *drinking is considered macho:* Iwamoto et al.

152 *many men already feel . . . :* See, for example, Barry; Iwamoto et al.; Wells.

152 *A junior in Iowa . . .. joining the fraternity:* Interview with the author.

153 *the more a boy is concerned:* Wells; Iwamoto and Cheng; and Iwamoto et al.

153 *men who embrace . . . masculinity:* Wells; Iwamoto and Cheng; and Iwamoto et al.

153 *to moderate consumption . . . :* Scott-Sheldon et al.

155 *"People drink because . . . ":* Interview with the author.

Chapter 5: Girls and Group Identity: How Chapters Can Influence Guys' Attitudes

170 *University of Southern California:* Margaret Hartman, "Frat Email Explains Women Are 'Targets,' Not 'Actual People,'" *Jezebel,* March 8, 2011.

170 *North Carolina State University:* See, for example, Tasneem Nashrulla, "NC State Fraternity Suspended After Alleged Pledge Book with Rape, Lynching Jokes Is Found," Buzzfeed, March 20, 2015.

170 *University of Central Florida:* Kim Bellware, "Frat Suspended After 'Rape Some B*****s' Comment Caught on Tape," *Huffington Post,* August 15, 2015.

170 *University of Richmond:* Petula Dvorak, "Time to Dismantle Fraternities and the Sexism, Rape Culture and Binge Drinking They Encourage," *Washington Post,* September 15, 2016.

171 *Cornell:* Elise Solé, "Cornell University Frat Ran a 'Pig Roast' Contest with Points Earned for Sexual Conquests," *Yahoo Lifestyle,* February 3, 2018; Cleve R. Wootson Jr., "Cornell Fraternity on Probation After a 'Pig Roast' Contest to Have Sex with Overweight Women," *Washington Post,* February 7, 2018.

171 *University of California at San Diego:* Kriti Sarin, "Fraternity Pledge Solicits Topless Pictures from Female Student," *The Guardian* (UCSD), October 15, 2015.

172 *groupthink . . . "importance of their doubts"*: Irving L. Janis, "Groupthink," *Psychology Today,* November 1971.

172 *feel less personal responsibility:* See, for example, Serge Moscovici and Marisa Zavalloni, "The Group as a Polarizer of Attitudes," *Journal of Personality and Social Psychology* 1, no. 2 (1969).

172 *an extension of the brain's . . ."becomes aware of it":* Gregory Berns, *Iconoclast: A Neuroscientist Reveals How to Think Differently* (Boston: Harvard Business School Press, 2008). *Iconoclast* is fascinating and fun to read.

172 *pressure to conform and comply:* See, for example, Meredith G. F. Worthen, "Blaming the Jocks and the Greeks? Exploring Collegiate Athletes' and Fraternity/Sorority Members' Attitudes Toward LGBT Individuals," *Journal of College Student Development* 55, no. 2 (March 2014).

172 *"independent thought . . . ":* Ibid.

173 *tend to dehumanize them:* Janis, "Groupthink."

173 *display more degrading . . . : ASHE Higher Education Report,* 2014; Cortney A. Franklin and Leana Allen Bouffard, "Sexual Assault on the College Campus: Fraternity Affiliation, Male Peer Support, and Low Self-Control," *Criminal Justice and Behavior* 39, no. 11 (October 5, 2012).

173 *objectifying images . . . sexual language:* Ibid.

173 *"these ideals likely":* Jozkowski and Wiersma-Mosley.

173 *Tufts University fraternity:* Ben Kesslen, "Abolish Fraternities," *Tufts Observer,* November 7, 2016.

173 *Indiana University's . . . :* Madeline Buckley and Justin Mack, "IU Fraternity Is Shut Down Less than a Day After Sex Video Emerges," *Indianapolis Star,* October 7, 2015.

174 *BGLO fraternity members, too . . . :* Rashawn Ray, "Sophisticated Practitioners: Black Fraternity Men's Treatment of Women," *Journal of African American Studies* 16, no. 4 (December 2012).

174 *possible that BGLO brothers . . . :* Ray, "Fraternity Life at Predominantly White Universities"; see also Rashawn Ray and Jason Rosow, "Getting Off and Getting Intimate: How Normative Institutional Arrangements Structure Black and White Fraternity Men's Approaches Toward Women," *Men and Masculinities* 12, no. 5 (April 2010).

174 *two women as International Board officers:* http://lambdaPhiEpsilon.com /executive-appointments.

174 *black fraternity members feel:* Ray, "Sophisticated Practitioners."

174 *"When I was pledging":* Interview with the author.

175 *compared to white fraternity men:* Ray, "Sophisticated Practitioners."

175 *"same to other women":* Interview with the author.

175 *Group polarization is . . . :* Moscovici and Zavalloni.

175 *juries whose individual members . . . :* Robert Bray and Audrey Noble, "Authoritarianism and Decisions of Mock Juries: Evidence of Jury Bias and Group Polarization," *Journal of Personality and Social Psychology* 36, no. 12 (1978).

175 *polarization happens for three reasons:* See, for example, Antony Manstead and Miles Hewstone, eds., *The Blackwell Encyclopedia of Social Psychology* (Cambridge: Blackwell, 1996).

175 *make students feel more negatively . . . :* D. G. Myers and G. D. Bishop, "Discussion Effects on Racial Attitudes," *Science* 169 (1970); D. G. Myers, "Discussion-Induced Attitude Polarization," *Human Relations* 28, no. 8 (1975).

175 *common in homogenous groups:* See, for example, Thomas Gilovich et al., *Social Psychology* (New York: W. W. Norton and Company, 2015), http://www.wwnorton.com/college/psych/socialpsych/reviews/ch02.asp.

175 *middle- to upper-middle-class:* See, for example, Kaitlin M. Boyle, "Social Psychological Processes That Facilitate Sexual Assault Within the Fraternity Party Subculture," *Sociology Compass* 9, no. 5 (2015).

176 *racist or sexist activities: ASHE Higher Education Report,* 2014.

176 *Kappa Sigma "Asia Prime":* Katie J. M. Baker, "Duke Frat Bros in Trouble for Racist Asia Rager," *Jezebel,* February 6, 2013.

176 *Baylor University:* Samantha Schmidt, "Baylor Frat Holds 'Cinco de Drinko' Party: Students Reportedly Dressed as Maids, Construction Workers," *Washington Post,* May 3, 2017.

176 *California Polytechnic State University:* Marwa Eltagouri, "Fraternity Brothers Posed in Blackface and Gangster Costumes, This College's Latest Racist Dust-up," *Washington Post,* April 10, 2018.

176 *Arizona State University's:* Tyler Kingkade, "Arizona State University Permanently Boots Frat Off Campus Following Racist MLK Party," *Huffington Post,* January 24, 2014; Javier Panzar, "8 More Fraternity Scandals That Made National Headlines," *Los Angeles Times,* March 9, 2015.

176 *In the Civil War:* John Hechinger and David Glovin, "Deadliest Frat's Icy 'Torture' of Pledges Evokes Tarantino Films," *Bloomberg,* December 30, 2013.

177 *In 2015, SAE's continued racism . . . :* Susan Svrluga, "OU: Frat Members Learned Racist Chant at National SAE Leadership Event," *Washington Post,* March 27, 2015.

177 *as late as December 2014:* Internet archives for the page http://www.sae.net /page.aspx?pid=756.

177 *pressure to be disrespectful toward women:* Boswell and Spade.

177 *"people don't get called out for anything":* Interview with the author.

177 *a New England house . . .* : Interview with the author.

178 *As students spend more time:* See, for example, F. Poulin and M. Boivin, "The Role of Proactive and Reactive Aggression in the Formulation and Development of Boys' Friendships," *Developmental Psychology* 36, no. 2 (2000).

178 *In the mid-twentieth century . . . wrong answer:* Solomon E. Asch, "Opinions and Social Pressure," *Scientific American* 193, no. 5 (1955).

179 *New research . . ."conform with the social norm":* Berns.

179 *Researchers in the Netherlands:* See, for example, Elizabeth Landau, "Why So Many Minds Think Alike," CNN, January 15, 2009.

180 *signal triggers . . . that triggers conformity:* Vasily Klucharev, Kaisa Hytönen, Mark Rijpkema, Ale Smidts, and Guillén Fernández, "Reinforcement Learning Signal Predicts Social Conformity," *Neuron* 61, no. 1 (January 2009).

180 *"Deviation from the group":* Landau.

180 *pull toward conformity is strongest:* See William Bukowski and Lorrie K. Sippola, "Groups, Individuals, and Victimization: A View of the Peer System," in Jaana Juvonen and Sandra Graham, eds., *Peer Harassment in School: The Plight of the Vulnerable and Victimized* (New York: Guilford Press, 2001).

180 *Compared to adults . . . :* See, for example, Philip R. Costanzo and Marvin E. Shaw, "Conformity as a Function of Age Level," *Child Development* 37, no. 4 (December 1966); see also Monisha Pasupathi, "Age Differences in Response to Conformity Pressure for Emotional and Nonemotional Material," *Psychology and Aging* 14, no. 1 (1999).

180 *according to group standards . . . :* See, for example, Franklin and Bouffard; Syrett.

181 *"the peer group has reinforced . . .":* Jozkowski and Wiersma-Mosley.

181 *"a high-tier sorority . . . know about it?":* Interview with the author.

181 *groups with high levels . . . conformist than other groups:* Leslie A. Gavin and Wyndol Furman, "Age Differences in Adolescents' Perceptions of Their Peer Groups," *Developmental Psychology* 25, no. 5 (1989).

182 *"Upon entry . . .":* Joshua Schutts and Kyna Shelley, "Modeling a Values-Based Congruence Framework to Predict Organization Constructs in Fraternities and Sororities," *Oracle: The Research Journal of the Association of Fraternity/Sorority Advisors* 9, no. 1 (Spring 2014).

182 *"showed increases in" . . . a year later:* Jeffrey B. Kingree, "Fraternity Membership and Sexual Aggression: An Examination of Mediators of the Association," *Journal of American College Health* 61, no. 4 (2013).

183 *do not polarize:* J. S. Fishkin and R. C. Luskin, "Bringing Deliberation to the Democratic Dialogue," in M. McCombs and A. Reynolds, eds., *The Poll with a Human Face: The National Issues Convention Experiment in Political Communication* (Mahwah, NJ: Lawrence Erlbaum, 1999).

183 *"Diversity helps . . . will be wise"*: James Surowiecki, *The Wisdom of Crowds* (New York: First Anchor Books, 2005).

Chapter 6: Looking Out for One Another—and "Helping the Fraternity Out"

202 *When boys first join . . .* : Jozkowski and Wiersma-Mosley.

202 *fraternity brothers are three times . . .* : See, for example, Foubert. See also Anna North, "Is College Sexual Assault a Fraternity Problem?" *New York Times,* January 29, 2015; Catherine Loh, Christine A. Gidycz, Tracy R. Lobo, and Rohini Luthra, "A Prospective Analysis of Sexual Assault Perpetration Risk Factors Related to Perpetrator Characteristics," *Journal of Interpersonal Violence* 20, no. 10 (2005).

202 *"rape a virtual inevitability"*: Jozkowski and Wiersma-Mosley.

202 *"luring your rapebait" . . . "American college"*: Foubert.

202 *on measures of sexual aggression:* Stephen E. Humphrey and Arnold S. Kahn, "Fraternities, Athletic Teams, and Rape," *Journal of Interpersonal Violence* 15, no. 12 (2005), cited in Boyle.

202 *"a few bad apples"*: Interviews with the author.

202 *Certain chapters across:* Sorority sister interviews with the author.

203 *chapter presidents (at Cornell):* Bogel-Burroughs.

203 *Baylor:* Associated Press, "Baylor University Phi Delta Theta President Charged with Sexual Assault," NBCNews.com, March 5, 2016.

203 *Temple:* Claire Sasko, "Temple Frat President Ari Goldstein Charged with Attempted Rape, Indecent Assault; Bail Set at $2 Million," *Philadelphia,* May 16, 2018.

203 *Utah State. . . . these types of violations:* Robert Boyd and Mark Green, "Fraternity Chapter Ceases Operations at USU After Former President Accused of Sexual Abuse," Fox13 (Salt Lake City), March 25, 2015.

203 *some adult Greek leaders:* Interviews with the author.

203 *In 2016 . . . accused rapist:* Tyler Kingkade, "Lambda Chi Alpha Fraternity Leaves National Umbrella Group Amid Controversial Lobbying," *Huffington Post,* October 27, 2015; Anna Merlan, "Frat Lobby Wants Congress to Block Schools from Investigating Rape," *Jezebel,* March 25, 2015; Joanna Rothkopf, "Frat Cuts Ties with Group That Lobbied to Make Campus Rape Harder to Prosecute," *Jezebel,* October 27, 2015.

203 *"This proposal is completely . . ."*: Tyler Kingkade and Alexandra Svokos, "Fraternities Consider Lobbying Congress to Thwart College Rape Investigations," *Huffington Post,* March 25, 2015. Campus proceedings are intended to determine whether a student violated the school's code of conduct, not whether he's guilty of a crime. As Know Your IX, a survivor- and youth-led organization, states, "A criminal trial is brought against a defendant by the

state—not the victim—in defense of the state's interests. That means that what the survivor needs is sidelined. In contrast, schools, unlike criminal courts, are focused on the victim and are required to make sure he or she has everything they need to continue their education. Examples include academic accommodations, dorm and class transfers, and mental health support" (https://www.knowyourix.org).

204 *In January 2016 . . . "our claims"*: Interview with the author.

204 *"counterproductive tactics"*: Kingkade, "Lambda Chi Alpha."

204 *withdrew support . . . mandate:* Tyler Bishop, "Forcing Colleges to Involve Police in Sexual-Assault Investigations?" TheAtlantic.com, November 19, 2015.

204 *tougher to prosecute:* Ibid.; Tyler Kingkade, "Fraternities Hire Trent Lott to Lobby for Limiting Campus Sexual Assault Investigations," *Huffington Post,* October 14, 2015.

204 *University of Oregon study:* Jennifer Freyd, *The UO Sexual Violence Survey,* 2014.

204 *an "alarmingly high" rate:* Josephine Woolington, "UO Study: Rape Danger Higher in Greek Life," *The Register-Guard,* October 16, 2014.

204 *"When we saw the magnitude . . .":* Freyd, interview with the author. Some of the interviews and information in this essay were originally used in Alexandra Robbins, "Sorority Secrets: The Dark Side of Sisterhood That No One's Willing to Talk About," *Marie Claire,* August 2015. The class years of these sources are as of the time of the original interviews.

205 *despite her findings . . . "places for women":* Woolington.

205 *"There is high demand . . .":* Interview with the author.

205 *Freyd was stunned . . ."Greek system":* Interview with the author.

205 *John Foubert . . . assault:* Foubert.

205 *sexual victimization happens . . . fraternity house:* Jozkowski and Wiersma-Mosley.

205 *Police say it's easier . . . :* See, for example, Anna Higgins, "What I Hear Is That You Aren't Listening," *Cavalier Daily* (University of Virginia), April 10, 2015.

205 *The Greek system is known . . . either gender:* See, for example, Franklin and Bouffard.

206 *sorority members are sexually:* Lori A. J. Scott et al., "Health Behavior and College Students: Does Greek Affiliation Matter?" *Journal of Behavioral Medicine* 31, no. 1 (February 2008). Jacqueline Minow and Christopher Einolf, "Sorority Participation and Sexual Assault Risk," *Violence Against Women* 15, no. 7 (2009); R. Sean Bannon et al., "Sorority Women's and Fraternity Men's Rape Myth Acceptance and Bystander Intervention Attitudes," *Journal of Student Affairs Research and Practice* 50, no. 1 (2013).

206 *sorority sisters are four times . . . :* Minow and Einolf.

206 *The National Institute for Justice:* https://www.nij.gov/topics/crime/rape
-sexual-violence/campus/Pages/increased-risk.aspx.

206 *"Fraternities are accused . . .":* Interview with the author.

206 *Erin:* Interview with the author.

207 *decrease sororities' insurance premiums:* Danielle Paquette, "Why Frat Bros
Can Throw Parties but Sorority Sisters Aren't Allowed To," *Washington
Post,* January 22, 2016.

207 *Greek life commonly involves:* Interviews with the author. See also, for example, "Courting Belongs in the Past," *The Flat Hat* (William & Mary), October 23, 2014.

207 *"For Homecoming . . .":* Interview with the author.

207 *At a Missouri school . . ."with the sisters' ":* Interview with the author.

208 *When Erin wrote . . . :* Interview with the author.

208 *Sororities again silenced . . . her membership:* Joanna Rothkopf, "Report: Ole
Miss Sororities Banned from Speaking About Sexist Derby Days Video, 1
Sister Kicked Out," *Jezebel,* April 20, 2016; Joanna Rothkopf, "Ole Miss Investigating Sigma Chi Frat over Sexist 'Derby Days' Video," *Jezebel,* April
18, 2016.

209 *2015 Derby Days . . ."grabs the bat":* Jia Tolentino, "Welcome to Derby Days,
the Most Spectacular Con in All of Frat Philanthropy," *Jezebel,* September
30, 2015.

209 *"The event seemed . . .":* Meghan McCarthy, "I Fought Back Against My College's Sexist Fraternity," TheAtlantic.com, February 24, 2014.

209 *"Colonial Bros and Nava-Hos":* Julia Hickey, " 'Colonial Bros and Nava-Hos'
Frat Party Prompts Cal Poly Investigation," *The Tribune,* November 20,
2013; Kathryn C. Reed, " 'Conquistabros and Navajos' Party Faces Criticism," *The Crimson,* October 27, 2010.

209 *"ABC (Anything but Clothes)":* Interviews with the author.

210 *"Champagne and Shackles":* Anemona Hartocollis and Steve Friess, "Clamp-
down on University of Michigan Fraternities After Reports of Sexual Mis-
conduct and Alcohol Abuse," *New York Times,* November 11, 2017.

210 *at a North Carolina school:* Interview with the author.

210 *Some sorority members . . . rank will drop:* Ibid.

210 *All 250 to 300 of Reese's:* Ibid.

211 *Maryland graduate . . . "will exist":* Ibid.

211 *membership requirement:* Ibid.

211 *An Indiana chapter . . . together:* Ibid.

212 *Missouri sorority:* Ibid.

212 *some guys feel . . . :* Ibid.

212 *Michigan junior . . . :* Ibid.

213 *"Fraternity men were significantly":* Franklin and Bouffard.

213 *Lacey:* Interview with the author.

213 *why Erin turned:* Ibid.

214 *"We're pressured to get":* Ibid.

Chapter 7: The Brotherhood: Relying on a Second Family

245 *"The party's fine . . . ":* All police officers' words in Oliver's story are as remembered by Oliver.

248 *Travis:* Interviews with the author.

249 *brotherhood involves constant:* Ibid.

249 *recent Pennsylvania grad:* Ibid.

250 *Georgia freshman:* Ibid.

250 *Oregon chapter treasurer:* Ibid.

251 *Many of the rituals:* Ibid.

251 *"for the good of the fraternity":* Ibid.

251 *"gave him a hug":* Ibid.

251 *An upstate New York chapter:* Ibid.

252 *Teddy's chapter:* Ibid.

253 *Seton Hall University:* Ibid.

253 *Georgia Southern University . . . "in football":* Ibid.

254 *ninth value . . . "one of them":* Ibid.

255 *an Idaho campus . . . Latino students:* Ibid.

255 *"strolling" or "stepping":* See, for example, Jacqui Malone, *Steppin' on the Blues: The Visible Rhythms of African American Dance* (Champagne: University of Illinois Press, 1996); Marissa Armas, "Stepping, Strolling and Community: Latino Fraternities, Sororities Grow in Popularity," NBC News, August 23, 2017.

256 *LGLO membership . . . discussions:* Moreno and Sanchez Banuelos; S. M. Muñoz and J. R. Guardia, "Nuestra historia y futuro (Our history and future): Latina/os fraternities and sororities," in C. L. Torbenson and G. S. Parks, eds., *Brothers and Sisters: Diversity in College Fraternities and Sororities* (Cranbury, NJ: Fairleigh Dickinson University Press, 2009).

256 *gay/bi/trans/queer fraternities:* See, for example, *ASHE Higher Education Report,* 2014.

256 *"It gives me a space":* Ibid.

257 *rocky freshman year:* Ibid.

Chapter 8: What Makes a (College) Man: How Students View Masculinity

271 *stage at which . . . grief:* Capraro.

271 *pressured to be "masculine":* See, for example, Keith Edwards and Susan

Jones, "Putting My Man Face On: A Grounded Theory of College Men's Gender Identity Development," *Journal of College Student Development* 50, no. 2 (March/April 2009); Michael Kimmel, *Guyland: The Perilous World Where Boys Become Men* (New York: Harper Perennial, 2009); Niobe Way, *Deep Secrets: The Hidden Landscape of Boys' Friendships* (Cambridge, MA: Harvard University Press, 2013); Worthen.

271 *Masculinity is a performance . . . forms of masculinity:* See, for example, Frank Harris III, "College Men's Meanings of Masculinities and Contextual Influences: Toward a Conceptual Model," *Journal of College Student Development* 51, no. 3 (May/June 2010); Richard de Visser and Jonathan Smith, "Alcohol Consumption and Masculine Identity Among Young Men," *Psychology and Health* 22, no. 5 (2007).

272 *11 prevailing expectations of masculinity:* James Mahalik, "Development of the Conformity to Masculine Norms Inventory," *Psychology of Men and Masculinity* 4, no. 1 (2003). See also Iwamoto and Smiler.

272 *"There are lots of ways":* Mahalik, correspondence with the author.

272 *doesn't mean all men:* Berkowitz.

272 *accepted by other men:* Kimmel.

272 *"Most men don't want":* Berkowitz.

272 *are rewarded while those:* See, for example, Franklin and Bouffard.

273 *Most men want to . . . will drink:* Berkowitz.

273 *most college guys don't endorse:* Ibid.

273 *guys who are considered:* Interviews with the author.

273 *"you gotta be very fit . . . more masculine":* Interview with the author.

274 *men who endorse traditional . . . :* See, for example, Wells; Will Courtenay, "Constructions of Masculinity and Their Influence on Men's Well-being: A Theory of Gender and Health," *Social Science and Medicine* 50, no. 10 (2000); Harris.

274 *and commit sexual assault:* Edwards and Jones.

274 *is common for men . . . rate for girls:* Way.

275 *Delta Sigma Theta:* https://www.deltasig.org ("Better Men. Better Lives").

275 *Delta Sigma Phi:* https://www.deltasig.org/fraternity/the-better-man.

275 *"To better the man":* http://alphasigmaphi.org/Websites/alphasigmaphihq /images/Better_Man_Program/TBTM_Manual.pdf.

275 *"whole man":* http://kappagamma.com/mission-statement.

275 *"resolute man":* https://www.thetachi.org/resolute-man.

275 *"the highest ideals of manhood":* http://sigtau.org/tag/our-heritage.

275 *"The initial transition . . .":* Interview with the author.

275 *"Guys are more expected . . .":* Ibid.

276 *"Dragon's Breath":* Ibid.

276 *An Iowa fraternity:* Ibid.

277 *Self-disclosive friendships . . . and feelings:* Way.

277 *engaged black adults:* See, for example, the aforementioned works of Rashawn Ray. See also Rashawn Ray and Jason Rosow, "The Two Different Worlds of Black and White Fraternity Men: Visibility and Accountability as Mechanisms of Privilege," *Journal of Contemporary Ethnography* 41, no. 1 (2012).

277 *Men can also join:* See, for example, Ray and Rosow, "Getting Off and Getting Intimate."

277 *"what black masculinity is":* Interview with the author. As a BLGO member told University of Oklahoma higher education professor T. Elon Dancy II, his fraternity gave him a "blueprint" for manhood, providing guidance and examples. T. Elon Dancy II and Bryan Hotchkins, "Schools for the Better Making of Men? Undergraduate Black Males, Fraternity Membership, and Manhood," *Culture, Society and Masculinities* 7, no. 1 (Spring 2015).

278 *more restrictive:* See, for example, Boyle; Jozkowski and Wiersma-Mosley; Scott-Sheldon et al.; Chadwick Menning, "Unsafe at Any House? Attendees' Perceptions of Microlevel Environmental Traits and Personal Safety at Fraternity and Nonfraternity Parties," *Journal of Interpersonal Violence* (October 2009).

278 *Fraternities are . . . "extremely masculine":* Worthen.

278 *eventually change his mind-set:* See, for example, Schutts and Shelley.

278 *endorse casual sex:* See, for example, Worthen; Scott-Sheldon et al.

278 *objectify women:* Jozkowski and Wiersma-Mosley.

278 *accept aggression toward women:* Worthen.

278 *pressure peers to hook up.* Syrett; Kingree.

278 *"hypermasculine":* See, for example, Charles Corprew III and Avery Mitchell, "Keeping It Frat: Exploring the Interaction Among Fraternity Membership, Disinhibition, and Hypermasculinity on Sexually Aggressive Attitudes in College-Aged Males," *Journal of College Student Development* 55, no. 6 (September 2014).

278 *College men . . . emotionlessness:* Iwamoto and Cheng; Wells.

279 *Scientists have discovered . . . "emotional situations":* Lise Eliot, *Pink Brain, Blue Brain: How Small Differences Grow into Troublesome Gaps—and What We Can Do About It* (New York: Houghton Mifflin Harcourt, 2009). Thank you to Lise Eliot for further clarifying information for me.

279 *close, solid friendships . . . younger boys:* Cynthia A. Erdley et al., "Children's Friendship Experiences and Psychological Adjustment: Theory and Research," *New Directions for Child and Adolescent Development* 91 (Spring 2001).

279 *"suggest that boys . . .":* Erdley, correspondence with the author.

279 *"we gender and sexualize":* Way, interview with the author.

280 *"they are depressed":* Erdley, correspondence with the author.

280 *non-Western cultures:* Way, interview with the author.

280 *"to be to his fraternity":* Syrett.

280 *"They attempted to . . .":* Ibid.

280 *appearing feminine or gay:* A long-standing issue. See, for example, R. A. Rhoads, "Whales Tales, Dog Piles, and Beer Goggles: An Ethnographic Case Study of Fraternity Life," *Anthropology and Education Quarterly* 26, no. 3 (1995).

281 *seminude all-male rituals:* Some fraternities haze pledges by making them watch gay porn. See, for example, "Fraternity at University of Kentucky Suspended for Hazing," CBS News, April 27, 2016.

281 *desire them . . ."vulnerable relationship":* ASHE Higher Education Report, 2014. See also Scott Fabius Kiesling, "Homosocial Desire in Men's Talk: Balancing and Re-creating Cultural Discourses of Masculinity," *Language in Society* 34, no. 5 (2005).

281 *could be an overcompensation:* See, for example, Worthen.

281 *"precarious manhood" . . . try to regain it:* Jennifer K. Bosson and Joseph A. Vandello, "Precarious Manhood and Its Links to Action and Aggression," *Current Directions in Psychological Science* 20, no. 2 (2011); James R. Mahalik et al., "Gender, Male-Typicality, and Social Norms Predicting Adolescent Alcohol Intoxication and Marijuana Use," *Social Science and Medicine* 143 (2015).

281 *revolve around joking:* Capraro.

282 *"There's a lot of fear":* Interview with the author.

282 *"boys feel effeminate":* Kimmel.

282 *stifled by these narrow gender norms:* See, for example, Berkowitz.

282 *"the mask of masculinity":* William Pollack, *Real Boys: Rescuing Our Sons from the Myths of Boyhood* (New York: Random House, 1998).

282 *"This performance" . . . "own emotions":* Edwards and Jones.

283 *fratty . . . "for a camera":* Interviews with the author.

283 *Kirk's two chapters . . ."refugee crisis":* Ibid.

284 *male teenagers prioritize work:* See, for example, Iwamoto and Cheng; Brian Sweeney, "Party Animals or Responsible Men: Social Class, Race, and Masculinity on Campus," *International Journal of Qualitative Studies in Education* 27, no. 6 (2014).

285 *"the view" . . . a feminist:* Ibid.

286 *"I had really bad":* Ibid.

286 *fewer than half of US states:* Maggie Jones, "What Teenagers Are Learning from Online Porn," *New York Times Magazine,* February 7, 2018.

286 *guys I interviewed agree:* Interviews with the author.

286 *Their smartphones . . . expected to perform:* Jones.

286 *"The over-the-top":* Interview with the author.

287 *2014 study . . . college men:* Frank Harris III and Shaun Harper, "Beyond Bad Behaving Brothers: Productive Performances of Masculinities Among College Fraternity Men," *International Journal of Qualitative Studies in Education* 27, no. 6 (2014). Thank you to Frank Harris III for clarifying information for me.

287 *"love and respect":* Interview with the author.

288 *"We look for leaders":* Ibid.

288 *"productive masculinities":* Harris.

288 *"There's a correlation . . .":* Interview with the author.

289 *"You want to forget . . .":* Ibid.

289 *"These partying behaviors . . .":* Edwards and Jones.

290 *Many college students . . . hard work:* Sweeney.

290 *"We're college students . . .":* Interview with the author.

290 *"If someone is completely . . .":* Ibid.

291 *weren't always that way:* Syrett.

291 *popular and influential:* See, for example, Worthen; Harris.

291 *"the embodiment of ideal masculinity on campus":* Ibid.

292 *"hierarchy of masculinities" . . . sports:* Ibid.

292 *Programs, presentations:* See, for example, Harris and Harper.

292 *"In these specific ways" . . . with others:* Edwards and Jones.

293 *"it's really liberating . . .":* Interview with the author.

293 *"The day-to-day things . . . outlet":* Ibid.

Chapter 9: Good Fraternities vs. Bad Frats: How to Tell the Difference

324 *"If fraternities were a franchise . . .":* Interview with the author.

324 *Massachusetts school . . . "should happen":* Ibid.

325 *midwestern university . . . slurs at its members:* Ibid.

325 *"gives a sense . . . help and report":* Kiss, interview with the author.

326 *historically white national fraternity:* We included the historically white NIC fraternities, Tau Kappa Epsilon, Lambda Chi Alpha, Kappa Sigma, and Phi Delta Theta.

327 *training sessions or prerequisites:* Interviews with the author.

327 *"As college students evolve":* Interview with the author.

328 *"What is the alcohol culture like":* Ibid.

328 *"ATO was super sweet":* Ibid.

328 *a potential red flag:* Ibid.

329 *"Do they make" . . . "culture isn't present":* Interviews with the author.

329 *Dartmouth banned. . . . financial aid:* Philip J. Hanlon, "Moving Dartmouth

Forward: The President's Plan," Dartmouth College, Office of the President, January 29, 2015.

329 *Since Dartmouth enacted:* Author's database research.

330 *"If there's one intrinsic . . . values are"*: Interviews with the author.

331 *"hazed as much as freshmen"*: Interview with the author.

331 *"Every chapter is going . . ."*: Ibid.

332 *LGBTQ ally programs:* See, for example, Worthen.

333 *moving furniture around . . . :* Erin Zagursky, "Study Finds That Space Matters for Student Learning in Fraternity Houses," https://www.wm.edu/news, December 17, 2015.

333 *"alumni initiates":* Advisor, interview with the author.

333 *An Iowa fraternity . . . :* Interview with the author.

334 *"Rarely, if at all":* ASHE Higher Education Report, 2014.

To find updates on the characters, or to book Alexandra Robbins for speaking engagements, appearances, or consulting work, please visit www.alexandrarobbins.com.

ACKNOWLEDGMENTS

My deep gratitude goes to Jake and Oliver, who were generous with their time and candor, and patient with me during hours upon hours of interviews. Thanks also to Kirk, Ben, Teddy, and the countless other fraternity brothers and alums whom I pestered frequently with questions.

Researcher Amy Lin worked tirelessly to help compile the information for our database of fraternity incidents. I am indebted to her for her hard work and valuable insights.

I'd also like to thank Ariel Fishman for assisting with statistics Kiersten Murphy for her invaluable sourcing help, and Nathan Holic for his thoughtful, knowledgeable responses to my many inquiries. His students are lucky to have him. I'm grateful to Al B., Morgane G., and the rest of their merry office gang for providing a fun, stimulating environment in which to revise. And I was thrilled to have the opportunity to work with the awesome campus super-team of: Kelli B., Sharon C., Kimberly L., Arianna N., Kathleen O., Ian R., and Hannah R.

You cannot write effectively if all you do is write, and so I'm grateful to my GNO girls and walking buddies for pulling me out of my book cave: Chrissy M., Laura R., Laura D., Jesse D., Charlotte P., Meaghan F., Alex J., and Stef D. (and forever Amy L. from afar).

Knowing Jill Schwartzman, cheerful and wise, is a pleasure; working with her is a blast. Her big-picture and structural suggestions in particular helped make this book much better than it was. Also at Dutton, I thank Christine Ball, John Parsley, Carrie Swetonic, Elina Vaysbeyn, Amanda Walker, Emily Canders, Susan

Schwartz, Alice Dalrymple, Melanie Koch, Bonnie Soodek, Yuki Hirose, and Marya Pasciuto. I feel so lucky to work with this creative, enthusiastic, motivating team.

At the Ross Yoon Agency, my appreciation goes to the one-of-a-kind Gail Ross for deftly shepherding this project from the start, and Howard Yoon for his ideas and inspiration. Special thanks to Dara Kaye for her brilliant notes on the essays and to Dara, Katie Zanecchia, and Anna Sproul-Latimer for their assistance in formulating this project at its inception. Thanks also to Michael Prevett for working to get these issues addressed on television.

Ellie A. and my brother were helpful with word choice suggestions; I appreciate their efforts. I'm also grateful to my parents, always supportive, who suggested research avenues, sourcing, and leads. I thank my sister for the time and thought she put into giving me the kind of sharp-eyed manuscript read I requested, the kind only a sibling can give.

No one can write books without a support system. My family has my heart, if not all the time that I wish I could give them when I am deep in what my patient husband calls "book mode."

You, reader, also have my gratitude. I'm fortunate to have a community of supportive readers who offer suggestions and feedback, jokes and comments, and who generally brighten my day. Feel free to join us on social media at:

www.facebook.com/AuthorAlexandraRobbins
www.instagram.com/AuthorAlexandraRobbins
www.twitter.com/AlexndraRobbins

ABOUT THE AUTHOR

Alexandra Robbins is the author of five *New York Times* bestsellers, one of which readers voted Best Nonfiction Book of the Year in the Goodreads Choice Awards. An award-winning investigative reporter and speaker, she has written for outlets including *The New York Times*, *The New Yorker*, *Vanity Fair*, *The Washington Post*, and *The Atlantic*. Among other honors, Robbins, whose books include *Pledged*, *The Overachievers*, and *The Nurses*, has received the John Bartlow Martin Award for Public Interest Magazine Journalism and the Heartsongs Award for "contributions to the mental health of children and young adults."